Part of the Family

Pathways through foster care

Acknowledgements

I would first like to express my very sincere gratitude to the 40 young men and women who kindly agreed to be interviewed for this project, gave me their time and shared their lives with me so fully and often so movingly. I hope that I have been able to do justice to their stories.

I would like to thank Professor David Howe, whose knowledge, support and enthusiasm for this project and for all of my research and writing endeavours over the last 12 years has been invaluable. I have been very privileged.

I have also been very fortunate in having an excellent group of colleagues at the University of East Anglia and would like to thank them for contributing their different areas of expertise to my understanding of foster families, permanence and qualitative methodologies; in particular Mary Beek, Professor June Thoburn and Dr Liz Trinder.

Finally, I am very grateful to Julia Warner for her care, efficiency and patience in helping me in the final stages of producing this manuscript.

Gillian Schofield
December 2002

Note about the author

Dr Gillian Schofield is Deputy Director of the Centre for Research on the Child and Family at the University of East Anglia. An experienced social worker and guardian *ad litem*, she now has special teaching and research interests in attachment, resilience and the welfare and development of children growing up in foster care. Her most recent books are *Attachment Theory, Child Maltreatment and Family Support: A Practice and Assessment model* (Macmillan, 1999 with David Howe, Marian Brandon and Diana Hinings) and *Growing Up in Foster Care* (BAAF 2000, with Mary Beek, Kay Sargent and June Thoburn).

Part of the Family
Pathways through foster care

Gillian Schofield

British Association for Adoption & Fostering
(BAAF)
Skyline House
200 Union Street
London SE1 0LX
www.baaf.org.uk

Charity registration 275689

British Library Cataloguing in Publication Data
A catalogue record for this book is available
from the British Library

ISBN 1 903699 28 2

Cover photographs posed by models
Designed by Andrew Haig & Associates
Typeset by Avon DataSet, Bidford on Avon
Printed by Russell Press Ltd (TU), Nottingham

BAAF Adoption & Fostering is the leading UK-wide membership organisation for all those concerned with adoption, fostering and child care issues.

Contents

Preface

PART I INTRODUCTION 1

1. **Background** **3**

Long-term foster care 5
The tasks of the foster child 7
Attachment, resilience, risk and protective factors 8
"The crowning insult" 11

2. **The study: design and methodology** **14**

Research design 15
Defining and recruiting the sample 17
Some characteristics of the sample 20
Conducting the interviews 22
Data analysis: defining pathways 24
Confidentiality 29

PART II PATHWAYS 31

3. **Close and special** **33**

Legacy 34
What the children brought with them to these foster placements 34
Foster family care 38
Warm welcomes 38
Real mums and dads 39
Belonging to the family – valued and treated the same as other children 47
Shared fate 50
Self-efficacy 52
Turning points 54

4. **Testing out** **56**

Legacy 56
What the children brought to these foster placements 57
Childhood selves in the foster home 58
Foster family care 62
Fitting in and belonging 66
Birth mothers 67
Turning points 70

5. **Distant and self-reliant** **73**

Legacy 73
What the children brought to the foster family 74
Foster family care 80
Adulthood 85
Partners and parenthood 89
Turning points 91

6. **Anxious and fearful** **93**

Legacy 93
What the children brought to this foster placement 94
Foster family care 100
Part of the family 105
Adult life and adult selves 108
Young unattached adults 105
Parents 112
Turning points 115

7. **Breakdown and rebuilding** **117**

Legacy 118
What the children brought with them to these foster placements 119
Foster family care 120
Discontinuity of care: the placement breakdowns 125
Rebuilding foster family relationships in adult life 132
Turning points 134

8. **Rescue, relief and recovery** **142**

Legacy 143
What the children brought from birth families 144
The first long-term placements 146
Foster family care in their final placement 156

New placements/children feeling in conflict and coped with 166
Anger with social workers 169
Reflections on the adult self 173
Turning points 177

9. **Hurt, angry and disappointed** **178**

Legacy 179
What these children brought to their placements 180
Foster family care 185
Telling and not telling 192
"Extra" families 195
Transition to adult life 197
Parenthood 199
Adult relationships 201
Turning points 203

PART III CONCLUSIONS AND IMPLICATIONS FOR PRACTICE 205

10. **The significance of a secure base: towards a psychosocial model of long-term foster care** **207**

To love 209
To act 214
To think 219
Thinking about the experience of separation and loss 222
Thinking through and managing memories and/or stories about the birth family 225
To belong 229
Family solidarity 229
Family ritual 231
Family relationships 232
Family identity 232
Shared family culture 234
To hope 235
Implications of this model for social work practice 237
Policy and practice in long-term foster care 238
Strengths and limitations of this study: the need for further research 242

Bibliography 244

Index 251

Preface

My interest in long-term foster care came about originally because of my professional concern about some of the children for whom, in the late 1980s and early 1990s as a guardian ad litem, I had recommended a care plan of "permanence in a substitute family". This meant either *adoption*, a plan which I subsequently saw in action as guardian ad litem for the adoption proceedings and which had some clear legal status as a "new family", or *long-term foster care*, an option about which very little seemed to be known – except for the fact that in many cases it only became the plan after adoption had been ruled out. I became increasingly concerned that, although I was recommending long-term foster care in some cases, I had little certainty about what it would mean as a family for life for the vulnerable children whose difficult histories and high levels of need and damage I was emphasising so forcefully in my reports to the court.

Associated with these two permanence options appeared to be two contrasting pictures. Adoption was a "forever family", whereas long-term foster care seemed to be linked to worrying stories about what happened to children who were "lingering' or "languishing" in care. These dichotomous views, promulgated by the media and politicians during that period and seeing a significant resurgence within the political context of the Adoption and Children Act (2002), were to some extent supported by concerns in the research literature. The Rowe and Lambert study (1973) *Children Who Wait* was still reverberating in practice as the worst case scenario for drift and delay, with other research raising concerns about long-term foster care (Rowe *et al*, 1984). Thoburn (1991) threw some doubt on this negative view of foster care by her finding that breakdown rates in permanent foster care were similar to adoption, once age as a factor was taken into account, but this message was not widely accepted nor acted on in terms of policy or practice development. Long-term foster care has continued to be seen very often as the last resort, rather than as a positive option.

In spite of this negative view of long-term foster care, I knew anecdotally that the image of foster care as transitory and far removed from the family for life offered by adoption was not the whole story. I visited foster carers of young children who told me about their adult foster sons and daughters, who had grown up in their family and were still in touch. I taught a post-qualifying social work student in her 50s who told me that she had a foster sister in her 60s. I then supervised a research student who was investigating the experiences of adults who grew up in Barnardo's care and had just been given access to their records (Pugh, 1999; Pugh and Schofield, 1999). These men and women were now in their 50s, 60s and 70s and often talked of foster parents as "real" parents for them in childhood, as well as through their adult lives. This set me on the trail of thinking not only that we needed to know more about long-term foster care, but that adult sources might have a great deal to contribute.

My sense that the retrospective approach would yield very powerful information was also based on my own previous research experience of interviewing women in their 20s about what it had meant to be a "school girl mother" and discovering their pride in disproving the negative expectations which had been associated with that particular stigmatised role (Schofield, 1994). This added an extra dimension to the idea of a long-term foster care research project with adult subjects, in terms of giving a voice to those who had also experienced a potentially stigmatised childhood identity as a "child in care", but who were now, as seemed quite possible, leading ordinary adult lives.

At the same time as these ideas were forming into a possible research project on long-term foster care, I was teaching child development to social workers and drawing quite heavily on the work of Vera Fahlberg (1988, 1994), with her emphasis on attachment as a way of making sense of children's experiences of separation, loss and relationship-building in new families. When I looked at the attachment research literature from developmental psychology and psychopathology, I discovered that this field of study outside of social work offered a rich framework for making sense not only of separation and loss, but of many of the complexities of the emotional and behavioural legacy of maltreatment for foster children. It also provided possible ways of understanding how that legacy interacted with the foster family environments into which they came.

At that point I had the very great good fortune to work with David Howe, Diana Hinings and Marian Brandon from the University of East Anglia and a group of social work practitioners and team leaders from Norfolk Social Services Department over a two-year period, testing out the usefulness of this more complex attachment framework in making sense of the social workers' most worrying family support and child protection cases (Howe *et al*, 1999). It was an obvious next step to think about how this work could be moved on to thinking about children once they were in foster care. These children's pathways would include not just the birth family, but very possibly a series of substitute families, in which relationships and the development of the self in interaction with family environments needed to be understood.

The coming together of my awareness of the gaps in our research and practice knowledge about long-term foster care and the opportunities presented by the theoretical framework of attachment to get behind the statistics and understand family relationship experiences and meanings led to two research projects. Researching long-term foster care and addressing relationship questions is always going to require a perspective that takes into account changes over time. This offers two broad choices of approach – the prospective and the retrospective. On this basis two studies were planned. The first was a prospective, longitudinal study of children placed for long-term foster care (Schofield *et al*, 2000). The second was the study that is the focus of this book, a retrospective investigation of the experiences of previously fostered adults. The opportunities offered by prospective and retrospective approaches are very different, as these two studies demonstrate, but there is always the possibility for overlap and integration at the level of theory and lessons for practice.

For this study I was interested in adult stories, what they might tell us about the experience of foster care, and how they might help us think about foster care as a family form for children who need a family for life. Apart from Triseliotis (1980), there was little research in the UK that had addressed these issues with adults. A study designed around talking to previously fostered adults about their lives seemed to offer an important opportunity for an in-depth exploration of the "family for life" question from social work research and practice, alongside an analysis that could take advantage of developmental theories, such as attachment and resilience.

During the period of this study, long-term foster care has remained a significant challenge for policy and practice, but one that perhaps is beginning to be acknowledged more widely. Kelly (2000) has suggested that long-term foster care has persisted even though it does not fit easily into simple categories or offer easy solutions. But as Lowe *et al* (2002) have put it most recently, long-term fostering has become rather a "Cinderella option". They go on to say:

> *There needs to be an overall nationally co-ordinated coherent policy for all children who are not going home – both for adoption and long-term fostering. There is a need for policy and planning for long-term fostering to be sharpened up – with clear answers as to what it is and* positive *reasons for its use*. (Lowe *et al*, 2002, p. 107)

This policy development needs to be built on the best and most up-to-date evidence on current procedures, practice and outcomes from prospective longitudinal studies, but it can also benefit from a more theoretical understanding of how long-term foster care is experienced as a family for life. It is hoped that this study may play a part in generating ideas that can contribute to the larger debate in policy and practice.

Part I

Introduction

1 Background

In social work practice with children and families, there is a necessary interest in children's varied developmental pathways. We need to make sense of what happens to children as they grow up in different kinds of birth family or as they move through foster care, residential care and adoption. We know that although children are born with a specific genetic inheritance, the environments in which they grow and develop, physically, emotionally, intellectually and socially, will affect their capacity to lead successful and fulfilling lives in adulthood. Differences in environments and the impact of these differences on the development of children in the short, medium and longer term, must therefore be central to our understanding of the different pathways which children will take.

The child is not, however, a mere passive recipient of environmental influences. Our model needs to recognise the interactive nature of the person–environment relationship. Knowledge about those interactions contributes not only to our understanding of children but also to our understanding of the legacy of childhood in adult life. Although many kinds of environment, including the physical environment, will play a part in this developmental and interactional process, the relationship environment is of particular interest to social workers in understanding the emotional and social development of children. This is especially the case when the children in question are facing the major developmental and existential challenge of being separated from their birth family and looking to a long-term foster family to meet their needs for family life. It is this experience in this relationship environment that was the primary focus of this research.

Research in many disciplines has addressed the question of what might be thought of as the range of "normal" (as culturally defined) relationship environments which act as a context for children's development. But much has also been learned from the investigation of adverse and atypical environments. This has included research on the environmental impact of *extreme adversity*, as in the case of Genie (Curtiss, 1977), a child deprived of normal social contact with people until the age of 13, or environments generally felt to be *undesirable*, such as an infant's experience of multiple non-related carers in institutional care, or hopefully *benign* environments, such as the attempt to replicate normal family life in adoption by strangers. Such research has, for example, taken the form of the investigation of the outcomes for separated identical twins placed in different adoptive environments, effectively natural experiments on the interaction of genetics and caregiving environments (Plomin, 1994). Most recently, there has been the intensive programme of research on the group of children adopted from Romania (Rutter *et al*, 1998), an important piece of research which is providing data on the short- and longer-term effects of both early deprivation and remedial family environments. These studies allow researchers to comment on the unusual and specific nature of particular environments and their consequences for developmental pathways, but they also promote understanding of what might be features of all pathways – such as the importance of social relationships in infancy or the nature of genetic factors in development or the impact of adversity at certain points in a child's developmental history. Even the use of the language and concept of *pathways* suggests the way in which each individual will follow a route through life that will be affected by nature and nurture in a particular pattern (Sroufe, 1997). Sroufe uses the metaphor of a tree to capture this diversity, with individual routes through the tree depending on a multiplicity of interacting factors, with forces that sustain continuity and forces that produce turning points of discontinuity, for better or worse.

Although there is always more to learn about the precise nature of these person–environment interactions and pathways, different relationship environments have been found to have both short-term and long-term consequences for children's welfare and the quality of their relationships in adult life. The acceptance that adult social relationships are influenced by relationship experiences in childhood has fuelled our continuing interest in those experiences in themselves and in the extent to which they are transmitted into adult life – and, inevitably, how they might be transmitted across the generations through subsequent parent–child relationships. It is for this reason that different disciplines, each with their own perspective on ways of understanding and researching social relationships, pursue the detail of specific environments and the healthy development which they may promote or prevent. Social work research has had to learn from developmental psychology and psychopathology in many respects in this field, but it can also make its own contribution to the knowledge base.

This study focuses on experiences of one particular environment that has commonly been looked to as a form of remedial intervention, but has also raised questions as to whether it can meet the needs of psychologically damaged children separated from their birth families – the long-term foster care environment.

Long-term foster care

In the UK, most children who are unable to be brought up in their own families are likely to end up not in adoptive families nor in residential care but in local authority foster care (Department of Health, 2002). This environment represents an attempt by a professional bureaucracy to provide a family in the community who will meet the needs of these children during their childhood. It is an artificially created family, as in adoption, but unlike adoption, the adults who act as parents do not have legal rights, they do not have "parental responsibility" to use the rather telling expression from the Children Act 1989. Parental responsibility is either held entirely by the birth parents (CA, 1989 s20) or shared between the local authority and the birth parents (CA, 1989 s31), who continue to have contact in most cases and attend meetings where decisions are made about a child's life. Ordinary parenting roles, such as attending school parents' evenings or giving medical permissions, become a matter for negotiation between the "parents".

What is more, even where the placement is expected to last through childhood, there is no expectation that the foster "carers", as they are called, will continue to provide parenting or a family base into the adult life of the fostered child of the kind that birth and adoptive families generally provide for their children. The official sources of their link with the child, i.e. the legal responsibility of the local authority to place the child and the payment of allowances to foster carers, both cease at the age of 18 if not before – although there is an expectation that some financial and other support might be offered up to the age of 21 (CA, 1989 s24). Thus, as the young person enters adulthood, he or she may face a dilemma in terms of where to have Sunday lunch (Thoburn, 1994) or to spend Christmas. It may be that several households or none have a place at their table to which the formerly fostered adult feels they have a right.

So foster care is a very distinctive and distinctively different family environment in which a child grows up and from which a child moves into adult life. In addition, the children who are entering this form of family care are themselves likely to be distinguished from the majority of children by the nature of their childhood experiences prior to joining the foster family. By the time children have found a long-term foster home in which they feel able to settle, they are likely to have experienced a combination of adversities which may threaten their healthy development. Since the implementation of the Children Act 1989 in England and Wales and the Children (Scotland) Act 1995, family support services have been designed to enable all but the most intractable of difficulties to be resolved with the child remaining at home. The troubled children who are looked after now by the local authority in a long-term foster family are likely to have experienced abuse, neglect and/or have parents who have mental health difficulties, difficulties with alcohol or drug misuse (Schofield *et al*, 2000; Sinclair *et al*, 2000) or have themselves suffered in adult life from unresolved traumas in childhood (Howe *et al*, 1999). The children are likely to have significant emotional or behavioural problems, which will have made them the focus of multiple professional investigations. In addition, these children are likely to have suffered a number of moves and separations, both within their birth families and within the care system, before finding and settling in a foster home where they are able to stay until they are adult (Schofield *et al*, 2000; Sinclair *et al*, 2000). Thus their overwhelming experience will be one of loss and separation, in addition to their previous adverse experience of being parented.

It is therefore the case that children who are placed in this kind of family environment, the long-term foster home, will have come with the history of a developmental pathway which is likely to lead to some degree of developmental risk, and some increased chance of emotional, behavioural, educational and social difficulties in their lives. Even though some of these children may have had the benefit of certain genetic or environmental protective factors (such as high intelligence or positive grandparental care), the experience of foster care has to be seen in the context of the likelihood of one or more previous adverse environments.

The tasks of the foster child

The tasks of the foster child are many and will be explored in detail later, but fundamental to their situation are some very difficult questions, among which is the following:

> *I keep asking how we are supposed to live a normal life . . . and no one gives me an answer.* (Fostered child in Parker, 1980, p. 146)

All fostered children have to find answers to such questions if they are to overcome the psychosocial risks to which they have been exposed and achieve a "normal life" and healthy development. When thinking about the relationship environments from which they came, it must be remembered that these children bring those environments with them, intact and largely unresolved, in their internal worlds. They are negotiating relationships and finding a place inside the foster family while retaining their identities and loyalties to the real or fantasy birth family. Such tasks are both emotional and cognitive. Children draw on difficult memories and stories that require mental accommodation. The child who can half remember shadows in the bedroom or waiting outside the pub with her baby brother for her mother to emerge or reading the newspaper report that her parents were imprisoned following the death of her baby brother (three examples from this study) will be locked into an energy-consuming and emotionally complex task of absorbing that information into their story about themselves. The familiar questions for all children, 'who am I and where do I belong?', need to be addressed and answered by these children in a way which enables them to move on with their lives. As the foster child sits curled up on the settee watching his new but strange (to him) family get on with their lives around him, his mind is unlikely to be still. Through to adult life, that child will be managing these thoughts and feelings, with new environments providing both anxieties and opportunities.

Attachment, resilience, risk and protective factors

An investigation of the experience of growing up in long-term foster care will therefore have to consider not only the specific nature of the new environment, but also the ways in which environment D can accommodate, build on or reverse the developmental legacy of environments A or B or C – or the cumulative consequences of all three.

One particularly useful theoretical framework for considering the forces that maintain continuities or achieve discontinuities in children's internal worlds has been attachment theory (Ainsworth *et al*, 1978; Bowlby, 1969, 1973, 1980; Crittenden, 1995; Main, 1995). According to attachment theory, children will have formed internal working models, mental representations of themselves, others and the relationships between them (George, 1996; Howe *et al*, 1999). They will bring these into the new set of relationships in the foster home – relationships not only with the adult carers, but also with the other children in the home, the extended family, the neighbours, the teachers at the new school and so on. Given the histories of these children, it is likely that these internal working models will reflect their adverse relationship experiences. Working models are likely to derive from experiences of anxiety about their own lovability, which the child will have needed to defend against. The insecure attachment histories of these children will produce particular patterns of relating, based on beliefs and expectations of the lack of availability of sensitive care from others (George, 1996; Howe *et al*, 1999). Those who have experienced consistent patterns of rejection may have learned to deactivate their proximity-seeking attachment behaviours and demonstrate an avoidant attachment pattern. Those who had insensitive, unpredictable care may have learned to hyperactivate their attachment behaviours and demonstrate an ambivalent/resistant attachment pattern. Many maltreated children who have experienced particular kinds of frightening *and* unpredictable environments will have developed representations of caregivers as dangerous or neglectful and will have found it impossible to organise a strategy for coping. They may demonstrate a disorganised attachment pattern. All of these children are predominantly anxious and angry, confused and suspicious but may also be controlling and frightened. Even though some are travelling in hope of a relationship, they may often feel that their very survival is under threat.

Life in the foster home for such troubled children may be experienced as an opportunity to revise these negative internal working models or as confirmation of them. They are unlikely to have experienced the secure base effect in infancy and early childhood that would free them to explore, to learn and to make the most of life's opportunities at home and at school (Bowlby, 1969, 1988). Their capacity to develop rewarding relationships, even when these are offered, will depend on a multitude of factors. How did they cope with the adversities in their lives to date? Have there been protective factors in previous environments which have left them with a raised self-esteem or some capacity to accept and reciprocate care? Perhaps there was a special relative or a specially committed social worker. Do they have a sense of humour, a capacity to share a joke, to see the funny side of things? Have they been intelligent enough or focused enough to earn success at school, in spite of everything?

Much has been said about the sources and importance of *resilience* (Gilligan, 2000; Haggerty *et al*, 1994; Rutter, 1985, 1999). Rutter (1999) has defined resilience as 'relative resistance to psychosocial risk experiences'. He has also emphasised that resilience is not a fixed characteristic of the individual, but will vary in relation to different stresses.

> *Resilience does not constitute an individual trait or characteristic. Moreover children may show resilience in relation to some sort of stresses and adversities, but not others; similarly they may exhibit resistance to some sorts of psychopathological sequelae but not others.* (Rutter, 1999, p. 135)

Sroufe (1997, p. 256) suggests that there is a need for a *developmental* model of resilience. He contrasts this with the rather too common "trait" interpretation of resilience.

> *Within a developmental perspective, in contrast, resilience is not something some children "have a lot of". It develops. A capacity to rebound following periods of maladaptation (or to do well in the face of stress) evolves over time within the total context of developmental*

influences. The capacity for staying organised in the face of challenge, for active coping and for maintaining positive expectations during periods of stress are evolved by the person in interaction with the environment across successive periods of adaptation. And even as an acquired capacity it is not static, but is continually influenced by ongoing changes in context.

Within Sroufe's developmental model there are features that suggest the persistence of individual strengths and weaknesses, but there is always the possibility of change and increased capacity to cope. "Changes in context" will include moves into or away from secure family placements or supportive schools.

It is important to note here the conceptual overlap between resilience and attachment theory, since the terminology from both will feature in the analysis that follows (see also Schofield, 2001). In so far as the internal working model develops and evolves in response to the quality of the caregiving environment, then it can be seen as compatible with Sroufe's developmental framework for understanding resilience. The concept of adaptation lies at the heart of attachment theory as it does of resilience. It is the way in which the child adapts to the caregiving environment which will determine the pattern of secure or insecure attachment (Ainsworth *et al*, 1978; Howe *et al*, 1999).

Both resilience and attachment theory see the child as an active participant, an actor in his or her own life, subject of as well as subject to the events that make up his or her life story. Attachment theory would suggest that, from the earliest hours, days and weeks of life, the child is interacting with the caregiving environment and having an impact on it as well as reacting to it behaviourally and internally processing and dealing with it. Adaptation begins rapidly as infants learn to utilise, cope with or, at the very least, survive their caregiving. These adaptations organise themselves into patterns of behaviour. Even older so-called disorganised children have to find ways of controlling and manipulating their environments, particularly if they are being maltreated, in order to survive (Crittenden and Ainsworth, 1989; Carlson *et al*, 1989; Crittenden, 1995; Howe *et al*, 1999). Their adaptive strategies may be destructive in certain respects, they may not look like resilience mechanisms, but in the sense that they are functional they may be necessary (for a more detailed discussion of resilience and maltreatment see Mrazek and Mrazek, 1987).

One further conceptual overlap is that both frameworks rely on systems theory as a way of describing the complex interactions which lead to different outcomes for children. Although attachment theory is most closely associated with caregiving relationships and resilience is sometimes seen as reflecting relationships with the wider world (Gilligan, 1997), both frameworks, properly understood, take into account all levels within the ecological model (Bronfenbrenner, 1979) from the internal world of the child through different caregiving environments and on to wider environmental considerations, such as the context of social pressures or supports that can affect the development of children for better or worse. This theoretical model is consistent with the *Framework for the Assessment of Children in Need and their Families* (Department of Health, 2000) and is equally important when we think about the layers of interacting factors, from home to school to peergroups, that will affect the outcomes for fostered children.

The mechanisms by which a particular child acquires resilience, manages to develop a sense of his or her own worth and efficacy in the face of abuse, neglect and separations from attachment figures, are the subject of very great interest when we are seeking to understand long-term foster care. We need to know how children's self-esteem and self-efficacy are raised in the context of secure, sensitive care beyond infancy. In contrast, the resistance of some children to change, even when offered the best possible care, is a source of great frustration and concern. Outcomes are always likely to be the result of an interaction between the child and the environment, but the balance of influence from the child or the planned remedial environment or the factors external to both will vary.

"The crowning insult"

In addition to the application of developmental theories to our understanding of long-term foster care, we need also to think about the meaning of family membership and the significance of separation from birth families for children. Failure by birth parents to care for children leaves those children with a burden. There is a lot of explaining to do – to the self and to others. Fanshel and Shinn (1978, p. 3) spoke of the relative impact of impoverishment, racism, malnutrition and ill health in childhood but described the absence of parents able to care for a child as being 'the crowning insult'. This suggests that, not only do the individual child's circumstances which led to them coming into care affect a child, but that the *meaning* of being fostered is profoundly linked for all children with the cultural expectation that children will be brought up within their birth family, most usually by one if not both of their birth parents. This theme moves the issue of being fostered into a much broader domain, where we have to consider what we mean by the blood tie or the significance of birth families in our society. As research demonstrates, for many (though not all) adopted and fostered people there is a powerful urge to know about, and in some cases meet, their blood relatives (Beek, 1997; Howe and Feast, 2000; Pugh, 1999, Pugh and Schofield, 1999). It is a given of foster care that most children will struggle to some extent with divided loyalties. We cannot ignore the possibility that there is a cultural imperative about blood ties which has to be considered alongside the notion of beneficial emotional ties based on an attachment relationship. Family relationships and family membership are not simply a private matter – they have a public face which fits or fails to fit with cultural expectations that children themselves will have internalised. A further test of foster care must therefore be whether it can provide not only emotional growth but also family membership.

However well planned or stable the long-term foster care placement (and evidence suggests that this is very variable, see Berridge and Cleaver, 1987; Fratter *et al*, 1991; Rowe *et al*, 1984; Triseliotis, 2002) there remain some fundamental challenges, given the issues described above. Yet there is some evidence from recent studies (Schofield *et al*, 2000; Thoburn *et al*, 2000) that long-term foster families can and do offer *parental* care that includes sensitive responsiveness to the child's developmental needs and encompasses giving the child a sense of belonging as part of the family. We cannot ignore the concerns expressed about instability in long-term foster care and the extent to which long-term foster care can meet the welfare needs of children relative to adoption (Rowe *et al*, 1984; Triseliotis, 2002). But it is more constructive, given the fact that many children will continue to grow up in foster care, to move on from seeing long-term foster care as the default permanence option outside the birth family when adoption is not achievable and start to understand more about what long-term foster families are able to offer children who need a family for life. This study was designed to contribute to that process by taking the opportunity to hear from adults who had experienced long-term foster family care and to learn from their experiences.

2 The study: design and methodology

Some key research questions emerge from the combination of practice concerns about the future of children in long-term foster care, the social work research literature on long-term foster care, and a particular interest in developmental theory.

- How can/does long-term foster care meet the needs of children for family life and family relationships?
- What are the different pathways through childhood in long-term foster care and into adult life?

This study takes a particular exploratory approach to those questions, through listening to and analysing what previously fostered adults tell us about their experiences. We have to bear in mind that we are dealing here with at least four different kinds of data.

- What happened – the reality or "truth" about their childhood.
- What they remember – that reality or "truth" as processed at the time and since.
- What they have been told or remember that they have been told about childhood – again as processed at the time and since.
- Who they are now – their adult lives and their adult state of mind, with its complex roots in the childhood reality, the memories, the stories told to them and the processing.

All of these realities are laden with meaning, as experience is evaluated, put in boxes, made to connect with other things (Howe, 1998). In addition, for fostered children and adults, the experience of remembering, forgetting and telling their stories is complicated by the often traumatic nature of these stories and by the incomplete and fragmented picture that they often have because of movement and change (Mollon, 2000; Toth and Cicchetti, 1998). Their minds are often the only place where their full history is "known". Yet so much is unknown to them or partially known or only known about through what can seem to be a process of telling and re-telling among the families and professionals around them in which the "truth" can get lost. These layers and uncertainties needed to be thought about as the stories unfolded in each interview.

Research design

As the research question was about how long-term foster care had been experienced and the meanings which had been attributed to those experiences by adults, it seemed that the use of an interview that could be analysed qualitatively would be the best fit (Cresswell, 1994; Mason, 1996; Seale, 1998). The research question was one which invited the telling of stories and the variety of these stories needed to be captured in ways that survey questions would be unlikely to facilitate. I wanted to meet the men and women who had had this experience in childhood and hear their stories in the language in which they wished to tell them.

A single interview was conducted with each person. This choice of a single rather than multiple interviews was made for several reasons. First, I hoped that these adults would take me through their lives from birth to the present in an uninterrupted conversation – to have had the story divided up in, say, two parts would have led to the possible mental separation of childhood from the adult present. I hoped that the baby, the little girl, the teenager, the adolescent, the "care leaver", the adult and, in most cases, the parent would pass before us in a continuous flow, which would allow echoes and connections across ages and stages to be thought about and discussed. Secondly, a second interview may have been a way of gaining further information or sharing the analysis, but may also have risked suggesting the need to check the "facts" – not an impression I wanted to give. Thirdly, I did not believe it was advisable to promote the idea of building a relationship, which second or subsequent visits might have implied.

Although I was not always entirely at ease with leaving these young men and women after one revealing interview, I decided that suggesting that I was available for greater involvement represented more of a risk and would be unhelpful and misleading. I knew from the system of obtaining the sample (see below) that each person had access to at least one person with whom they could discuss the research interview, if they wished. I had some informal feedback from referrers saying how much young people had felt they had benefited from the experience. The fact that this interview was rewarding or at least survivable seemed in itself to be a sign for some that they were now able to face the past and move on. However, the risk of leaving someone with a number of raised but unresolved issues meant that I took great care in how I managed the most difficult discussions and especially in how the interview ended. I did not, for example, pursue disclosures of sexual abuse but accepted the story as told. To end the interview I always focussed on a specific final question, which was 'What advice would you give to a social worker working with a young person in foster care?' This reminded them of the constructive use to which the interview would be put and, without denying the sadness and loss that had often been a feature of at least part of the interview, ended the interview on a more emotionally neutral note.

For this study, with its developmental approach, an interview was needed which covered the *chronology* of life to date and also explored current circumstances and hopes for the future. In planning what to cover in the interview, the topics fell into two broad areas. First there was the question of the development of the self in the context of relationships. These relationships were primarily with caregivers, but were also with siblings, peers, partners and children. This section therefore included discussion of all relevant families, birth, adoptive, foster and current – but could also include residential care or friendship networks. The role of education and other areas of activity that would have impacted on the self and relationships were seen to be an important part of the narrative. Secondly, there was a social work strand in the interview which addressed memories of social workers, reviews, decisions to move placements, the question of adoption, and so on. The overlap between self in relationships and social work lay on the one hand in the possibility that relationships with social workers might also have been significant and on the other hand in the need to discuss what "being in care" or being a foster child had meant to their developing identity.

In looking for suitable interview questions and formats it was decided to use the questions from the Adult Attachment Interview (AAI) (George *et al*, 1985) to tackle the relationship-based issues. Deceptively simple questions, such as 'can you give me five words to describe your relationship with your foster carer when you were a child?' followed by examples for each word, yields rich material. Although the AAI questions were not used to classify the attachment patterns of adults in this study, they did provide a useful framework that could focus on core attachment concepts and to which could be added questions about social work practice and what it meant to be growing up as a child in care.

Defining and recruiting the sample

The criteria for the sample were not obvious. It was important to build in some comparability in terms of age and experience but also allow for some variety. An age range of 18–30 was chosen because this would include adults whose memories of childhood were still vivid but who would have gone through adolescence and be establishing themselves as adults. The maximum age of last admission to care was set at 12 years, because of the way in which adolescence presents challenges to foster care placements, and it was thought useful to see how that period had been managed as a life stage. This also conveniently overlapped with the upper age limit for our prospective foster care study (Schofield *et al*, 2000), thus offering the prospect of some comparisons.

Setting the criterion for the length of time in foster care was a difficult decision. The study started with a criterion of five years in one foster family on the (false) assumption that any less would not be enough to see whether the placement had become permanent or a real family in which to belong. Once referrals started to arrive, it became clear that strict application of this criterion might lose some excellent cases and so the criterion was changed to three years in one family. There were adults, for example, who had come into care young, been in a number of placements, perhaps including a failed adoption, and ended up in a foster placement in their mid-teens, but had become a member of the foster family and was still part of that family in their mid-20s. Similarly, some adults had experienced multiple families of three years or even less, all of whom were still around in adult life. These stories were just as remarkable and perhaps more unexpected than placements that had started young and lasted till adulthood. There were also other referrals where foster placements had led to adoption in the late teens – but it felt as if this was still essentially a foster family experience.

Very rapidly I realised that it was the diversity that was providing the insights – exceptions that did not so much prove the rule but offered the possibility of more flexible and creative "rules". However, it was not possible to know, except informally at interview, if these placements had been planned as long-term placements at the outset and so the sample was retrospectively defined in a way that is most similar to that of Rowe *et al* (1984).

Identifying adults who had spent a period of time in one foster family was by no means straightforward. Local authorities often do not keep complete records for very long after children have left care. The eight local authorities that were part of our prospective study (Schofield *et al*, 2000), including four shire counties, one unitary authority, two London boroughs and one large metropolitan authority, gave permission to approach their social workers (child care, family placement and, where possible, Children's Rights Officers) who might be in touch with foster carers and care leavers. Where possible I tried to meet groups of workers and carers personally, so that they would feel more comfortable about mentioning the study to the young people, many of whom were still at quite vulnerable points in their lives and all of whom had stories that were difficult to tell in many respects. Not surprisingly, most contacts came via workers and carers that I had met personally. Social workers were sent letters to circulate to carers and young people. Advertisements were also placed in the National Foster Care Association (now Fostering Network) magazine and at the university where I teach. The former route produced just one referral – but this was one of the most intriguing in a sample of very intriguing cases. The latter route also brought some very interesting cases, students who had been fostered or whose family had fostered and suggested I approach their sister or brother. I was also contacted by post-qualifying social work students about cases and, most fortuitously, I met a social worker in a lunch queue at a conference who suggested I might like to meet his adult (foster) daughter, who now had a family of her own.

It became apparent at the initial telephone contact with the young adults, and was confirmed in the interviews, that there were a number of reasons for participating: the wish to tell their story to help other foster children; a sense of gratitude to their foster carers or social workers (or in some cases a sense of anger and outrage); simple curiosity; an interest in talking it all through. Some felt a justified pride in the way in which they and their children had turned out, given the disadvantages that they had faced, and wanted me to know that survival and even success were possible. They wanted to correct negative stereotypes of children in care. Whatever their primary reason, they were all keen to know that the research would be used to help social workers understand more about what it felt like to be a foster child.

The commitment on their side was to let me have up to one-and-a-half hours of their time, at their homes and at a mutually convenient time. My commitment as a researcher was to ask them a series of questions about their lives to date as a basis for discussion, but to move on if they did not want to answer any particular questions and to end the interview at any time if they felt uncomfortable. The tape recording of the interview was discussed at the time of the interview. None of the 40 people objected to this, once I explained that they would only be heard by myself and that any quotations that were used in the final report would not identify them or their families – although there were some who felt that their foster carers deserved a medal and might have liked their praises to have been sung more publicly. My explicit commitment to them was also to make good use of what they told me and do whatever I could to help social workers and children in foster care on the basis of the research. I had to explain that it would be several years before the full research was published (which disappointed several), but in the meantime I would be using their ideas to help me in teaching social workers.

A small fee was offered in a thank you card. I suspect few would have done the interview for the money alone. Two people were rather offended by the offer, saying that they really valued the opportunity to do the interview and would give the money to charity. Their sense that I was buying their life story rather than that they were giving it freely and altruistically made me doubt the wisdom of the fee. However, other people seemed to feel that it was important to get financial recognition.

Some characteristics of the sample

The age distribution of the eventual sample was particularly helpful to the study (Table 2.1). I had anticipated having a sample dominated by recent care leavers, because I had imagined that those would be the people most likely still to be in touch with agencies or carers. The opportunity to talk with people in their mid and late 20s, who were established in careers and often in families of their own, was very valuable. The range of ages had various implications for the life stages that they represented, though the age/life stage match is never exact. Twenty-three of the sample, including some teenagers, were parents. The young mothers of 18 or 19 may have had less in common with their age peers just completing a college course and living at home than with mothers in their early and mid-20s. But the more recent role of social workers in their lives, for example, or the more recent experience of organised birth family contact represented some kinds of difference between younger and older people.

Table 2.1
Age, gender and ethnicity

		N = 40	%
Age	18–19	4	10
	20–22	10	25
	23–25	15	37
	26–30	11	27
Gender	Female	30	75
	Male	10	25
Ethnicity	White British	32	80
	Minority ethnicity/ cultural origin	8	20

NB. Not all percentages add up to 100.

The gender split was not even. I had been unsure as to whether men would be less likely to be in touch with foster carers or less likely to be available or to volunteer for such a study. In fact several of these men were very much in touch with their foster parents and very keen to tell their story.

I had not set any target for numbers of adults from minority ethnic/ minority cultural groups but 20 per cent was quite high given that most participants were from the shire counties. There were six children from African-Caribbean, African and mixed ethnicity parentage backgrounds – five had originally come from London. The other two children were of minority cultural rather than minority ethnic groups, coming from families of Southern European origin. All were placed in white British families (see Thoburn *et al*, 2000, for an in-depth discussion of the specific permanence issues for these groups of children).

Age at final admission to care (Table 2.2) seems worth highlighting here, since many of the children came into care young – 25 out of the 40 at age five or less and seven at less than a year, several of these at a few weeks old. The question of adoption had been around for some of these very young children, but where they were adopted it was often much later – one woman had been placed at six weeks and was adopted at 17. Such figures tell us very little about meanings – for one person adopted as a 16-year-old the adoption was a matter of indifference and she cut most ties with her adoptive parents as soon as possible. In contrast one person adopted at 17 had been desperate to be adopted for some years and only felt safe finally from her birth parents at that point.

Table 2.2
Age at final admission into care

Age	*N = 40*	*%*
0–12 months	7	17
1–2	11	27
3–5	7	17
6–7	5	12
8–12	10	25

NB. Not all percentages add up to 100.

Contact with at least one foster carer was almost universal (Table 2.3), not surprisingly given the sources of referrals to the study. The two who had no such contact were two of the three who had spent time in prison. The contact itself varied from those who lived at home or, when older, phoned home every day, to those who just sent and received Christmas cards from carers.

Table 2.3
In contact with foster or birth families

		N=40	*%*
Living with or in contact with at least one foster carer	Yes	38	95
	No	2	5
In contact with birth parents	Yes	27	67
	No	10	25
N/A parents deceased		3	7

Contact with birth families was the majority experience, even for some who had been removed after serious neglect in infancy and remained in a stable foster family placement since. Presence or absence of contact bore little relation to the quality of specific experiences or relationships in their history, although the absence of contact (ten cases) seemed to be more likely where there had been violence or sexual abuse, where children were entirely abandoned in childhood, or where young people themselves were angry with parents who they felt had let them down.

The process of recruitment alone was such that the sample for this study could not be described as representative – mainly because it was biased in favour of those who were still in touch with a carer or an agency social worker. However, the range of individuals and stories, as the rest of the book will detail, was rich and varied.

Conducting the interviews

The interest and even enthusiasm in some cases to participate in the study, expressed in the preliminary discussion over the phone, did not mean that all the young men and women were equally comfortable about revealing their history to a total stranger once I was in the room. Some gentle preliminaries had to be gone though before we engaged in the interview itself. Indeed some were very preliminary – two of the young mothers had been watching for my car and, carrying their babies, came out to where I was parked to greet me and introduce me to their child. Where the young adults were parents, there was a great deal of shared enjoyment during the interview of the exploits of their babies and young children or appreciation of the older children's school photographs, as these children got their mention in their mother's or father's story. Several young adults wanted to share their life story books with me. For one young woman this included some very sad pictures of her appearance before and after a step-mother came into her life, cut off her hair and dressed her in jumble sale clothes. Another young woman showed me the picture taken when, as part of life story work, her social worker had taken her and her siblings to visit, for the first time, the grave of her infant brother who had died following neglect by their parents – the grave had no headstone, just a number. This sharing of their lives with me, the ordinary as well as the traumatic, was always very touching and very challenging. It often seemed as if I was being put to the test to see how I would respond – perhaps just as they thought they were being tested by me or perhaps to see whether it would be safe to talk to me. In short, a range of interpersonal social work skills were as necessary as research skills, or perhaps need to be included in our definition of research skills. The similarity and differences between research interviews and first interviews as a social worker or guardian ad litem were striking. Similarities rested in the rapid collection of sensitive information and history. Differences arose from the fact that this would be the only visit and that I had no power over what happened in their lives – only an interest in learning from it.

In most cases I was struck from the beginning of each interview by how intrusive such an interview might/must seem. I was a stranger and they would only be seeing me the once, with me taking their life story away on tape. The fact that I was a stranger and knew nothing about them might in some ways have been anxiety-provoking for them, but it may also have helped in reducing anxiety. I had no preconceived ideas and could open with the question – 'I don't know anything about you apart from the fact that you lived for a part of your childhood in a foster family – so can we go back to the beginning? How old are you? Where were you born?' This starting point meant that, unlike meeting other professionals in their lives, they had control over my knowledge about them – their version of their history would be all I had. This was quite liberating for both of us, but a few people found this rather strange and wanted to make sure I had the truth, for example, saying that they wished their foster father or mother could have been there to fill in some of the gaps in their memories. For a few young adults, the idea that I was interested in them now and how they saw things now was perhaps rather more anxiety-provoking than that sense they had of a regularly told childhood story that could be handed over complete, as a package, without too many questions asked.

Data analysis: defining pathways

The interviews were transcribed in detail, including every repetition, the length of each pause, each linguistic uncertainty and every interruption from the babies and young children.

At this point I had two sources of information. The official "research data" was the transcribed interviews. The unofficial data was the experience of meeting and spending time with the 40 young adults. I saw their homes, I met their young children or saw photographs, and I had a powerful sense of the men and women as they were during the interview – there was even a different atmosphere with each person. Listening to the tapes subsequently brought back those 40 events. Although working primarily with the text, the words on the page, I could never lose the person as I had met them and heard them. Although I was not using a realist approach and testing the interview content against other sources of data (Silverman, 1993) nor taking the more naturalist, feminist approach in using the personal interaction as data (Stanley and Wise, 1993), the process of accessing these stories or narratives as text was inevitably accompanied by an awareness of the interview itself, which was hard to separate from the story in the spoken words and on the page.

My particular interests in terms of attachment, resilience and the existing literature on foster care and its outcomes were also a feature of making sense of the interview data. As Fetterman (1989) puts it, researchers need to have 'an open mind, not an empty head'. This interest in certain frameworks is appropriate – why else review literature in framing the research question and methods unless we want to be knowledgeable? Why else would practitioners do research in their existing areas of expertise? In my case, "knowledge" about family placement biased me towards an interest and alertness to themes that connect with the themes that were present in the literature or perhaps, more correctly, in my choice of literature. These were around what adults would have experienced in terms of foster family continuity, foster family membership and foster family relationships.

In reviewing all the stories it seemed that there were some key elements that might assist in grouping them for analysis, ways in which different pathways could be defined. The analysis of narratives has increasingly been valued as a way of analysing qualitative data (Reissman, 1994). As Coffey and Atkinson (1996) suggest:

> *Narrative as autobiography describes the way in which people articulate how the past is related to the present (Richardson, 1990). Time is placed into a personal history, where the past is given meaning in the present. Social actors organize their lives and experiences through stories and in doing so make sense of them* (p. 68).

In making sense of the interviews, it seemed relevant to consider the most obvious of characteristics first – notably did the adults have the experience of a family that lasted them through childhood into adulthood and how did they describe what that meant to them? Continuity and discontinuity, as explored in the family placement literature (Berridge and Cleaver, 1987; Fratter *et al*, 1991 among many others) has always been a first choice measure of outcome, but is also a major feature of any story that has a beginning, a middle and an end. The sample could be divided into continuous and discontinuous placement experiences. Apart from being an indication of successful foster care or successful social work practice, continuity also equates conceptually to some degree of "normality" – the greater the proportion of a childhood that had been spent with one set of foster carers/parents and the greater the continuity into adult life, the more the foster family might be seen as approximating real biological families. It seemed possible to trace these stories in ways that addressed not only continuity but also the psychological dimension of security or emotional closeness *and* the more psychosocial dimension of "real families" – which drew on a telling combination of family relationships and family membership.

This process of searching for stories that had patterns relating to these core categories or dimensions led to the division of the 40 cases into seven groups, each reflecting different pathways. The young adults who had experienced continuous care and membership were allocated to four pathways that drew on other, less measurable discourses about relationships and their meanings to individuals. These pathways also reflected differences in how individuals defined themselves. In summary, the first continuous care group had felt special and close to their foster families, as "real families" who had set them up well as relatively comfortable and confident adults. The second group described more tension in the foster families, at least in part because they had been difficult and challenging children, but they also credited their foster carers with coping with them, sticking by them, and being a "real" family for them. The third group seemed rather more distant, one step removed, grateful to carers but not having the same sense of close emotional involvement as Groups 1 and 2, in spite of the qualities in the foster families and the continuous membership into adult life. They were not describing them so emphatically as "real families". (As it happens, all the transracially placed children are in Groups 1 and 3, but given the nature and size of the sample, this suggests only that such placements can be stable, not that any particular proportion will be.) The fourth pathway concerned a group of rather fragile adults who had almost certainly benefited from the continuity of care, the quality of care and the sense of family membership in real families, as they were the first to admit, but who still seemed to be struggling with the demons of early childhood experiences and questions about the value of the self.

Turning to those who had experienced discontinuous care, two particular patterns emerged that were very striking in the complex pictures that needed to be understood. In particular, in spite of placement endings, they both had significant elements of continuity into adult life. So the fifth pathway of the seven was of placements that had lasted into adolescence but had then broken down, with teenagers experiencing a range of troubling difficulties. However, this discontinuity was moderated by the fact that they remained in touch with their original long-term families, contact being initiated by both parties at different times, and so family *membership* was continuous into adult life even though family care, in terms of residence, had been discontinuous.

The sixth pathway was of histories where children had experienced poor or abusive care in the birth family, followed by at least one long-term foster or adoptive placement with poor or abusive care, prior to a move to a placement which then offered continuous care and membership into adult life. These were third-chance families for older children who were angry and distressed at how they had been treated previously. Again, the hallmark in adult life was continuity with these new families and there was particular gratitude to carers.

A final pathway included those for whom, whether from continuous or discontinuous placement histories, there had been problems in placements, and in adult life there was no sense of a foster family provided by the local authority that felt like a "real" family or that offered reliable care and support.

This division of the sample into seven pathways is not intended to suggest that these pathways represent all possible stories of adults who have grow up in long-term foster families. For this reason and because the sample is small, numbers of cases in each pathway are not specified as this might give a misleading impression of proportions in the long-term foster care population as a whole. As is not uncommon in qualitative analysis, these groups are not even wholly distinct from each other – human experience is not that easily divided up and there are overlaps. The pathways did, however, give a useful shape to the material. They produced what I think are life story patterns that practitioners would recognise. But they also made it possible to apply ideas from the research and theory to look beyond and behind what might be a specific story to generate theory to be applied to other foster care stories.

The purpose of the pathway analysis, therefore, is to look at how combinations of the various dimensions of continuity of placement, continuity of family membership and emotional security could help to conceptualise processes in foster care and to work towards a model that practitioners would find helpful in making sense of the stories they hear. In each of the seven chapters that follow, these dimensions are tracked, but they are also interwoven with other themes that interact with these dimensions: social work practice; stigma and care status; experience of education, employment and friends; the long-term consequences of abuse and neglect; the interaction of foster family and birth family. These were not headline issues for the analysis but they presented their own share of interest, and often surprises, along the way. It is to be hoped that this richness and diversity of issues can be addressed without losing the core threads that tie these stories together.

The seven pathway chapters will trace these key elements in the story across a number of cases. The shape of each chapter is chronological to reflect the developmental pathway approach and draws on attachment theory as a framework for understanding the process of interaction between the individual child and the social environment. It also draws on the patterns identified in the language of resilience, the turning points and the "chain reactions" that have led to upward or potentially downward spirals across childhood and into adult life.

In each chapter the key characteristics of the children will be described first, to clarify what the children in each pathway group brought with them to the foster homes. Then there will be an analysis of the various ways in which those characteristics interacted with the quality of foster family care offered in the caregiving environment of the foster family. The legacy in the adult lives of this interactive process will also be explored. Throughout there is a sense of how these adults mentally represent themselves and their families (birth and foster). The evidence available is entirely as seen through the eyes of the adults as they look back over their lives and so it will be their memories, the language they use to describe and define relationships, and the links to developmental theory made by the researcher that provide the core material on which the pathway analysis is based.

The final chapter of the book then offers a model of long-term foster care with associated messages for practice.

Confidentiality

In describing each pathway, quotations from the interviews are used to illustrate the different characteristics, but also to give a voice to the subjects. Their choice of language and speech patterns are reflected in the quotations where possible, with pauses indicated by ellipses. In very few cases have lines or phrases been left out of quotations, and then only to protect anonymity. It has been a particular challenge of this study to tell stories in sufficient detail to capture the fundamental elements without making individuals identifiable. Some valuable but rather too distinctive stories and quotations have not been used, in order to reduce the possibility of recognition. For the same reason, pseudonyms have been used, with at times different pseudonyms for the same person in some chapters or pseudonyms being alternated with indefinite labels, such as "one young mother". This does break up some of the stories, but it seemed to be a necessary cost. It may appear that some extreme examples, positive or negative, are identifiable, but in fact more than one foster father gave away his foster daughter at her wedding, more than one young woman had experienced the death of a sibling at the hands of a birth relative, and so on.

All stories and quotations are treated as respectfully as possible and have contributed to lessons being learned that will be used to enhance practice. It is therefore hoped that if any young person involved were to read this account and recognise themselves or their words, they would feel that the purpose for which they had participated in this project had been achieved.

Part II

Pathways

3 Close and special

Pathway summary: Continuous care, continuous membership, rewarding close relationships with foster family members and heartfelt gratitude to foster carers as parents.

This first group of adults went to their foster families from abusive or neglectful birth families, sometimes via other short-term families, and remained throughout childhood. They were close to those foster carers in childhood and saw them as their "real families" in adult life. The age at placement ranged from six months to 12 years. The families were busy foster families, with foster and birth children. These children had special status as long-term children, but a sense of shared fate with other fostered children, long and short term. They typically described their foster carers as offering a special relationship in which they felt valued and respected but also felt treated equally and as a full member of the family from the beginning. They often reported closeness to siblings, birth or foster, in the family. Most but not all referred to the carers as mum and dad and were treated as/described themselves as sons and daughters/brothers and sisters. This was true also for transracially placed adults of minority ethnic origin in this group. Relationships were seen as uncomplicated for the most part and credit was given to the foster carers as loving parents. For some the most powerful memory of family feeling was the sense of close relationships with the foster carers, but for others it was the range of close relationships within an intimate extended family group.

Although most had contact with birth parents, it was not highly significant emotionally. Contact had not been highly conflictual or anxiety provoking, although some adults described being let down or birth parents not really interested in them or family circumstances that would not have suited them. Such feelings reinforced their sense of the difference between birth and foster families. Care status was not a problem and they were matter of fact about it and the role of social workers. The key here was the powerful feeling of family and of fitting in and belonging.

Legacy

As adults, they had a fairly relaxed, comfortable approach to life and to themselves as people. They called on their foster carers and specific siblings for family rituals and special occasions and were clear about the merits of foster family over birth family. Continuing contact with birth families varied – some having no contact but others experiencing membership in the two families in parallel, with each serving very different functions. They were all in work or education or were full-time parents of young children. Life may not have been trouble free, but their capacity to cope as adults was consistent with the secure, special relationships and family ties that had developed.

What the children brought with them to these foster placements

As with children across the sample, these children had experienced a range of neglect and abuse in the birth family, which affected their presentation and behaviour at the point of meeting their foster carers. Neglect was a major factor, either as a consequence of general lack of care, for example, birth parents leaving babies and children unsupervised, or as a result of parental alcohol problems. The neglect, as they described it, could be associated with high anxiety or fear in the child when even supplies of food were unpredictable, when dangerous events ensued from the lack of supervision or simply because the lack of availability of an attachment figure for extended periods caused states of chronic anxiety which could not easily be resolved or defended against.

Where children had been neglected for extended periods, they had had to adapt and fend for themselves. Stephanie (25) had the experience of living with an alcoholic mother who did not offer availability or protection. She remembered wandering the streets looking for food and going into strange houses. She described being forgotten as a child.

> *My Mum would just forget, because of the alcohol because she would just forget to pick me up from school and I'd always know if there was a police car in the car park that it was there to collect me to take me home.*

Stephanie was used to going to neighbours' houses for food and perhaps company, which she remembers vaguely but favourably.

I can't picture myself going into the houses, but I can see like the open arms. Things like I can picture the parents – sort of willingly bringing me in.

The lack of support at home and the increasing sense of a need to rely on herself were reflected in her tendency to run away.

I must admit I've always been very, very independent and that may have something to do with the fact that my mother was an alcoholic – you get on with it yourself, don't you? I can't remember exactly how old I was but one day I put all my clothes in carrier bags put them in the pushchair and walked down the street. It was before I was nine years old. I knew how to run away and things like that then.

Stephanie presents this picture rather matter of factly, as she does her account of causing a fire and putting herself in danger.

I was being very careful. I lit a fire on a metal tray, like you do when you experiment when you are little. I put it out but I put it in a carrier bag and I tucked it in the spare room and it all set alight again . . . I remember that because I really tried to waken her (birth mother) up 'cos she was downstairs and I was shouting at her and I can see myself shouting – she just wouldn't wake up, she just sort of sat there mmm I can't remember how that resolved either . . .

This is a powerful "episodic memory" (Crittenden, 1995) and is used to represent the nature of that relationship and her childhood experience within it. This account of "seeing myself shouting", the unresolved crises and a mother who was unavailable, is also given without too much sense of feelings attached. Stephanie's story of the self as she entered foster care is of a self-reliant, defended child. She minimises the seriousness of the situation and normalises her own behaviour e.g. 'like you do when . . . you are little' as a way of dealing with the memory.

Experiences of fear mixed with violence in the birth family could lead to very quiet, watchful children, like Kay, who said that her mother had 'broken my arms and legs' and that she had spent most of her first year of life in hospital. But family violence could also lead to a more chaotic, less controlled or even violent child. Phil (30) had the experience of both being assaulted and acting aggressively, even as a toddler. He described his behaviour by way of an explanation for the fact that his mother could not cope with him.

> *I was mucking around with one of my brothers and split his head open. And I was only about two-and-a-half then – or three. And he was turning up to one.*
>
> So why do you think you were like that?
> *I don't know. I think it was something to do with my old man really.*
>
> Mmm.
> *He threw me down stairs a lot. I think that just turned me violent.*

It is not clear if this is a memory or is part of the story he tells about himself based on accounts given to him by adults, but it gives him both a simple explanation of his own behaviour and good reason to be grateful to the carers who cared for and coped with him.

Exceptionally in the sample as a whole, Patrick (24) reported having had some good care in his early life, prior to his mother's death when he was five. The memories are of episodes that left him with some experience of the availability of caregivers.

> *An excellent grounding. We kept very close, just her and me. She used to sit me on the back seat of her bike and take me back and forth to playgroup. I remember that and we had a show and tell and at the time I had a black and white panda bear that went everywhere with me and I'd left it at home and I was distraught through the day and the school phoned my mum at work and she went home to get it and brought it into school. That is my first real memory.*
>
> A nice memory.
> *Of her bringing my teddy bear into school for me.*
>
> So do you think you had a pretty good start?
> *Oh yes – I think that's where the basis was – I grew up – I got the*

grounding of the pleases and thank yous . . . the way to behave and what's the difference between right and wrong . . . so . . .

Do you have other memories?
Being in the bath when I was two or three and splashing about and when we were at St Catherine's there was like one post office selling ice creams and she was very friendly with the post master and the post mistress. And I used to take forever to tie my shoelaces and pretend I couldn't do it and she says, 'You do one shoe, I'll do the other and if you do yours quicker than mine you can go and get an ice cream down at the post office'. It always worked. She used to drive me to Greenview Primary School, the first school, the little one, and I remember her driving me there, picking me up, me running across the playground to meet her.

These are classic images associated with the dimensions of secure caregiving as defined by Ainsworth *et al* (1971). This is a mother who goes out of her way to be *sensitive* and to soothe a distressed child at school; a mother who *accepts* the child being needy of comfort or being difficult about tying his shoes; a mother who rather than get into a confrontation with a child is *co-operative*; a predictably *available* mother at the child's reunion after a separation. These are apparently random memories and yet not only did Patrick have the experience and the memory of those experiences, he also knew the importance of such experiences at an instinctual or feeling level and had selectively remembered them, another powerful "episodic memory". As an adult he can draw on this remembered model of relationships in addition to his good experience of foster carers.

Following the death of his mother when he was five, these caregiving experiences were replaced for Patrick by emotional neglect and physical abuse from his alcoholic stepfather. He reported frequent beatings by his stepfather, going to school with a black eye, and so on. He remembered, however, defending his stepfather.

There was one time he had beaten me quite badly at the flat in Queen Street, I'd got a massive adult's handprint all down my face and a black eye. And I was at school and I used to sit right in front of the teacher. And he said 'what have you done?' And I said, 'I fell downstairs'. And it was that weekend that I came into care and Paul (his best friend) *said, 'Your dad's knocked you about' – but I was still trying to protect him. I used to think it was my fault.*

So even for Patrick, by the time he arrived in foster care, his view of himself had become distorted and negative. Like the other children in this group, the move into foster care by strangers was still viewed with suspicion. 'I erred on the side of caution', as he put it. Uncertainty and anxiety about their own physical and emotional security were features for all of these children.

Although this group of children had not experienced sexual abuse, there was a range of neglectful and abusive experiences, in addition to the major separations and losses, which had shaped their internal working models of the self and the meaning they attached to the move into the foster family where they were to stay through childhood. Whatever the specific detail of their backgrounds, their models of the world and their mental representations of the adults in it were of people not to be trusted. Looking after number one, whatever form that took, was part of their survival strategy.

Foster family care

Warm welcomes

In spite of the difficulties presented by these children, their stories told of their arrival in families who greeted them warmly, made them feel at home, and gave them predictable care. Their notion of these families as real families is built on this sense of welcome that had to do with acceptance, warmth in relationships and, as will be explored below, family membership. These quotations from Sally (24) begin to capture the picture of this first experience:

So I suppose I was very shy when I first came here but . . . I don't know. Because it was a very friendly, homely environment, I just picked up on it so well that I just sort of let myself go as such and I just enjoyed what I was seeing and what I was doing. I just became happy I suppose.

I remember snuggling into a nice, warm bed and knowing that my clothes were at the end of my bed and knowing that really because the boundaries were there I accepted them because of the other things which I had.

For Sally, aged nine at the time of placement, the sense of warmth and predictably available caregiving in this first foster family enabled her to *let go* to some extent of the self-reliance and the barriers she had put up to defend herself from the experience of loneliness and lack of care. She had to give up her previous "freedoms", such as wandering the street, in return for the care and boundaries offered by the foster family. Woven in here are a number of other themes that come up commonly as the young adults attempt to capture for the researcher some idea of what they remember as significant. First, there is the sense of this foster home as offering *normal* "homely" family life, the first time that Sally had experienced this. There is an important sense that the world was predictable, not only in terms of the more abstract emotional consistency, but even at the concrete level of the clothes at the end of the bed.

The qualities of the new foster family were therefore a contrast to previous caregiving in ways that even as a child she could understand and perhaps appreciate or value. Although through the literature on children in care runs the important theme of loss, there was a sense here that this was more like a rebirth – in significant ways life, as Sally now knows it, began at that point.

Real mums and dads

Fascinating in the accounts given of what "families" of different kinds had meant to them was the way in which the language used had to be constantly modified and explained to the researcher, to ensure that meanings were understood. These attempts at clarity of language and definition of people and relationships within the interview seemed to reflect the way in which such definitions had to be thought through over time, as adults introduced themselves to others and told this same story of who they were.

> And how long have you been in this family?
> *Since I was two-and-a-half. Quite a long time really!*
>
> It is.
> *I mean I know my foster parents as mum and dad.*
>
> Do you call them mum and dad – and always have as far as you know?
> *Yes.*
>
> What do you know about the first two-and-a-half years of your life?
> *Not very much really. Only what I've been told through foster care. Mum and Dad used to own a pub – like my real parents – and things just went from bad to worse really.* (Craig, 19)

Here we see how Craig, in this opening discussion of the interview, talks of the people he "knows" as "mum and dad". He thinks of them that way, talks *to* them and *about* them (an important distinction in some cases) using that language. He mentally represents his carers as parents. But his contact with birth parents throughout childhood, and in adult life, means that they too have those labels. Indeed he introduces them here as his "real" parents. As the interview progressed and it was possible to pick up on Craig's terminology, the discussion settled on the term "parents" as consistently meaning the foster carers. It was then possible to return to the relative importance of his mums and dads. He talked, for example, of the importance of contact with his mother, whom he had seen quite regularly but who died of an alcohol-related illness when he was 14.

> Do you think it was good that you carried on seeing them?
> *Yes it was. Because if I hadn't I'd still be wondering now – if I'd never met her – what was she like? Even though I don't know that much I'm just glad that I was kept in touch.*

In his mind he separated out the different parents, but there were overlaps in terms of his sense of connection to both. Although he is clear that his birth parents did not make a good job of looking after him when he was a baby (i.e. he does not idealise them) nevertheless, they both had the capacity to be kind in different ways. The test in distinguishing between "parents" comes with important questions about the different roles they played in his life. It was his foster parents who were there when Craig needed an advocate at school because of his dyslexia. There is a picture of consistent availability and parents who were partial.

> So if you were upset about something?
> *I could talk to Mum but that was always Dad that was sent up the school. She'd be on my side whatever the matter was. I was never wrong. Unless it was something that I'd done deliberately and I got punished for.*

> What about your dad?
> *He's great as well. He helped me out with loads of things that I've got into really. Especially with school. He was always there to help me out.*

As an adult he had a meal out with his other dad (birth father) from time to time but lived at home with his (foster) family. A further test of this real family membership came when he moved out in his teens to live with a girlfriend's family but needed to come back, 'It was nice to know that if I wanted to come back I could'. When he thought about his future, it was this foster family who would be his family. As he put it, 'I'd never go out of the family – I could never see that'. But he also saw an ongoing relationship with his other (birth) dad.

> *Oh yes . . . I wouldn't shut him out now.*

> How does it feel to have two dads?
> *I only really know one . . . I don't know really . . . it's confusing . . .*

> Very different from each other?
> *Oh yes.*

> Which would you rather be like?
> *This one . . . If I'd never been taken into care, I would never have had the opportunities, you know, the comfort of life I have now.*

Within the concept of "family" in this group of adults is the sense that this foster mum and dad offered something special and the continuing presence of the birth parents in their lives was important but confirmed this distinction. The concept of parent has multiple mental representations but in ways that are not necessarily confusing – they are simply different models to those of children and adults for whom all parental roles are wrapped up in biological parents.

Other adults had developed a language for describing the process by which family relationships are defined and represented. In Luke's interview, he says of his foster family, 'I would *class* them as my family. More than I would any of my normal family.' Luke is not alone in using the word "class" as a way of describing for the interviewer the distinction between what the world might think or expect and the way in which *he* defines his close relationships. When he starts to describe the foster family he says,

> *There was who I class my brother, Jack. He moved in and my mum fostered him as well. And she had her own son, Richard . . . he's about six or seven years older than I am.*

The use of the words "mum and dad", "brother" and "own son" here play an important role, but for Luke, classification is by feeling rather than status:

> *Ever since I moved in I called her Mum. I don't know why but I suppose that's the way she made me feel.*

> Can you think of five words to describe your relationship with Maureen (carer) when you were a child?
> *Mother and son. She looked at me as her son and I looked at her as my mum sort of thing. Even though when you're 18 you officially leave care but we kept in touch. We go round there for dinner, she comes round here. She classes my children as her grandchildren.*

Perhaps it is in itself interesting that in a first response to this question taken from the Adult Attachment Interview, Luke offers not the emotion words that are more commonly offered as a description of relationship, but words reflecting *family roles* as socially defined. His first thought in expanding those role definitions is to talk about how they "looked at" each other, regardless of how others from outside might have "looked at" a foster carer and a child in care. The second is to mention the continuing relationship into adult life as being the "unofficial" but more "real" stage of being a family. This is rounded off with his usual use of the word "class" applied to his foster mother's view of his children in another social role, as "her grandchildren".

The long-term family membership and relationship continuity into adult life are reflected in many small ways in the interview and in particular in the choice of language. For example, this opening description of how one man's short-term placement became long-term is repeated later in the interview.

It was only supposed to be for a long weekend. Yes. It was supposed to be from Friday to Monday. I don't know what happened but I stayed there since – that's been a running joke that have!

The notion of "a running joke" suggests that this is a familiar, much repeated and much enjoyed, shared family story of the kind family members do tell about themselves when gathering with other family members and confirming their shared and inclusive identity. Here is perhaps the sense of the process of staying on as having been accidental, unplanned (as if he just never got round to leaving), even magical. Something happened, but they do not know what, that made this family his family for life.

It was common in this group to maintain the use of the mum and dad labels for both foster and birth parents, while having a clear sense of the differences between the two. The label "mum" and the special relationship with the foster mother that went with it is reflected on by Paul, who had troubles in his teenage years as a result of alcohol problems that led to some minor offences.

She still kept in touch?
Oh yes . . . I think more of her than I do my own mum.

And you always called her mum as you were growing up?
Yes. (roared with laughter) *Still do!! To grow up in her house, from the age of five . . . that's 24 years – can't sort of change it now and call her June can I? After 24 years!*

So her official role was your foster carer and yet here you are at 29?
Oh yeah!

So it's not like a social services thing?
No. It's like a mother kind of thing.

Paul was at boarding school after the age of 12, but his family membership and the strong sense of his foster mother as a "secure base" persisted. As an adult he lived independently in a flat and had a steady job. He visited his birth mother weekly to see how she was, but said that she did not show the same interest in him as his foster mother.

One of the tests of the foster family as secure base came when foster children became parents themselves. Whether this occurred while they were still living at home or after leaving and getting married, the ongoing support was critical. Norma, now in her late 20s, said that her foster father still popped in at the end of each day to see her children. Fiona, a teenage mother, found that it was the support of her older foster sisters as well as her foster parents that had helped her get past her anxiety about herself as a mum.

I always get worried because I think, will I be like how I am with my real mum, you know, distant?

The idea that foster carers went beyond their designated role was strong in several interviews. Stephen (24) when asked for his five words to describe the relationship with his foster mother said, 'It was what I wanted – a mother–son relationship'. Stephen didn't come to live with this family until he was 12 and he used their first names rather than "mum" and "dad". But he was specific about the feelings and the parental role that they had and still have in his life. Later in the interview he talked of how this relationship has worked out in his adult life. He joined the navy and his carers came for his passing out.

I was proud to have them there . . . my senior officer and that knew the situation and going for interview . . . he said who's going to be there for your passing out and I said, my foster parents, they haven't just deserted me – so they were there. I was one of their children. And that was a really warm moment – when I came home and they'd decorated the living room and they'd put up the pictures of their three children and they said, but where's Steve? So they put my picture up.

Yes.
And the three of them – always, Xmas and birthday cards – dear brother.

Really – yes.
And like Pat and Tony – cards and flowers for Mother's and Father's Day.

So that has felt like . . . ? You come to this family late and yet they have become your family in many ways?
Oh yes – set me straight, accepted me.

Stephen has a strong sense of family membership and belonging, which in some senses, perhaps because of the relatively brief period of childhood when he lived with them, has continued to evolve and be confirmed in adult life. The examples he gives highlight how different family relationships are in adulthood – it is often the more symbolic contacts, the phone call before the exam, the birthday card from her to him and the mother's day card from him to her, that reassure from a distance and create the sense of pattern, emotional availability and family normality. The relationship was also more mutual. They held each other in their minds and indeed Stephen expressed concern about how overworked his foster mother was with the disturbed foster children she currently cared for. He wanted to see himself as now strong for her, as a son should be.

Later in the interview, Stephen talked of how his feelings are those of a child towards his parents and of his gratitude, the hallmark of this group, that his parents went beyond the role of foster carer.

It's only my very close friends that know that I don't live with my mum and dad. I live with my parents, my guardians, the people I call my parents. This is definitely home and anyone who wants me comes round here. People in town stop Pat and ask how I am.

A family?
I'm just so grateful . . . as a 16-year-old joining the navy, being discharged from care, if you wanted to be graphic and black and white about it – they had no longer any requirements or duty by me or responsibility but they've always been – you're welcome.

And that's after a relatively short period?
After four years.

Yet in a way although it's not a legal thing . . . a relationship thing?
A moral thing – moral might not be the right word, but in all but legal – if you were to be bold and brash about it, strictly define my relationship, you could put it down to me being a tenant and Pat my landlady – I rent a room. But if I'm at work and I'm having a bad week – the stress of my apprenticeship, my exams, then I'll ring her and she'll say, try, if you don't try you'll spend the rest of your life wondering.

So you can ring her?
Oh yes – the first person I'd turn to.

Each part of this interview was packed with language and turns of phrase that illustrate how these adults are trying to find a way to explain to themselves, perhaps, as well as to the interviewer, exactly what this unexpected and culturally different relationship means to them. In the process they try to distinguish the commonsense view or cultural role definition e.g. "landlady", from the emotional significance of having someone to turn to and the sense of a mutual "moral" commitment.

The closeness of these relationships between foster children and parents often focussed on mothers, but fathers also played a powerful role. For Luke it was the sense of availability and shared activity which was at the heart of the rather traditional father–son relationship.

Frank used to, when he used to come home, he used to make sure he had loads of time to spend with you. He used to help us fix our pushbikes and then when we got older he used to help us. And he used to take us down to the docks all the time and I used to get to know people he worked with.

So he was away when he was working but when he was there his time was yours?
Oh yes. He wasn't one of these people who say, oh, bugger off and watch telly. If you got your scalextric out or playing cards or whatever

– he'd always find time. Even if it was, 'Half hour and I'll be with you' . . . but he always used to find time.

Luke also has childhood memories of missing his foster dad when he was at sea and of reunions, when the children, birth and foster, would watch for the boats coming in from the cliff top and run down to meet their dad.

When he was away we used to miss him. Like a normal dad . . . sort of thing. Used to look forward to seeing him when he come home. We just used to wait for him, stand on the quay and then used to run up to him with your arms open and that.

The feeling for his dad as a "normal dad" was mixed with his sense of him as a role model, a feeling shared with Patrick (described above).

I admired him I did. I wanted to be like him.

Belonging to the family – valued and treated the same as other children

Although relationships with carers were valued very significantly for the way in which they provided warmth and security from childhood through to adulthood, what was also central in defining a real family was the experience of being treated the same as other children – particularly birth children of the foster carers. It was important to be seen as equally loved and lovable with the message – 'You don't have to be a blood relative to belong'. As in Stephen's example above, having your photo put up alongside the birth children was mentioned by a number of people across the sample as highly significant. This kind of visible equality of treatment was seen as the test of how equally valued they were by foster carers, but also as a test of whether this was a *normal* parent–child relationship. The important element here appears to be the need to define the relationship in a way that relieves the stress or stigma of plainly not being a *real* i.e. biological or legal child of these parents, but in fact being legally the child of the local authority. The power of foster family relationships to build self-esteem and to shift the negative self-images brought from birth families needs to be associated with an ability to help children deal comfortably with their care status, their sense of difference.

Pete's foster family included a range of boys with different biological, legal and emotional relationships to each other and to the foster carers. There were also different foster care statuses, with some being long-term and part of the family and others being short term. Pete described processes in which family membership was defined and operated that shed light on the dynamics of "real families" in this pathway.

> *I was the first one she fostered. Before she had Jon she sat me and her other son, her own son, down and said we're thinking of fostering another child, what do you think? She classed me as family so she brought me into the discussion as well.*

Pete was five at the time but has the memory that he was part of the family that was taking on this new child and was treated as having feelings and views about it. The use of the language again here is pointed – her "own son" becomes her "other son". This is linked to equal treatment.

> *She treated you as her own sort of thing. Just like a normal mum would be. We didn't get treated no different. Because like she had her own son and we were treated no different to him.*

He explained that he would have to share his bedroom with any new arrival and that is why his feelings counted.

> *Instead of just getting someone and chucking them in with you, she explained to you.*
>
> That made you feel?
>
> *That included me – brought us closer like a family. She's a very understanding lady.*

When asked if he minded having short-term foster children in the family, he said that sometime he felt a bit of resentment but:

> *It didn't spoil our family because we knew who we were and she wouldn't say, 'this person's coming to live with us', she used to say, 'I'm fostering this person for two weeks or two months' – so we knew beforehand. I mean every time she fostered someone – it didn't matter how many kids she had already, she always used to sit us down and ask if that was OK.*

Here again there is an interesting semantic distinction between "living with" and "being fostered". The account that Pete gave was of parenting that made him feel a member of the family. In some ways the sense here of *them* and *us*, with the coming and going of the short-term foster children, reinforced the privileged status of the "us". Consulting the children was the kind of respectful parenting that clearly acknowledged his personhood. Again it was sensitive, accepting, co-operative and accessible as defined by Ainsworth *et al* (1971). The foster carer took into account the child's feelings and anxieties. In particular the sense of being both *understood* and *comforted* is real for Pete.

If you said something to her, she'd sit down and have a good conversation with you, ask your decision on things. So that if she asked you something and you didn't think that was right and said no, she coped with it, she tried to understand.

And if you were ill or upset, what would you do?
I'd go to her – she comforts you when you're upset. She helps you.

The slip to the present tense probably does reflect Pete's sense of this care as ongoing.

Apart from the memory of good things that were shared equally, the sense of equal punishment was mentioned as further compelling evidence of family membership. Tom had described how bad behaviour could lead to no dinner – just tea and biscuits in your room.

Did you feel you were treated the same as you grew up?
Yes we all got treated the same – no one got special treatment!

So he (birth son) would have got the tea and biscuits treatment?
Oh yes – and he was often grounded as well. They done it for all of us.

The fact that this punishment is done "for" them rather than "to" them seemed to suggest that such punishment was for their own good – so everyone had to have it. Although in some other groups strict discipline was reported negatively, discipline in this group was simply viewed as part of the strength of the caregiving, being associated with three other core elements – first, the foster carers were very emotionally available and protective of them; second, the strictness was seen to be fair and to have benefited them; and third, the carers were seen as treating foster and birth children the same.

Shared fate

Although in some senses more difficult to tease out, it did appear that adults in this group were generally quite relaxed about being "in care" and that this may have been linked with the busy foster family experience of being surrounded by foster children, at home and at school. Brother and sister relationships were often between two children, birth or foster, who took to each other or had something in common – being a similar age, for example. At school, older or stronger foster children from the same family looked after younger or more vulnerable children in the playground. Tom described wading in to protect his "brother" who was a similar age but smaller. For these large families it was not easy to be accommodated as guests visiting ordinary families, so their social life often revolved around other foster families. This also enabled birth siblings placed in different families in the area to meet and to see themselves as part of an extended family of "aunts and uncles".

These foster family patterns meant that having a social worker was "normal" and the fact that some were better than others was all part of the normal mixed hand that life might deal you – perhaps like having some teachers at school who were better than others. The good social workers stayed for years and sent you Christmas cards for years afterwards. The bad ones were those who did not turn up or who appeared to be pressing you to "dish the dirt", as one person put it, on your carers. But they were not central to life – that role was taken by the family itself and the membership and relationship continuity that were available.

Important in these pictures of what might have seemed an idyllic or idealised picture of childhood is the fact that the account was quite balanced and the mixed experience viewed again as "normal".

> *Every now and then we'd get on each other's nerves and we'd end up bickering and fighting. But it was just like a normal family. We treat each other like brothers.*
>
> So some of those relationships have continued?
> *All of them have really.*

Do you see more of your birth brother and sisters or foster?
I always see more of my foster brothers than my birth ones.

There are several significant themes here. First, there is the important recognition that life has its ups and downs, but these can be managed within a normal family as he felt his was – a key part of healthy emotional development. Second, there is the sense that the sibling relationships, which feature frequently in his and others' stories, are an important part of what makes this a "real" family – both as part of the evidence that the carers treated the foster children the same as their birth children and because these sibling relationships have been important in themselves and have continued into adult life – as they do in other families. The fact that he sees more of his foster than his birth siblings is another piece of evidence for Luke that important relationships are the ones that have intrinsic merit or are between people who grow up together rather than between genetically related children or adults. Even the possible stigma of care could be dealt with in this framework.

And what about friends?
Because I grew up in foster care, a lot of the people I knew at school were fostered or part of a foster family – and their friends got to know us – there wasn't a lot of people at school that I didn't know.

Was any stigma attached to being fostered?
You get the odd one every now and then but I never used to let that worry me because I always felt that I was better off than them.

So for you being fostered you said meant – a bigger family, outings?
Yes – I suppose it made me feel a bit more superior to the ones that lived with their own natural parents.

Did you ever wonder why, as you were growing up, why you couldn't live with your own mum and dad?
No . . . I don't think so, because I felt more happier with my foster mum and dad than if I lived with my natural mum and dad.

What is striking here, of course, is that the constant emphasis on what was "normal" about his family and the "realness" of family relationships and the family itself is only necessary because Luke must be aware that in society's eyes this is far from a normal childhood and a real family. In many ways these large, changing, busy foster families were some of the least like "real", "normal" families in the sample. Holidays for Luke meant a coach going to a holiday camp with other local foster families and having fun en masse. They had social workers visiting the house frequently. Birth parents were either absent or had something called "access" at fixed times. Yet the feeling was that this offered what he needed from family life.

Self-efficacy

Although much of the caregiving contributed to raising the child's self-esteem as a member of the foster family, the fact that this group turned into conscientious workers in adult life seemed to be something to do with the promotion of independence, self-efficacy and the value of work. Even the experience of being consulted about new foster children coming into the family was part of this, but so also were high expectations in terms of contributing to the family by doing chores and so on. Similarly, discipline was part of high expectations of behaviour but also fulfilling your role in the family. The fathers acting as role models also seemed to have operated in this area. But there were a number of specific examples of carers preparing children to be independent or confident in their abilities, an important resilience characteristic.

How confident are you in yourself?
I'm very confident.

Why do you think that is, when you look back?
Because I should say Mum and Dad showed me so many things and if I got stuck I knew I could ask them for help and they would help me. And they're not one of these people who take over and do it for you. They're one of these people who will tell you how to do it and then you do it . . . They'd never, if you were stuck or something, for instance if you got a puncture on your push bike they wouldn't say, oh fair enough, I'll go outside and fix it for you, they'd take you outside, tell you what to do and then you'd fix it while they sat there and watched you . . . that's why I'm so confident.

Pride in achievements was also used in adult life as a counterbalance to the threat of stigma. Patrick (23) talked about an experience of defending his care identity.

> *They're trying to put a stigma on it. There is a lot of stereotyping – to some extent there's a lot of prejudice. I had a run in with a middle-aged lady at a party somewhere. She said something sweeping – 'Kids in care, they grow up and they'll be robbing grannies and that' – I overheard – and I'm not exactly the most backward in coming forward person – I just turned round and said, 'Well actually, I grew up in care, I'm in the Royal Navy, I've been in six years. I'm the third youngest in my rank in a 45,000 manned service. And I grew up in care – what are you going to say about that?' She sort of stood there flabbergasted – I said, 'There are people in care who have horrible problems – but there are decent members of society.' And I walked off.*

Although foster families in this group appear to have met the emotional and family needs of the troubled children who came to them, one young man told the story of needing additional help as he hit adolescence. He saw an independent counsellor, whom he trusted because she was outside the system and whom he recommended to all children who subsequently came through the foster home. He saw her for six weeks only, but felt that it had turned him around in contrast to other attempts at life story work or therapy.

> *And I thought, because I'd been beaten as a child, I was going to be violent. And, that's the only way I know to deal with anything . . . playing up. The other children here, if they were annoying me I'd thump them – I was a bully, not at school, but it was raising concerns the way I was being at home.*
>
> So what was special for you about (counsellor)? You said it was not stigmatised like a psychiatrist – but what was it about what she did with you?
>
> *Friendly, relaxed, comfortable environment – you know. She didn't preach to me – I could open up to her, definitely in confidence there. She made my life like a road and said, 'Right, let's walk down this road together and tell me what you come to'. It was then me that come to it and I could get there in my own time.*

This group of adults were managing adult lives quite successfully. They were all in work or education and choice of employment often followed the employment patterns of the foster carers in terms of skills levels. There were skilled working-class families in which having a trade was valued and "grafting" for a living was expected. Adults from various families had gone on to further professional training and education, such as NNEB, business qualifications, nursing or a degree. Much was expected in order to conform to the family norms, but high expectations had beneficial effects in the context of emotional support.

Turning points

It seemed clear from these stories that placement in this foster family had been the major turning point of their lives. These had not all been planned as "permanent" placements, often starting off as for a weekend or short term, but as a result of the interaction between what the child brought and how the carers met their needs, the caregiving relationship *and* the sense of belonging in this family, the "placements" lasted to adult life. Although the arrival in this home was presented as having almost magical qualities, the gradual settling in as a member of the family also came across strongly. It was this developing relationship with foster family members, primarily carers but also new brothers and sisters, that appeared to have warmed up the cool children and calmed down the wild children. The effect of treating children sensitively, and with warmth and affection, providing a secure base while also setting boundaries, was to launch a chain reaction in which the children moved confidently into their own comfortable relationships with peers and with each other in the family. The striking closeness of older adults, women and men, to their foster parents seemed to be the most conclusive evidence of the way in which childhood family experiences had provided not only an internalised secure base, but also an ongoing pattern of supportive relationships.

Although the accounts given of close, special, individual relationships with the carers were often detailed and reflect the caregiving qualities associated with secure attachment, there appeared to be an added ingredient here for the troubled young child in terms of the foster family as a stable *group* which can contain all their complex behaviours and feelings. There is no talk here of excessive expectations of individual children, more the sense that, as in a small community, hard work, basic standards of decency, family membership and citizenship are taken for granted. The combination of the individual's experience of the caregiver's emotional availability and the support and values of the family group as a whole supported such resilience characteristics as self-esteem and self-efficacy, successful peer relationships, stable attendance at school and facilitated the move towards accepting the benefits and restrictions of the adult world and the world of work.

The thread running through these accounts was that of a paradox. These families were not "real families" in the usual biological or even legal meaning of that word. The constant emphasis on ways in which they were special and "real", as expressed in terms of the words "mum" and "dad" or being treated the same as birth children or just being experienced as "normal", simply confirms the difference from real families. Being grateful to one's parents does occur in ordinary families, but even that characteristic of this group reflects their sense of themselves as rescued children who were lucky. But this family *was* a special experience for them and somehow it had enabled them to become real people and to operate in the world with the knowledge that, whatever happened, like other people, they had a family to call their own.

4 Testing out

Pathway summary: Continuous membership, continuous care, family relationships are fairly close but children were "difficult" and credit is given to carers for coping.

This group was similar to Group 1 in having continuous care and membership in their foster families and remaining there throughout childhood. But there were a number of key differences. The adults describe themselves as having been more difficult and stubborn as children, with some conflict being more in evidence in placements. The foster families were also very different from Group 1. These were not traditional local authority foster families with multiple placements. The children were often the only fostered children and two went on to be adopted as teenagers in these families. They see these foster families as their family in adult life, calling parents mum and dad, but are less insistent on the notion of "real family". They report generally good relationships with foster carers, recalling carers as having high expectations, but themselves as having been difficult, testing, and some sense of being "coped with". They were more likely to feel different from adopted siblings/birth children. They valued the fact that carers taught them to be independent and gave them role models or middle-class lifestyle/aspirations. On the whole there is some sense of self-reliance, that they stubbornly did it themselves – decided to behave, work at school, and so on. Birth mother contact was absent or much more complicated, for example, involving mentally ill mothers, threats of abduction, opposition to adoption in this family, and so on.

Legacy

In adult life these adults are successful socially, but they describe themselves as independent people who do not trust others easily and continue to test out relationships in some respects. They are rather more troubled, with some anxieties about rejection, although they also have some clear strategies for dealing with these. They see their foster family as important, the place to be for Christmas or to provide grandparents to children. Where there is still contact with the birth mothers, they feel a little torn and guilty about how to meet their needs or perhaps control their involvement.

What the children brought with them to these foster placements

The combination of neglect and abuse in early childhood was not dissimilar to that described in Group 1; however, the addition of mental health problems in parents and some fundamental existential fears did seem to make these stories more alarming – both in term of actual experiences and, a key factor in any reflective account of childhood, as a story to tell oneself and others about one's origins and roots.

Laura had had the experience of serious maltreatment in infancy. By the time she entered her foster family at 18 months, she had experienced caregiving from her birth mother, a foster family, hospital and a second temporary foster family. The account she gave was that her birth mother had post-natal depression and added, 'It came out that my mum tried to take my life a few times – she was really unstable like that'. The fear of being trapped under a duvet cover, which she remembers from early childhood, could be traced to the fact that her mother was said to have attempted to suffocate her on more than one occasion. In the foster home where she went after being removed from her mother, she was neglected to the point that she needed extended hospitalisation. As she put it:

> *But they* (the foster carers) *didn't look after me very well. And they sort of left me in a cot and didn't take any notice of me. And they thought I had cerebral palsy because I couldn't really move my legs but that's because I hadn't been stimulated.*

The language here suggests a minimisation of the harmful parenting, she does not use the word neglect, for example, but the image of herself as an infant who was thought to have a disability captures the extreme nature of the situation.

Maternal mental health problems were also the major feature of Claire's history, although she too had a complex experience of maltreatment in that her father had physically abused her as a young child.

So you were quite frightened of him when you were little?

Sort of – but angry towards him as well. He was quite physical towards me if I was naughty or whatever. I used to get belted with a belt like – even by other members of the family. Like my godfather.

He would belt you?

Yes – because I would never eat my food – actually I remember that. I used to sit there and just not eat anything! I was a funny child really. Strange. I think my dad punched me in the stomach. I was living in the same house at that time and I was actually with my mum – because I used to sleep with my mum a lot – and he said I was actually making a noise but we were just going through a catalogue and he came in for no apparent reason and hit me basically – quite winded me. I think I was six or seven at the time.

Such children had either memories or stories of fear to defend against, although a disorganised insecure attachment in this "funny child" would have been a likely response to a violent family life.

Childhood selves in the foster home

The behaviours shown by these children in their new placements included a range of characteristics that would be predicted, using attachment theory, from such early experiences. Laura (24) offered a series of pictures of her very young self.

They said I had absolutely no attachment to anybody in particular. I would go to any adult. Absolutely indiscriminately – it didn't matter. I'd go to any adult. They had to keep a watch on me all the time because I would just disappear off and be talking to the nearest tall adult. But they said that when I came at 18 months I could fully bath myself and take complete care of myself.

This combination of self-reliance and indiscriminate approaches to adults from her pre-school days suggests that she has a defensive behavioural strategy, not surprising in a child who has experienced multiple carers, some hostile and others, as in hospital, constantly changing even in the course of a day. Although the context is very different, this pattern is not unlike Stephanie's account (previous chapter) of going to neighbours' houses looking for food when her mother was drunk. However, Stephanie was more self-reliant in her presentation, whereas Laura was more inclined to seek out others indiscriminately. Stephanie's experience had at least been consistent, allowing her to develop an organised defence, while Laura might well have been unattached, having had no experience of selective attachment prior to this foster family and effectively, as she put it herself, institutionalised. Adaptive behaviour in the hospital, where smiling randomly at strangers might have proved effective, can be a barrier to the development of attachment relationships with new carers, but also potentially a source of risk and danger. Fortunately her foster family was able to provide stable care for the time it took to build new attachment relationships in their family.

Laura's next image of herself in this foster home is as a child that used to steal and lie, not untypical in unattached or formerly maltreated children. Like several others across groups, she stole at school and at home.

> *I know at infant school I used to steal things a lot because I hadn't had many possessions. Really I did – they had quite a lot of problems with me . . . because I used to steal a lot.*

For Laura, stealing was not a random behaviour. She had an idea that there was a reason for it, that is to say she had not had possessions before. She also had a memory of planning the thefts.

> *I think I did tend to think things out myself a lot. When I stole this pound, I planned it all out really carefully. Like – I planned it with my friend what I was going to buy with it and the times I was going to do it and everything . . .*
>
> Yes.
>
> *It was really thought out and my mum's friend came round with a list of what I was going to buy and showed them this and said it was me, I'd planned it all.*

Although her behaviour might have appeared indiscriminate or impulsive, Laura as a young child had a purposeful approach. Although being a planner can be seen as a resilience factor, evidence of planning a theft must have appeared to the foster carers to be worse than an impulsive theft. What was being stolen or, equally significant, lied about i.e. food was also interesting, given her history of neglect in infancy.

I did lie a lot – especially about food. I used to throw food away a lot. They caught me throwing food away down the drain on the way to school. Quite sneaky I think in my behaviour. They used to make me toast and I used to put it behind the radiator.

The primitive need to survive is associated with physical rather than emotional need. The use of the word "sneaky" suggests again the kind of behaviours that foster carers find most difficult to deal with. The account though also suggests that as an adult she can reflect on the fact that she was not an easy child.

I don't know. . . but I did used to do sneaky things . . . I had like a hair dye packet and I dropped it everywhere in the bathroom.

But even with this kind of behaviour, which appears more impulsive than the planned theft, she can think about why she did it.

I think I was just curious. I think I did it because I wanted to know what was in this packet. After I'd done it I felt really guilty. Even while I was doing it I knew I shouldn't be doing it and when it dropped on the floor I felt I totally deserved it.

How old would you have been then?
Four.

She also thought through at the time how best to manage the situation to minimise upset to herself.

What was the foster carers' reaction to that?
At first it was real horror because it was bright orange on a white rug. Then they did say – don't worry about it because I did say I'd been worrying about it upstairs for two hours and, I could hear the television

and I'd been thinking, they're downstairs shall I tell them about it or wait for them to find out about it.

This account paints the picture of a child sitting thinking in response to stress, rather than panicking or running to a foster carer as a source of reassurance. Her thinking was productive in that by telling her carers that she had been worrying about it for hours they are disarmed and tell her not to worry about it any more. She demonstrates here a degree of mind-mindedness – a capacity, operating in a quite unconscious way, for "mind reading" and for anticipating other people's reactions and therefore being able to control the outcome. These incidents become in themselves small turning points – what was potentially a major incident is defused and Laura learns that this is the way to survive in relationships. But what they demonstrate is perhaps the thin line between "manipulation" and "planning". The former is generally seen as a negative survival strategy of maltreated children, whereas the latter is a productive source of coping and resilience in the longer term. This young woman proved to be a skilled thinker who also went on to significant academic success.

"Stubborn" was a word that cropped up several times in this pathway, but there was also aggression and anger in the mix. Rachel described her typical behaviour while with her birth mother and how this continued in placement.

So what kind of little girl were you when you were with your (birth) mum? If I had met you when you were seven or so?
Oh, strange apparently. I was a bit strange because I was living with a mentally ill person. Because she's schizophrenic. I knew that as normal behaviour so I was quite a strange person – well very quiet and into myself.

Were you? So if you were upset about something as a little girl, what would you do?
I don't think . . . something . . . I don't remember really . . . mmm . . . I think I tended to sulk quite a lot.

So you wouldn't tell somebody?
No. I'd go off in my own little world.

Although quiet and withdrawn as a way of coping, she was still an angry child at heart, needing to survive. Rachel described situations where she would manipulate and attack others to get what she wanted.

> *I used to try and pull Sheila's* (foster mother) *hair out – terrible. Horrible child – being very physical towards them. I punched Jack* (foster father) *in the stomach and he's actually got asthma. I nearly killed him or Sheila thought I'd nearly killed him. Terrible. Horrible child!! All that anger – I was that angry. Why towards them I don't know.*

Rachel's accounts of childhood here show her difficulty as an adult in managing this rather negative image of the self as a child. Although events were treated almost humorously, in the way that adults often do recall childhood misdemeanours with some humour, the anxiety of being like her mother she described as 'always there at the back of my mind'. Such anxieties make it more difficult to revise the internal working model towards a more positive view of the self.

Foster family care

It is important to consider then how these foster families dealt with and cared for these rather controlling children. The bottom line was that the placements lasted and the families offered continuous membership and relationships into adult life. The context of the family placement is relevant here. The foster families were not busy local authority foster families of the kind described in the previous chapter. They took these children to be part of their families, either with a view to adoption at some stage or with a sense of taking in this specifically needy child. The carers were approved by local authorities and social workers did feature to a greater or lesser extent, but they were not fundamentally part of the local authority workforce, available to take on allcomers. To this extent they were more like ordinary nuclear families with relatively closed boundaries.

The difference in the carers' motivation and expectation of this placement was likely to make an impact on the relationship with this child, but the differences from the first group in terms of the whole family experience for the child also came across as very marked. Such factors need to be looked at in more detail in order to understand why, in the face of a situation that more closely approximated "real families", they did not stress this as clearly as Group 1. Is it the case that when you *are* in a recognisably real family you simply do not have the same need to emphasise its realness? Or is it a more complex mixture of the child's personality and attachment strategy, the family circumstances and the birth family stories/contact that leads to this particular kind of adult description of the family experience?

All the young adults were asked a broad opening question about their foster families. Their responses often revealed interesting priorities in terms of what they chose to tell first.

OK, Lynette, could you tell me about your foster family?
They're lovely, like middle class – compared to my mum's it was such a difference. I went somewhere where there was loads of toys, playing instruments, helped me out with my work, at school. She was there for us. It was really nice!

Nice house?
Lovely house. She's still there – I've just been. Lovely house – big house and they were all like obviously more like middle class.

And you remember liking that then?
Oh yes – nice atmosphere. Ben (carers' birth child) *playing the piano.*

This answer reflects Lynette's pleasure in the sheer physical environment and the contrast to the disrupted, chaotic life she had led previously. The availability of the carer, 'was there for us', 'helped me out with my work' gets a mention but as a memory of those first impressions, the simple comfort and stability was of great significance. The sense of wanting to be like this family and belong with them is very strong here and elsewhere in the interview.

Your relationship with your foster carer?
Yes – argumentative – we still are now. Nice though – daughter... mother and daughter. She considers me her daughter...

How does her being like this affect her relationship with you?
Well I'm the kind of person who gives things up easily – and say I was

doing a hobby, she'd push me to do things. She pushed me to do things – quite an amazing person.

As a sulky but occasionally angry child, Lynette needed to be "pushed" to do things. This is seen by her as a potential source of tension, but also valued as a way of promoting self-esteem and self-efficacy, enabling her to do some of the activities that she admires the carers' own child for doing. These are defined as normal activities in a normal family, in contrast to her birth family experience, which was "disappointing".

You also talked about being disappointed with your mother?
Yeah I was. I wanted a normal family, normal relationships – although thinking about it, it's affected me for a very long time and still affects me now.

Does it?
Yes – because I do get very insecure.

Do you?
Although my foster parents I think are . . . I've never seen my mum as a role model. I see my foster mum as a role model because she's quite a strong person. Very strong person. And I look up to her. And if I have any problems, if I had any major things, I go to her not to my real mum because I consider her the person who has made me the way I am, really independent. I was quite dependent on her.

Although there was some encouragement to become active and independent, she could be dependent in the process. She was seen as the recipient of care in the parent–child relationship rather than as the caregiver, which had been her previous experience with her mentally ill mother. The "strength" of the foster carer was therefore necessary to take back the parenting role in a way that Lynette describes.

I was just glad to be there and for someone to actually care for me. I didn't have to have them depend on me – it was the other way.

So more like a child?
Yes. I got my childhood back.

Lynette is capturing here the essential paradox of a secure attachment relationship. The process of being cared for, being dependent on this strong carer was an important step to exploring, to becoming appropriately independent. However, important here is the theme, which is also key in attachment and resilience frameworks, that the caregiver actively promotes self-efficacy by encouraging the child to take responsibility. This process here seems to be less straightforward than in Group 1, which may reflect some differences in both the children and the families, but nevertheless the core mechanism is the same. It is a factor for Lynette, as for others in the sample generally, that being placed at 12 meant that forming the new attachment relationship was taking place at a time when separation was also imminent through the normal maturational process of adolescence.

The developmental task for Miranda was rather different. As a toddler she would go to any adult for attention or comfort and in middle childhood retained some of her controlling behavioural strategies. Not surprisingly there were family tensions in this context. It was not easy to define these complex relationships with carers.

> *So hard . . . mmm . . . I don't know . . . I really like them both definitely . . . yeah positive I'd say . . .*
>
> OK. So positive relationship . . .
>
> *Quite a lot of arguments. And she* (foster mother) *used to teach me a lot of things and I used to not want to learn them . . . So there was a lot of that. Mmm . . . I don't know. Oh gosh. She's my confidante – I tend to tell her things before I'd tell Dad. She will then tell Dad. Especially if I'd done something wrong. I'd go to Mum first . . . I just don't know. I mean, she was my mum . . . totally. Anne* (birth mother) *wasn't my mum.*

Here the two strands of her childhood were woven together as the conventional, rational and respectable foster family were dealing with or at least coping with this wild little girl, who was indiscriminately affectionate, who stole, lied and refused, initially, to accept the family expectations that she excel academically. But in attachment terms there is a clear sense of an available mother who was there to confide in. When stuck for words she also reverts to the "real" family discourse, 'She was my mum totally'.

Although the family feeling grew, the strains persisted too. This from Stella:

It was good, as far as I was concerned, how a family should be sort of thing do you know what I mean? It felt OK but it was put through a lot of strain obviously by the way that I was playing up and stuff like that.

Playing up was a problem in adolescence particularly, with concerns about the prospect of the girls putting themselves at risk through sexual activity. Alongside the fears about the inheritance of parental mental illness could come fears about sexual acting out and early pregnancy. As another young woman put it:

They were just in despair as to what to do with me. They thought, we've done everything but she's still like this . . . it must be in her genes, it must be natural, she must just want to go and do it whatever we say. But in honesty I wasn't thinking that and I hadn't done anything and I think that's partly why it worked out because I said to my mum, we had a talk, and I said for all that, I haven't done anything and I wouldn't. When it comes down to it I am quite sensible and I can see it's stupid. Because I said I know these boys aren't really interested and I could look at it like that. And I won't do it. I wonder now if I was just pushing them to see how far I could go because they had been so strict.

Such tensions were similar to normal adolescent conflicts, but with the added concern about genetic inheritance. However, her capacity to think and to talk things through with the help of her carers defused the situation enough for the placement to hold and for her to find her own way back, through academic success. This became a turning point for her.

Fitting in and belonging

Although the adults in this group do not use the term "real family", they described a strong sense of being part of the family.

Yes, all the family you would know if you were sort of born into it. Yes there was all the nannies and granddads and aunts and uncles.

Being adopted into the family at a later stage could confirm this family membership but was not essential to a feeling of family continuity.

Experiences of fitting in relative to siblings in the family were rather different from Group 1, especially where foster carers had high expectations or had own children who were very successful academically. However, it was also possible for these children, with their wild ways as one put it, to bring something fresh into the family – challenging but at some level to be enjoyed.

> *He* (foster father) *liked that I was very sociable, because when we used to go to church and everyone would be hello, here she is and I'd be chatting to everyone and I think he liked that because my brothers were a bit shy, a bit sensible. I think what my dad's always liked about me is that I've got a bit more emotions. I was a bit more impulsive, showed my emotions more . . . more tantrums and that.*

In this family it appeared that the goodness of the fit lay in the emotional complementarity and in the placement of a baby girl to follow on from their own two boys and complete the family. The family survived some difficult times together but she did indeed follow in her brothers' footsteps and went on to do a degree and then further degrees at university.

In some cases the differences between siblings became part of the bond, particularly in adult life when the rivalries from childhood were over and, as happened in one case, the foster carer's own daughter became a very fond aunt of the fostered adult's children. In adult life the sense of belonging was confirmed by the continuity of expectation that they were a member of this family, with all that this entailed in terms of family ritual and family availability. Many of the conflicts became resolved as difficult teenagers went on to become graduates, nursery nurses or wives and mothers. Battles between stubborn "mothers" and "daughters" became more of a family joke.

Birth mothers

One tension remaining for the young adults, however, was how to manage their birth mothers. Memories of contact in childhood contained some strong and uncomfortable images. This description is of contact with a mother with mental health problems.

On the way to see me she'd often been sick because she was car sick so she often smelled of vomit and she sort of came in her slippers in the daytime and she was dressed a little bit oddly . . . I just wasn't really very comfortable.

I see . . .
It was everything . . . her hair . . . was always wild and like she forgot everything – like in the house, she'd ask where the toilet was . . . six times in a visit – or where the door was . . . she was on a lot of medication so she didn't know where she was . . .

So as a child were you quite confused?
It was so strange when she came and I was always glad when she went.

This detailed description of Patricia's mother's appearance was accompanied by an account of the range of measures that were taken to protect Patricia from harm and, at certain points, abduction by another family member. In spite of the high level of supervision she had a strong memory of her mother secretly whispering to her.

It was a bit strange. When my mum used to come and visit me at my parents – my natural mum – she would get me on my own and say, 'When are you going to come back and live with us – we've got the room for you' . . . and . . . when she left. I used to say, 'I don't really want to go back and live with her' . . . and they (foster carers) *said, 'You'll be staying here, she's not looking at it very realistically'. So I knew really from a young age that she wasn't quite right in her mind.*

Here again we see the way in which even as an adult Patricia remembers how the foster carers helped her to think through the reasons behind her mother's behaviour in ways that did not threaten the child's self-esteem or the stability of the placement. The relationship with her birth mother was limited.

Did you feel you had a relationship with her?
Yeah . . . some sort of relationship . . . she really still thought of me as

> *her child . . . like close to me and I was coming back to her. But I didn't see her as my mum but as somebody I knew . . .*

In spite of such difficulties with contact in childhood, this was still a relationship in adulthood that needed attention, by phone at the very least. There could then be divided loyalties, as Lynette described:

> *I've always wanted a proper mum. And the thing is I feel a bit disloyal as well – I feel more as if Janice* (foster mum) *is my parent rather than . . . you know?*
>
> I see – and if you had good feelings towards Janice, then that feels like disloyalty?
>
> *Yes – and that's why it's difficult with my foster mum to show, 'Ooh I love you', to my foster mum. I never used to say that to her. It was somehow being disloyal to my* (birth) *mum – but at the same time I couldn't really say that to my* (birth) *mum because I was just angry about the whole situation.*

Feelings about childhood harms had been resolved to some extent, but just as there is no available cultural script for family relationships with a foster family in adult life, so there is no available cultural script for managing relationships with a birth mother from whom you had been separated by court order early in life. The extreme circumstances of their early years coupled with the lifestyle difference between themselves and their biological relatives added to the uncertainty of how to manage this relationship matrix.

As adults, they tended to mentally represent themselves as survivors and yet to minimise the parenting abuse and neglect to which they had been exposed. They wanted to move on and not dwell on the past. Their account of themselves as difficult or naughty rather than bad or disturbed children allowed them to feel that as adults they have simply grown out of the naughty behaviour, as normal children do, and are therefore able to face life on a level footing with other adults. This kind of switch was confirmed by foster families comfortably accepting and finding things to be proud of in their now adult foster children.

The extent of the switch from troubled child to settled adult seemed to vary to some extent, with the one young woman who had had a series of short-term foster placements prior to her long-term placement still having some questions about the "naturalness" of her childhood and her lovability in childhood and as an adult.

> *So even though you might not like things that happen or whatever it's just natural. Like now I would say well my past doesn't bother me sort of thing because to me it was my childhood, I didn't know any different when I was growing up.*
>
> So you had nothing to compare it with really.
> *Now I obviously know you are supposed to have like, well not supposed to but you know it's ideal to have like two parents, you grow up with them and that's it, but as a child you don't know that.*
>
> So it felt like a family, you didn't have questions?
> *No the only thing I used to think of was like sort of, I don't know, I suppose if you get a bit low or whatever you think well nobody wanted me, my natural parents, you didn't stay with your natural family sort of thing and then you went through foster families sort of thing and that wasn't necessarily that they didn't want you, it could have been that they were just a foster family or whatever sort of thing but you just think like nobody would want you.*

Even as adults the sense of an occasional need to test out others, especially in close relationships, remained but this is viewed as a difficulty to be overcome rather than as a source of depression or deep-rooted concern about the self. The fact that feelings had been expressed through the naughty behaviour of childhood and contained by carers had offered security.

Turning points

In these stories the point of arrival in these families was a clear-cut turning point in which permanence and continuity were on offer. Although the children's behaviour was difficult in a range of ways, this was weathered. The memories of childhood are more of a series of their misdeeds or battles, each of which might have led to a downward spiral towards placement breakdown but in the event did not. These are interspersed with the picture of carers not only offering a secure base, but also trying to move children forward academically and socially, away from the more destructive behaviours towards fitting in, not just with this family but in society as a whole. Children had been helped to manage their behaviour and their past memories. Even the difficult contact could help confirm family membership if put in context by carers. As in Group 1 there was a sense that they had been rescued from a difficult fate and introduced to a different lifestyle that had given them a new identity. Even being in care was worth it and ways could be found of explaining this away, as Laura described.

How did it feel you being in care . . . being a fostered child?
I didn't mind it.

School knew . . . ?
Yes – everyone knew – and people used to say, 'Oh that must be awful', and I used to say, 'No – I don't mind at all. I've got two mums.' And I used to make a joke – 'I get double Christmas presents' – and that was my way of saying about it. No I didn't think it was – I knew it was different – but I didn't think it was bad and probably Mum and Dad – I don't know if this is a good thing . . . but I always had the feeling that I was better off than if I'd stayed with Mum. Even at 14, I knew I didn't want to be with my mum and that wouldn't be good for me.

Perhaps the most interesting continuities are in the children themselves; the needy child, the wild child and the child who somehow rescued situations by the capacity to charm and to think. As adults, there may still be troubled thoughts but there are also strategies for dealing with them.

So how do you manage that, manage anxieties now? What do you do, Laura, if you are really worried about something?
I plan everything out very carefully. That's definitely how I deal with things. I get a piece of paper out and really – I'm very practical . . . I write – problem and solution. The only way I can manage it is to think out exactly what I'm going to do.

So that's your strategy, you sit down with a piece of paper . . .
I do speak to people – I have picked that out about myself. I am one of these people who likes to speak to a lot of people about my problems – sometimes indiscriminately – I really must stop doing that! But I feel that the problem isn't resolved until I've sat down with a piece of paper, no matter what other people say.

So do you think you are the most reliable source of an answer?
Yes – it's terrible! It sounds like I don't think a job's done properly unless I've done it myself.

It is possible to see some striking similarities to behaviours that might have appeared dysfunctional in childhood but had the seeds of quite functional, organised behaviour in adult life.

The differences between Group 2 and Group 1 may not appear great, since both offered security in relationship and family membership. Yet the stories in each pathway highlight the interplay of different factors in the child and the placement and differences in how, as adults, the self and family life are represented.

5 Distant and self-reliant

Pathway summary: Continuous membership, continuous care, foster family relationships are less intense or intimate. Foster carers described as caregivers rather than parents.

Individuals in this group had similar experiences in some respects to those in Groups 1 and 2, in that they too experienced continuous care in their long-term foster families. But here there is some sense of distance and separateness. These were later placements and although the sense of family membership in childhood continued into adult life, the family experience seemed less intense as recalled in adulthood with no strong sense of parent/daughter or parent/son as a way of defining the relationship with carers. There were few accounts of actual discrimination between children in the family, but a less explicit sense of sameness/shared fate than Group 1, even where there were other fostered children. Although attitudes to the birth family varied – one had rejected them entirely, another had had no contact since leaving at six, a third had consistent but unsatisfying involvement with her distant mother – the sense that the birth family was nevertheless their real family, for better or worse, is more persistent.

Although distance in the foster family was a factor in relationship terms, difference was a factor in social terms, with middle-class children with academic aspirations placed in working-class foster families and children of minority ethnic origin placed in white British families. However, these kinds of difference featured in other groups also, so that the interplay of emotional distance and social difference was not easy to unpick.

Legacy

In adult life they were socially successful – in responsible professional jobs (e.g. trainee solicitor, nurse, scientific officer) or a full-time parent and married to a partner who was in a professional job. Although the foster family is not described in adult life as "my real family", for shared family occasions such as weddings or a foster carer's birthday, they still join their siblings to celebrate. Similarly, when foster carers were in poor health or bereaved there was a strong sense of shared family concern. The unsatisfactory birth family and some distance/separateness in the foster family appears to have left them with the wish to distance themselves to some extent from the past altogether and start afresh as adults. There is a pride in independence and a tendency to take a sometimes resentful, sometimes regretful, but rather robust and even dismissive approach to the question of their past. Arrival in this family had been important in setting them on the right road socially, but key for them was the move into adult life – to be themselves more fully. As one woman put it, being an adult allowed her to make choices at last.

What the children brought to the foster family

The predominant experience described was of neglectful mothering by birth mothers who seemed unable to provide good care or emotional availability. The memory of childhood is reinforced by the continuing sense of a mother's negativity, 'She wasn't an attentive person. She never said she loved me at all.'

Anne could remember being left alone sometimes when her mother went to work.

> *I was on my own a lot of the time because Mum was working. My mum came home to see me sometimes swinging on the garden gate in my pyjamas and Wellington boots . . . but I mean . . . I was an eight-year-old.*
>
> And she was away all day?
> *Yes – and sometimes at night. In fact a lot at night. Yeah . . . I sat on my own a lot. I think that's why I hate being on my own at night really. A fear of being on my own at night.*
>
> So you can remember nights when your mum was out?
> *I do yeah. I used to absolutely hate it. I'd sleep with the light on. Very lonely.*

Her view of her mother was summed up as:

She was just somebody who shouldn't have had children . . . as much as it hurts me to say it . . . mmm. She shouldn't have had children really, but there you go.

The tone is one of sadness rather than anger and she has been able to reflect on and put her mother's lack of attentiveness in some kind of context.

I think my mum's had quite a hard life. (Really?) *Yes – when I look back . . . she's had quite a hard life. Some of it . . . I think she could have helped herself a bit but I think you go with the circumstances a bit.*

Similarly, Paula described quite sympathetically a combination of her mother's mental health and housing problems as the cause of her coming into care. She even took some of the blame herself for being a difficult child.

I have brief memories of living with my real mum up to the age of five and her giving me up for adoption because she couldn't handle looking after me because we were living in a one-bedroom house. She was a single parent with me and my brother . . . and I don't think we were the best-behaved kids possible.

Paula hung on to some more positive memories of her mother reading to her and looking after her. Even the point at which she came into care was described with tolerance.

I went to a children's home for a while after my mum . . . because I remember my mum shouting at social services that she can't manage her kids, she doesn't want her kids. And it was shortly before the time when she was evicted from her house.

So at the time, did you know why you'd gone into care?

Because basically my mum was evicted from the house and she couldn't manage two kids. Loads of people say how much of a hassle it is looking after one kid . . . but when you're not in a stable relationship and everything!

These more sympathetic images were not available for Nick who felt that his mother had had no excuse for rejecting and disowning him.

> *My mother was . . . not a good mother. I could certainly say. She was obviously more worried about herself than about her children.*

However, Nick's anger was mainly directed at the social services department, which had twice returned him to his mother from a settled foster home where he was making good academic progress.

Although these accounts were of neglectful parenting which could be construed as rejection, these adults seemed not to see the experiences in this way, but rather as sad or unfortunate. The impression left is therefore that they were not bad children and their birth mother was not a rejecting or deliberately unkind person. As stories, these seem to protect to some extent the image of the self as well as the image of the parent – my mother was not rejecting and I was not rejected and so I was not worthy of rejection. It is not possible to know to what extent this is a defensive strategy, minimising the blame and their own feelings of sadness, but what it led to seemed a robust and largely productive approach to life. However, the occasional intrusion of sadness into their adult lives (described below) perhaps suggests that there were personal costs and burdens to bear that have persisted from these childhood experiences.

There were some more extreme examples of frightening childhood experiences in this group, although they were associated with mothers' partners rather than mothers directly. These examples show how such memories linger as vivid images. Nick (29) described his memories.

> *We were put in care because her husband at the time threatened to kill her in front of us – knife at the throat over the sink in the house we used to live in. And I think we were taken into care . . .*
>
> Can you remember that?
>
> *Yes – I can remember watching that. That was something I do remember – I remember watching that. We were stood in the doorway while Graham I think his name was he held my mother down over the sink with a knife. He didn't do anything but very soon after that we were taken into care.*

Had he been violent to her at other times?
I don't remember specifics – but obviously that sort of thing sticks in the mind.

This scene was a memory of violence and fear which 'sticks in the mind'. It was not described by Nick as having had a permanent impact on his life, but his emphasis elsewhere in the interview on his "hardness", coolness and lack of emotionality suggests that this may have been one of the many childhood experiences that he needed to defend himself against.

A second example of frightening experiences was a young woman whose three-year-old sibling's death left a preoccupation with fearful memories.

My mum went off to work one morning . . . and mmm . . . I know it was in the winter . . . and mmm . . . he (mother's boyfriend) *got us ready and sat us on the floor and got our breakfast . . . and mmm . . . Owen, my brother's name was Owen, went to the toilet on the floor, just accidentally, and . . . I don't know what happened . . . And he* (mother's boyfriend) *just – I don't know, I just think he completely lost it. He picked him up and threw him, I remember him throwing him against the side of the bath and his head was just going back and forth.* (Right) *Yeah and the next thing I remember is seeing the sirens, the police siren going around the room . . .*

You were little then?
Yes – but I remember it clearly. My short-term memory's not brilliant but that incident . . . I remember how we were sitting and it was cold and it was early morning and it was still quite dark.

Such memories are not easy to live with. The picture remained in her mind over 20 years later and still demanded to be revisited and reworked, cognitively and emotionally. One consequence of that death was that she was sent away to boarding school by her mother at the age of seven, which proved to be the first step towards a more significant separation into foster care.

What these children took into the foster homes were therefore not experiences of physical or sexual abuse, but nevertheless they had anxieties and fears about what adults were like or were capable of and they had some difficulties in trusting. However, the lack of a clear sense of threat from the birth parents made the lurking question 'Why can't I live with my mum?' harder to answer. Paula described the distress she felt at the separation (at the age of six) from her mother, who had mental health and alcohol problems.

> *My mum had totally mothered me. I was on her lap . . . I didn't want to go to school. I wanted to stay home with her.*
>
> So if you had to think of five words to describe your relationship with your mum, what would they be?
> *Five words? I can say it in one, two. 'Very close'.*
>
> Very close . . . examples of that would be?
> *I was very clingy with her . . . I just used to follow her around. I didn't have a relationship with anyone outside my family circle. I had friends but . . . not best friends. My mother was the centre of my life basically. And I didn't understand what she was doing. I couldn't understand why we didn't go back to her. I used to cry really hard. I was crying and crying because I was only a little girl.*

Karen had a similar memory of being special to her birth mother and remembered how she continued to think she would go back to her.

> Do you remember what kind of little girl you were as a five-year-old?
> *Phew . . . I remember really loving my mum at the time but you don't know anything else . . .*
>
> So you remember loving her . . .
> *I remember I wasn't that upset . . . when I left her because I always thought I was going to go back to her. That's what I was told by social workers, that I was going back to her, and I was really upset . . . when eventually I got round to it . . . 'When am I going back to my real mum?' And someone said, 'You're not'. Like it wasn't explained to me. I think it should have been explained to me.*

Right.

I never grieved because I thought all through those years . . . I was going back.

There was an interesting contrast between those who were not upset because they held on to the idea that they were going home and those who declared that they simply did not care.

It depends on the individual. Some children come into fostering and they are vulnerable and want to be with their parents. But I didn't care so I did better.

This coolness and control was often associated with a child who was "good".

I must have been the perfect foster child because I wasn't – I didn't go off the rails, never in trouble – after the bit of shoplifting at Carol and Jeff's, never in trouble. I never used to steal from anybody, I never went out vandalising things, I was good. Better than some of the other foster children.

Did you get on well with any of them?

I used to get on with them – but again I was the snobby one – Martin – we see more of each other – our families know each other but I was always the posh one.

The not-so-hidden agenda here appears to be that he was different and felt both proud of it and a little isolated in the foster family as a result. He described himself as having been a "dungeons and dragons" kind of boy, but had found friends who shared his pleasure in such games.

The overall picture is of children who kept themselves to themselves to a greater or lesser extent, whether because they hoped to go home or because this was a defensive pattern brought from the birth family or because they felt different from other foster children or from birth children. The tendency to be self-reliant as a strategy had to some extent been forced on them by the circumstances of their birth family caregiving, but had been reinforced by the subsequent moves into foster families, where they were comfortable but not entirely emotionally committed.

Foster family care

Since this group turned out to be successful socially, academically and in career terms, credit was often given to carers for offering the security and stability that had made this possible – even if it meant reflecting at the same time with mixed feelings about what should have been available from birth parents.

> *I was given an opportunity when I was taken into care to have a normal decent life. To go to school, to go to college, the works. I wouldn't have had that when I was with my mum. But it also gave me the insight to see how she is and that it's not her fault. I think she's probably ill.*

This attempt at balancing blame with sympathy and understanding or forgiveness perhaps shows how this group have been able to use their ability to think through their past, to have insight, and come to terms with it, in some sense, to integrate the good and the bad. That perspective is in itself made possible by having foster carers who could act as sounding boards in developing reflective capacity. In the area of contact, for example, it was helpful when carers could talk though feelings.

> So do you think your foster carer helped you understand about your mum's situation?
>
> *Yes – definitely. I used to get upset, I used to talk to my sisters or go and sit with Trisha* (foster mother) *and talk to her. She talked me through it. I'd say, why is this happening, and she'd try to explain as best she could – or just give me a hug. Because that's often what you need at that age. But she used to be like my mother.*

For this group it was clear that one task of childhood in foster care had been to manage memories, ideas and a sense of connectedness with the birth family, while deciding how far to accept the offer of connectedness in the foster family. For some, including this young woman, even when there had not been a very close parent–child relationship with the carer, the foster carer played the parent role when it was needed.

At times, this delicate balance between family loyalties could be threatened by a lack of acknowledgement in the foster family of the previous life. For Jodie, subsequent adoption by the foster family was not particularly welcomed and contributed to what she saw as the family myth about her lack of a relevant birth family.

> *Everyone at home thinks – my present adopted family – that I didn't have any other family before I lived with them but that's not true.*
>
> So your foster/adoptive family didn't know much about your history before you came to them?
>
> *No – they do but . . . but they don't accept that I have a past life – it's like my life starts with them.*

It is impossible to know exactly what parts of her history (e.g. the fact that she was transracially placed) led to her sense of distance in the placement, but the quality of relationships with the carers was often strained.

> *She's very, very intelligent but very overpowering. I've got to be quite honest . . . I feel awful saying it because they have probably done their best for me over the years living with them but I don't think I have much of a close relationship with my foster parents. And that's being honest.*

That fear of being "overpowered" by carers and losing oneself was not unique to this group but did seem to link with the need for distance, which may have come from the birth family experience or from an interaction of a relationship past and a relationship present. For Jodie, the fact that the self was tied up with her birth family needed to be acknowledged. However, although there was some distance from carers, she did feel part of the foster family as a whole and enjoyed the other close relationships on offer with the siblings. So even for this young woman in this foster family, the sense of belonging is still significant. She said, 'I love my (foster) sisters implicitly'. She also felt part of the extended family, being very fond of her grandparents.

Lack of closeness could sometimes be associated with the sense that carers were not real parents for the foster child in the way they were for their own children – not because they treated the children differently but because it was simply not possible for that person to be a replacement "mum" or "dad" for someone who was not biologically a son or daughter. As Miriam explained:

> *I wouldn't say close. I can't say I had major fallouts with him* (foster carer) . . . *funnily enough, I remember thinking the others* (foster carers' children) *were so lucky because they had a dad and called him dad. I had never called anybody that. I just remember this tall person and the fact that they had a dad.*

However, even carers who were not emotionally close or "real" could still be given credit for the good care that was offered. This same foster father offered certain values and support in the face of racism, an issue for this young woman transracially placed and growing up in a particularly racist area.

> *But he was very fair and very kind and he gave us a very strong work ethic. I remember him being very good to me one day. It was when the "Roots" racism thing was happening and he said, 'I don't want you coming home crying tomorrow. You're black and I want you to be proud of your colour.' And I shall never forget that. He said, 'I want you to go in and hold your head up high.' They were both really positive about that.*

As well as such valued features in the carers themselves in terms of building self-esteem, there were advantages in the families in terms of the activities that children were encouraged to do. One young woman spoke enthusiastically about being 'such a busy teenager', doing ballet, swimming, horse-riding with other children in a busy family, 'It was brilliant we were all doing things – we all pulled together – we had to'.

There were some interviews where the language to some extent picked up on the "real families" discourse. Harry described his foster mother as 'the salt of the earth'.

> *They were really good – my happiest memories were with them . . . Excellent. They were perfect foster parents in my view. The house was bigger – we all had our own room. It was . . . perfect. If every foster parent was like that . . .*
>
> So what were they like as parents?
> *They treated us the same as their own children.*
>
> So that was important?

Definitely. There was never any favoritism. We all got the same money spent on us at Christmas and birthdays. They weren't worried if it was going to cost more than what they got from social services – that didn't matter to them. They were very happy that all the children in their care were treated equally.

Can you describe your relationship with them?
At the time it was very good. Personally, I'm somebody who doesn't bond well with people. I'm not an overly affectionate person – I never have been.

The sense of distance or coolness between child and carer was attributed by Harry to his own personality. He saw his coolness as a protective factor in his childhood and he contrasted his brother's preoccupied need for contact with the birth mother and displays of emotion as contributing to his brother's route into a lifetime of trouble of all kinds.

Whatever happened I'm hard and I don't let people in because of what happened to me. The only way I've survived as well as I've done is because I didn't let my emotions get hold of me like happened to David. He's an emotional child, he was an emotional person, and he couldn't cope because of it whereas I coped, maybe to my detriment in the end – maybe. I'm hard.

His choice of terminology was another way in which he established his definition of relationships.

I'm sure she (foster carer) *loved us. But I . . . as I say . . . I'm very wary of using words like . . . because I'm not overly a close person to people.*

So that would seem strange?
Yes – I would never call her mum – there was nobody I would call mum. Mainly it sticks in my throat to even think about my own mother as a mum. I don't like the word. Personally I don't like to use the words. I speak to Sam (son) *when he goes to bed and say – go and see your mum, but if I have to say to somebody about my "mum", I find that difficult. And conversations with people – and sometimes at work when I was still living at Rachel's* (foster mother's) *and at work you*

talk about your mum – I say that and have to clarify it – she's my foster mum. I don't like to use the word to be honest.

It is in these small ways that the task of coming to terms with the word and concept of "mum" caused difficulty to this man, as to adults in other groups. "Mum" may be too special a word to use for the carer, may be associated with abuse or neglect and therefore be an insult to the foster carer – or may simply already be attached to one person i.e. the birth parent, and is therefore not available for another.

Some adults could acknowledge that the definition of the parenting role was an equally difficult issue for carers. One young woman described her carer's feelings when, as an eight-year-old girl, she had arrived in the family.

She thought, 'It was so lovely to have my own little daughter'. But she was realistic. She was a realist. She knew I wasn't theirs. Well possibly not to stay. I wasn't her daughter.

In this placement, it was accepted, even by the foster children, that this foster mother would prioritise her own child over the foster children, and would fight to define and defend her own territory – her own food and toiletries, for example.

So with Audrey (foster carer) – words to describe the relationship – "strict" you said and "hard"?

Very hard. I lived with her. I get on with her lovely now but I used to hate her when I lived there. I loved her and she used to comfort me and she became my second mother, but I partly resented her because I was with her not my mother and she was very strict and I didn't like that. But in the long run it's been very good because now I don't have to live with her, I don't have to do things her way. It doesn't matter if I use someone else's toothpaste. She was very territorial. I don't have to put up with that now so I can see the nice side.

There seemed almost to be a battle for selfhood here, with the carer being as anxious about being overwhelmed by the demands of the children as some children had been anxious about being overwhelmed by carers. Defending the self in this way contributed to distance. But so also did the child's continuing feeling that 'my second mother' could not replace 'my mother'. The blowing hot and cold in this account reflects the love–hate, close–apart, real–not real, hard–soft, nasty–nice dualities that have to be lived with and managed. This description also suggests how, in foster families, like adoptive and indeed birth families, relationships continue to evolve in adult life and, with luck, past hurts can be healed through the benefit of age and a little distance. In this group, though, there was enough of a memory and an experience of a secure base in childhood, in spite of the complexities in the relationships, to build on as they worked towards different adult roles.

Adulthood

Although people in this group all continued to have relationships with foster families in adult life, there was not the same sense of intimacy or sometimes dependency that was in evidence in the first two groups. Sandy described how she broke out and was on her own.

> *Then at the age of 18 I went to Birmingham . . . I feel really awful because this was a period when I had a first big major falling out with my foster parents and I can't think to this day what happened . . . we had a row and it was one of those rows and I didn't call them up and they didn't call me up . . . and it was like three years had gone by . . .*

Where foster carers had been experienced as overpowering it became important for young adults to assert themselves. Jodie said, 'I just found a job as soon as possible and got out'. In both cases though, these experiences of breaking out were not total breaks – for Sandy, during that three years of separation, mutual friends made sure that each had news of the other. Although the job took Jodie away from the area where her carers lived, she still went back for family occasions and Christmas. It was perhaps also important for these two young women, both of minority ethnic origin and in transracial placements in white communities, to find themselves a niche in more multi-ethnic communities. Race and racism had been an issue for them, especially at school, and black culture was something they were both now more comfortable with in adult life.

Getting a good career had clearly been an important goal for all young people in this group. It was not easy for them to be sure that the career was the right one, but nevertheless it was impressive that there were young adults who had either stuck at education, going on to skilled or professional training and university, or had since returned to education at an advanced level after having children. The career could offer self-esteem, but also new kinds of supportive relationships. Harry described his laboratory work and how important it was for him to work in a team, a structured environment for relationships.

> *Although I'm a loner I do need a quiet nudge now and again. If you're working in a team you're getting the support from the others.*

Choice of education or career route highlighted some differences between foster children and carers. Harry had academic expectations of himself that were not part of his foster family culture. Unusually, it seemed, he had been influenced by time in a previous foster placement from which he had been returned home. In this previous placement the foster mother had encouraged him to use his intellectual ability to achieve academic success. Although some of this momentum had been lost when he was returned home on two occasions, very bad decisions in his view, when he finally came back into care to stay, it appears that he hung on to these expectations and was the only foster child not to take the skilled manual route more common in his foster family.

Another unusual story was of Julie, a girl from a middle-class birth family where the mother had mental health problems. Julie and her sisters all went to university, untypically in their working-class foster family. More remarkably, she told how the foster carer's birth son had left school to get himself a trade, as expected by the carers, but after visiting his foster sisters at university decided to take that route himself and was at university at the point that the interview was conducted.

Although self-reliance and building a life for themselves in adult life was very much a theme, there was, as with more damaged individuals in other groups, still a certain legacy of childhood experiences which showed itself in nagging anxieties or a lack of confidence. One young woman had experienced not only feelings of isolation and lack of love in her birth family, but went on to experience extreme racism in the school and area where she lived in foster care. These blows to her self-esteem had persisted to some degree.

I had the experience of being bullied and . . . people think that it's just harmless fun but it can be very damaging – it is very damaging and it can last for a very long time well up into adulthood. And I think because I wasn't a confident child at all, I was really insecure, and I'm not . . . people say to me, gosh, you're so confident, but it's just a bit of an act. I'm a lot more confident than I was ten years ago.

At times those anxious feelings still came back to trouble her. Her representation of self as lovable was still a little shaky when she reflected on her difficult childhood. But she had gained in confidence during her 20s and could describe how being married and having children had given her a positive identity within her own new family.

Similarly, another young woman (age 21) who had been pleased to find "independence" in her nursing training struggled at first.

You know, the insecurities, thinking about this and that, having the need to be wanted and everything . . . That never occurred to me until I reached 18. I've gone through . . . it's taken me till last year to grow up and progress a bit further and make me a lot more stable . . .

So something important happens between 18 and 20, 21 then?

Yes – but that happens with everybody.

Her last point, that this is a normal experience, is important to remember and is an important part of reflecting, thinking things through. Here it is significant that this is the young person's perception. She explained how she felt that separation, being fostered and then adopted had had a "huge" effect on her as an adult. Her birth mother had not maintained contact with her.

I do have my depressive moments, that I don't know why I'm so down. That could either be me or my background. I don't know but I wouldn't go to a counsellor to drag it all up because you end up feeling worse!

The nagging doubt, 'was this a normal anxiety or did it have its roots in the poor care and uprooting of early childhood or in the fact of being a foster child in care?' was another perplexing and finally unanswerable question that all of these adults had to face. However, in common with others in this group, her response to these feelings is to try to "pull herself together".

The robust approach did not always work. One young woman described waking up crying and being simply unable to cope – again picking up on a common theme that in waking hours you could devise strategies for dealing with unwanted feelings, thoughts or memories that intruded into your life, but in sleep the unconscious had ways of throwing you and threatening your hard won composure. Feelings of being "troubled", "down", a "real worrier" were often described, but as adults they wanted and needed, for the sake of their careers or their current relationships, to keep these feelings under control. Two young women had eventually approached a counsellor to get help with this control, but found that it had the opposite effect – it 'opened up wounds that were too painful'. This is one of several similar accounts of trying to deal with depression and anxiety through counselling.

> *And mmm . . . I just found it very hard because I'd go in there (for counselling) and I'd just end up in tears and I'd come out and I'd have to go and pick up the children . . . I just couldn't cope with that . . .*
>
> So feeling overwhelmed?
> *Yeah – I found it quite hard – I do have moments when I do get down but not too much. I try not to think about it or I'd be permanently down . . .*
>
> Yes.
> *Now talking about this to you now my life sounds like one big sob story . . . I'm not trying to portray it like that but that is how it was. The reality is – that was my childhood.*

The themes that 'I haven't got time to grieve' and 'if I think about it I'd be permanently down' reflect the difficulties of fostered adults with such experiences of loss. However, unlike some adults in the next group, they do allow themselves to have memories of the reality of their childhood. The tendency to try to push it to one side in order to get on with life has not been associated with a pathological lack of memory. Although the pain is there, it is linked to specific events, losses and people rather than being in the form of intrusive but entirely nameless fears. To that extent, reason allows them the capacity to think through the memories – even if that thinking leads on to some degree of defensive exclusion, putting things on the emotional back burner to be dealt with later.

Partners and parenthood

The impact of these experiences in birth and foster families and the psychological strategies for coping with them could be traced by the adults in their accounts of their current relationships. Harry, who had described himself as emotionless and hard as a child, had found a partner in adult life who gave him an experience of a different kind of relationship from the good care but rather detached relationship he had with his carers.

> *I don't think I had a close relationship with anybody until I met my wife to be honest with you. That's the honest truth. I don't think I've been close to anybody that I can remember. Joan and Fred gave me a stable home, somewhere to live, all that I needed and were there when we needed them.*

In his relationship with his wife he accepted that his "hard" man, self-reliant image was now in the context of emotional dependence.

> *I rely on her for everything really. Emotionally I rely on her – but then again I'm not an openly emotional person – that sometimes gets me – I can't show emotion. She's the only person I can cry in front of.*

Some people fled from this kind of dependence and needed space, which created other difficulties. The experience of being on your own as an adult could in some senses be seen as liberating – especially where adults had felt constrained while being "in care". Succeeding on your own was evidence of self-reliance and the fact that other people were not needed – but it led to a tendency to end relationships when they seemed to be leading to commitment. One young woman was moving to a different area for a new job and was looking forward to a break from a close relationship. Paradoxically, insecurity led to the need to get away.

> *I am quite an insecure person. I can be quite strong and don't show it and I try to build my security up so I can't see it taken away. My mum went, my sister went, my dad went – if you get my meaning – my career, for example. And I like living on my own. I'm looking forward to moving, I like my independence. I like being single. I like to know I can make it on my own whereas my mum couldn't. I'm not doing it to spite her. It's just they're all signs of insecurity.*

She has anxieties about talking with people – and yet struggles with the question, perhaps this is just normal? Or is there something wrong with her?

> *When I'm talking to my boss I talk like I do to you but inside I'm thinking, is it all right? Does he think it's OK? Do you know? Maybe everyone's like that.*

Insecurity could lead to dependence or to self-reliance. Links were sometimes made back to childhood – if things had been different maybe this insecurity would not have been the legacy. But the aim was to minimise this by both normalising and looking firmly to a future of self-reliance. Perhaps in adult life there comes a point when moving on and drawing a line under the past is necessary.

> *I just want to show that . . . anything that happens now in my life I can't always put down to my childhood. I make my own mistakes and it's down to me personally and individually. I wish I'd been given the right start in life and I wish that . . . and I just came to the conclusion recently that it is just pure luck who you are born and how your life is going to be . . . I think that's the only way to look at it, I really do. I think if you are lucky enough to be born to parents who are able to look after you and love you . . . but unfortunately I wasn't.*

Parenthood would bring new dilemmas that connected with both the determination to "get it right" and the anxiety about why it was that some parents did not or could not. Although this group had experienced continuity in care and had confidence in some areas of their lives, fear of being like their own parents raised important questions and brought them back to their sense of how different it felt when you had not been brought up with your "own" parents.

My foster mum said, 'You won't turn out like your mum and your dad.'

Was that your fear?
Yeah . . . and like I remember thinking – how can some people have children and love them and other people have children and don't love them? At the end of the day, one of the common factors for children in care, they're all in care for different reasons, but one factor is that they can't live with their parents and that's one of the factors we all share, we all have together. I just remember I felt different from my sisters – apart from colour wise . . . they were with their mum and dad.

Here we see that being treated the same as birth children may not be enough for some children who have their own sense of the significance of the birth/non-birth distinction. The anxiety about performance as a parent was tied to this sense of connection to the birth parent who did not care for them enough – would they be a parent who could not love enough? This could lead to close bonds but high anxiety, even in those who prided themselves on their "hard" exterior.

Turning points

These foster families had provided family care through childhood and family relationships into adulthood. Carers were described as proud of how well these adults had done and were given credit for the way in which encouragement at school or just stability itself had made a contribution to success and stability in adult life. Some of the emotional distance and self-reliance could be explained quite simply as an avoidant defence that had proved rather protective in childhood. In adult life, moving on from such difficulties and relaxing such defences was necessary for partnerships, marriage and parenthood.

Such distance as there was in the foster families, the lack of emphasis on real families, needs to be seen in the context of the way in which these particular adults were negotiating their relationships with two families – birth and foster – if not on an everyday practical basis then in their minds. Where the older children had had powerful memories of relationships in birth families, whether good, bad or mixed, the foster families took on a different kind of role. They provided emotional and social care, role models, encouragement and a sense of family membership – but were not defined by the adults as "real families" in the insistent way described in the first group.

However, it may be that this more diffuse, negotiated and evolving relationship with both foster and birth families had its own merits. These were children/adults who were still troubled to some degree and yet they had got a pretty firm grip on their lives and knew what they wanted to achieve. They allowed themselves to reflect on the past, showing appropriate signs of sadness, anger, resentment and satisfaction. They had a fairly balanced view of the merits and demerits of birth and foster families. Their capacity to reflect on their own strengths and weaknesses freed them up to make choices to some degree. They struggled with the big questions – Why me? Are my feelings normal? But even when reflecting on the distance between themselves and the carers, they could acknowledge that there are variable degrees of closeness in normal families. As one young woman put it: 'even with natural parents you might never have that much of a bond'.

The availability of a stable (foster) family in childhood and access to parent and sibling figures in adulthood seemed to help normalise their lives. They may have brought different expectations regarding academic ambition, for example, from a birth family or previous foster family, but it was this foster family that made the achievement possible. Permission to keep the birth family in mind and in their lives was also helpful. They could keep contact with birth families, but know that they always had a place in this other family, the foster family who wanted to hear from them and cared about their welfare. Self-reliance had its advantages, but the foster family as a secure base, socially and to some extent emotionally, was still an important part of their lives.

6 Anxious and fearful

Pathway summary: Continuous membership, continuous care, positive relationships with/gratitude to foster carers as parents BUT anxiety/ fear/feelings of helplessness persist.

From a simple chronological point of view, these adults had similar experiences to the first three groups in terms of continuities of care and family membership, once they reached the family that is still their family in adult life. However, although these foster families are regarded warmly and the real family discourse applies, the serious harm in the birth family appears to have made it more difficult for the foster family to entirely heal the hurts, to right the wrongs. These interviews were sad accounts of serious physical abuse and/or neglect or being singled out for rejection in the birth family. All the histories had left them feeling unlovable, and in some cases frightened and alone, when coming into care and in some senses these anxieties persisted in adult life. The care-giving in the foster family, although mostly described as positive as in other continuous care groups, had not been able to restore their faith in themselves entirely or truly enable them to feel safe. There were accounts of being victims, bullied at school or by a sibling. Distinctive here is the tone of voice in which the story is told, which was highly anxious, helpless and, sometimes, hopeless. Although there is the sense that the parent–child relationship existed with carers and was important, it had not liberated them to security and mental well-being. Carers are described with some sense of them as parents but without detail – there was no vivid sense of the carers as complex people in their own right. They existed – rather as the adults themselves existed. For these adults, the minds of other people are rather a mystery.

Legacy

Although superficially coping, there was a high level of fretting about who they were and, for those who were not parents in families of their own, what they were to do with their lives. The 'why me?' question was a problem for them. Here we have to consider the two different subgroups in adult life – those who were still struggling to get properly started, at ages from 18–28, and those who were in relationships outside the foster family, with partners or children. For the former group, university or the forces or a range of careers and training courses had largely been unsuccessful. Sometimes the failure to find the right route was more extreme, in both groups. One committed burglary and had been imprisoned and another lost her job through fraud. In spite of all of this, the foster families remained available and helped them back on track. It could be difficult for the young unattached adults to move on in their lives. Peer group relationships were troubled and the prospect of sexual partners was daunting. There were experiences of failure by men to find or approach women and of women attracting violent partners. Those who were parents themselves had additional sources of security, through some combination of partners, children or work, but there was anxiety about how to hang on to it all. The only parent to have had a child on the child protection register was in this group.

The process and language of these interviews was distinctive in reflecting the young men and women's emotional fragility and cognitive uncertainty. But the helplessness was expressed in different ways. On the one hand, these could be lengthy, rambling, almost incoherent accounts. On the other hand, and more characteristic, were sparse accounts with few narratives developed, memories vague or the existence of memories repeatedly denied. This picture of a lack of strategy to deal with distress suggested fear and disorganised insecure attachment in early childhood and unresolved trauma and helplessness in adult life.

What the children brought to this foster placement

The range of maltreatment experienced in the birth families included extreme forms of neglect and some more extreme forms of sexual and physical abuse. These experiences had lasted a considerable period of time for some who came into care as late as six to twelve years old, although even those coming into care at twelve months were apparently in a poor state. Some accounts were detailed in their picture of an atmosphere of fear and distress. Graphic details of their neglected state featured in the stories subsequently made available to the children.

This was how it was for Adam, taken to hospital after being left as a baby with his three siblings, all under six. He was found by a policeman, one of several accounts of rescue as if from the brink.

I was eating wallpaper. I had a severe nappy rash and I had to be taken into hospital and had to have the nappy sort of surgically removed from my bum.

Vivid tales of being malnourished, underweight, dirty or with diseases such as scabies on arrival in care reflected the experience of neglect, but also provided the persistent pictures in the adult mind, photographic images of sad babies, which needed to be dealt with and integrated into the image of the self.

Sometimes the early childhood narrative develops in the telling. It is helpful to start with one example of what was a common story – a story of parents "not coping" that builds through references to neglect into an anxious, angry account of physical abuse and fear. Lorraine, removed from her birth family at the age of six, gave this account of her early years.

My mum had me when she was a teenager, so she had me when she was quite young. And she weren't working, my dad had like a part-time job, but it's not very well paid so they were quite a poor family . . . and . . .

Brothers? sisters?
Yes. Little brother he's two years younger than me. He was a little baby then but I got the worst of it.

Do you know what happened? Why you came into care?
They . . . when I was a baby they left me in the car . . . when I was . . . From birth onwards when they went to the pub they spent all their money on drink, something like that. They'd leave me in the house on my own with my little brother . . .

Right . . .
My dad had quite a few affairs. She always forgave him because she could not cope with all of us on her own.

Yes.
I can remember one incident when my mum gave me a 50p piece to get her some sweets from the shop, and I was about five years old, something like that, I went out and lost it down the drain. I went home and she said, you're not going to come in this house until you find that 50p piece . . .

And you can remember that?
I can remember that very clearly. I came back and it was pitch black dark and the doors were locked and the windows were locked and . . . I was five and I slept outside underneath the hedge and the next-door neighbour found me.

Yes.
There was no food hardly. I was quite small, underweight, and I had bruises – my dad . . . I had cigarette burns on me – according to the doctor's records, I can't remember that . . .

Who was it that hurt you?
It was mostly my mum. My dad was violent towards my mum and my mum took it out on me. Same thing really. She was pushed downstairs, or slapped round the face or hit.

Can you remember anything happening to your brother?
No . . . No . . . Cos I was trying to protect him – with me trying to get the worst of what . . . didn't want them to lay into him so I got the worst of it.

This story is quoted in full because here it is possible to see how Lorraine's mind roved over the evidence and the reasons for coming into care, both the remembered and the told. It began as a "not coping" story, a young mother and a poor family. But rapidly it moved to key images of neglect – as a baby being in the car on her own and then as a pre-school child left at home with her brother, while her parents spent their money on drink and, by implication, not on her. She was two years older than her brother and her feelings of responsibility for him must have begun very early. This story escalated into what is an act of emotional cruelty in which she was left in distress with the house locked against her at the age of five.

The neglect story in turn expands towards bruises and cigarette burns – always one of the more traumatic injuries, with its association with a kind of deliberate physical torture.

Lorraine's *appraisal* of these events or apportioning of blame moved from the more benign youth and poverty through to a hint of her sense of the unreasonableness of having responsibility for her brother, an arrangement which left her in the house without a source of adult care. Then she moved on to her sense of shock that her mother should lock her out – although she has no words, such as "unkind" or "cruel", that can evaluate her mother's behaviour or capture her own feelings. The domestic violence story absolves her mother of some blame, but is nevertheless seen as being at the very least unfair on her. Later in the interview she described having frightening asthma attacks for which her parents did not get any medication. She said that she had since learned that her mother was sexually abused in childhood and that was 'some of the reason why she's the way she is'. But she went on, 'I still don't think that's a reason to treat kids like that'.

Several other men and women commented on the violence between parents that was associated with their own abuse and these adults, male and female, seem to be some of the more emotionally fragile in the study. Fear seemed to be a shadow over these interviews, even though the children had been very successfully placed in foster families that had lasted. For these children, the experience, as reflected on, mixed physical pain with fear – although as Lorraine's account demonstrates, they seem to have difficulty in naming the feelings. The atmosphere in these interviews was, however, chilling. Tony began by saying that his mum could not look after him and that he had cut that bit out of his memory. But when encouraged to expand on this story, he said simply and rather flatly:

I think our dad was beating us up and he was beating her up as well.

Yes.

I think that's the main reason why . . . I was quite young when I was there so I don't really . . .

So it was your dad that was . . .

Beating me up, yeah.

No explanation is offered, both detail and explanation being lost behind what is either a block in his mind, a reluctance to talk about it in the interview, or both.

Dean (22), a particularly tentative young man, was removed at nine from his birth family and described why he had "blocked out" his early years.

> *They told me a few things. And I sometimes get bits and bobs thrown back. I get blackouts sometimes. When I'm doing stuff. And I talked to Mum and Dad* (foster carers) *about it and they think it might be related . . . a lot of things that happened that I do think now are related to then. But it's all basically blocked out. Because some of it was pretty bad apparently. I just blocked it out.*
>
> Do you know bad in what way?
> *Mmm – abuse and that sort of stuff.*
>
> Physical abuse?
> *Yes. Mainly to me I think by Dad. Because I think he's mentally ill or something.*
>
> Right. So do you have memories of him at all?
> *I have physical things like – I can't remember the situation really – but he hit me round the face with a frying pan or something and chipped my tooth. That's all I can remember. I can't remember why.*

Having spent the first part of the interview stressing how little he could remember, Dean came up with what may be memories of actual events. The stories have less detail than Lorraine's but offer the suggestion that his father's mental illness might be a reason. Dean had a memory that after leaving his birth family he was generally fearful.

> *I'm not sure why – it's more of a feeling memory. But why . . . I suppose it's probably because it was not long after we got out of it. I think everything probably scared me.*

For Dean, so many of his thought processes are confused that ideas come into his mind without him always being able to rationally deal with them or explain them. Nevertheless, this makes his speech at times quite spontaneous and intuitively accurate. It does indeed seem likely that these "feeling memories" are *procedural* memories, which are not attached to specific episodes or semantic labels and may be therefore all the more difficult to resolve.

Fearfulness often extended outside the family. It is perhaps not surprising that the worst example of being bullied and distress in peer groups came from this vulnerable group. Gary had been a victim of fear and physical violence in his birth family, but had also been part of a wider network of fear. Domestic violence had been a major source of anxiety inside the home, but in addition the birth family had been targeted on the estate where they lived, with objects being thrown at the house. This sense of fear, violence and victimhood had then extended into school, where he was continually bullied and threatened. This continued even after his foster placement.

> *Well – it was mainly people . . . and school . . . I didn't have a happy time. The people – everybody picked on me. Literally the whole school.*
>
> Oh.
> *Even in the fifth year you got first years going* (pulled a face) *But . . . err . . .*
>
> Really. Any particular reason do you think?
> *Because I take everything really seriously. I still do to a certain extent and I probably always will.*
>
> You take things seriously?
> *It might be because of what happened in the past. Subconsciously I suppose.*

Gary was physically and emotionally bullied, but was helpless to stop himself being everybody's target. To be a 16-year-old and still the victim of 11-year-olds was painful and humiliating. His explanation, that he was too serious, was quite plausible as was his explanation of the link to his childhood. He said that he wondered if he was unable to speak up for himself because of being hit by his father if he ever spoke up. The extent of his feeling of powerlessness was exacerbated by what he experienced as bullying by his younger sister.

> *I'm quiet and don't talk back to everyone. And she's just the complete opposite. She was like just everyone at school really. That's why we don't get on. I think that's a lot of the reason we don't get on. I got all the teasing and bullying and everything at school. And then come home and get the same thing from her.*

This account, which captures the sense of the world as a hostile place in which others have the power to intimidate and frighten you, was particularly poignant. What is more, the description lacks any associated anger. There are no adults, carers or teachers who can make this life any different for him by putting an end to the bullying. When asked what he would have done when he was upset:

> *I'm not sure really. I can't really remember. Sometimes I think I just bottled it up.*
>
> Did you?
>
> *Yes – at school . . . you know . . . they* (foster carers) *wanted to go to school to see the teachers and I didn't because I knew it would only make things worse . . . I just don't . . . I want the easiest way out. Yeah . . . I . . . if it's going to make it worse I just don't bother. Even if it would probably be the best thing to do. I just don't tell someone because I know it would probably be worse.*

This is an example of his lack of confidence in his own effectiveness or the effectiveness of other people, but also reflects the helplessness characteristic of unresolved adults (George, 1996).

Foster family care

Although the hallmark of this group is emotional fragility and anxiety, it was clear that the foster family they had arrived in was a real family as defined by their experience of the carers as parents, by being treated as well as other children of the household and, always important, by being offered family membership into adult life.

Some powerful images emerged from this group of starting life at the point that they entered this foster family. One 18-year-old woman, Amy, felt that she was immature because, 'I missed the first six years of my life'. Gary put it very literally:

> *To a certain extent I sometimes think that my life started – I was born, I suppose, at about 10.*

Fond accounts were given of loving, generous foster carers.

> *She was lovable . . . Kind and caring . . . and we were never without anything. I mean I know she used to get paid off social services . . . but they hadn't got much money. And we used to get big Christmas presents and we used to have presents upstairs and then we used to come downstairs and have a big main present each . . . like a bike . . . or something like that . . . mmm . . . I wouldn't swap her. If someone came to me and said, would you rather be in another foster home if I was younger than 18 I'd say no. You'd have to fight me!*
>
> So let's think about those words – she's lovable . . . can you give me an example of that?
> *I mean if you had a graze on your knee, she's always there for you . . . cuddles . . . plasters on your legs and that. She always used to welcome us with open arms when we used to come out of the infants school.*
>
> You can picture her in your mind?
> *Yes – crouching down and going like this! Mmm I don't know – she's just really loveable I think. It's hard to explain.* (Janice, 28)

As children, relationship-building was not always straightforward. Feelings of anger, distrust and fear about previous experiences in families seemed to contribute to children not showing emotion in appropriate ways and therefore making it more difficult to get their needs met. Often these barriers were themselves seen as an indication that possibly unknown harms had occurred to the child. For Wendy (taken into care aged two), the fact that siblings born to the birth family (after she was taken into care) were sexually abused as young children left some doubts as to whether this had been her experience also.

> *I wouldn't let anyone cuddle me. She* (foster mother) *was loving, always showing love, trying to show me affection but I mean I don't think I have ever been one to show affection back to someone.*

Yes . . .

When I was younger if either Mum or Dad tried to cuddle me, I would move away and I wouldn't have any sort of physical contact with anyone, which is why they think that maybe I was abused.

As a young child, she had shown signs of distress after contact with her birth parents. Her foster mother had described this for her.

Mum (foster mother) *said to me once that one time after I had been to see Mum and Dad for the day, like we did when we were younger, I came back and for three or four days I didn't talk or do anything and I cried, but I wouldn't make a noise when I was crying.*

This frozen state with silent crying was ambiguous and therefore particularly unsettling as a story. She could have been distressed because she missed her parents or because she was afraid of them – who was to know? What meaning could be attached to this story in terms of her sense of self – apart from this image of a sad child who held on to her sadness as if in a state of shock.

Some adults neglected in their birth families had been given vivid pictures by their foster mothers of themselves on arrival in the placement as scared, anxious little children.

I used to run and hide from her . . . I used to hide a lot my (foster) *mum would say, she'd go, you were like a little frightened animal . . .*

Right . . .

I was so petrified I used to hide . . . and shake a lot . . . not do it on purpose but take things and hide and like one Christmas I used to go to my bedroom a lot. And no one knew until Christmas when she went to get the huge tin of Roses out – the really big tin, and there was none in there. They opened my desk and all these sweet papers come flying out . . . I can remember that one. And . . . I used to sit there on the floor under the table and suddenly this hand used to come up like this and take something under . . . I used to hide and eat it. So I don't know what went on when I lived at home with my real mum and dad. (Stacey, 28)

The image of the child who only felt safe under the table with just her hand appearing is one of the defining images of Stacey's childhood. Here, in a way which was repeated throughout many interviews, it is apparent how these images of their early time in the foster home raised the question of just how bad the birth family might have been.

For Stacey, this negative picture is in contrast to her elaborate dream of what might have been.

> *I used to dream that I was the perfect child, I used to dream of real mums and dads. Not like . . . and I had this lovely house and we were all together and my sisters and my mum and dad . . .*
>
> You still had this dream after you'd been fostered for some years? Can you remember how old you were when you had that dream?
> *I'd be coming up to teenage years.*
>
> And what would be happening in that dream – your family – all together . . . ?
> *Yeah . . . either at the beach or in the pub . . . picnics and going out on the boats at sea . . . but that will never happen . . .*

Stacey is extremely dependent on her foster mother and appreciative of all that she does, but can remember fantasies as a child that reflect the constant ambiguity for children separated from birth families. They may be well aware of the lack of concern that birth families had for them and yet hold on to an idealised version of what a real (birth) family might be.

Alongside this kind of account, however, were some strongly worded descriptions of fear at the prospect of being sent back to the birth family. Well-founded fears of abduction made this seem like a real possibility. This is the account of Amy (18) of the pursuit and fear of pursuit that followed her into the foster family.

> I'm trying to get a picture of you at that stage – you said you were quite small physically . . . ?
> *Yes – and very frightened. I was frightened that my nanny would come and take me away. Because when I first came here no one knew where I was and nanny got a private detective to find me and she followed me up to the school and went to the school and phoned up that evening and said "I know what my grand-daughter was wearing, know what you*

were wearing – you took my grand-daughter to school . . ." and that really shook me up. I'm like . . .

Yes, so that was frightening.
I was so frightened – ever since before until I was adopted (aged 17), because now I know they can't take me away.

So you felt that because you were fostered, someone could take you away?
Yes. I was afraid that someone could take me away and back to my mum and I didn't want that.

Did your parents ever say they wanted you back?
All the time, all the time. They threatened to go to court to get me back.

In this context, bad experiences at contact could be threatening.

And I wanted to get out of my nanny's house and I said to my social worker, 'Come on let's go' . . . this was a few years ago, and my nanny said 'No, don't go', and I was at the door and she grabbed hold of my wrist and tried to drag me back in the house – and oh . . . my nanny, she was very, very, strong, she was very strong, and she's strong-minded as well, and she literally grabbed hold of my wrist and that really hurt, and I was really scared.

Such experiences were remembered and spoken about in the child-like voice of her small child self. They made Amy very anxious and throughout her childhood in foster care she had bad dreams.

Sometimes I slept OK but I when I first came I used to rock like anything. I used to rock heavily because they could hear me downstairs. The bed would literally move . . . Sleeping was a bit of a problem – I used to think that they (birth parents) *could come in at night, I used to have this dream where my mum would take me away. She locked all the doors and windows so I couldn't get out and no one could come in and get me. I used to have nightmares . . . Sometimes I still do.*

This memory of intense rocking at night dates from when she was six or seven years old and suggests that she was in rather an infantile state of regression and distress – which fits her own perception of herself as having missed those early developmental years. Persistent nightmares in the new family, however, threatened the development of a sense of security.

Fears of being sent back could lead to artificially compliant behaviour, as Wendy described.

You said you were quite a quiet little girl?

Yes . . . I think . . . because . . . I was fostered I didn't want to cause arguments sort of thing because I always had the fear of being sent back to my mum. So I was always quite quiet and not confrontational.

Many of the children in the sample described themselves as "quiet" children when they arrived in their foster homes. Various reasons were offered for this, but in this group the explanation was often explicitly linked to fear and compulsive compliance.

Part of the family

Lorraine, one of the most fearful children, however, saw at the outset that this was a home where she could belong. So, how did the transition from the birth family feel?

Yes, I did feel part of the family as soon as I came here. I came here and there were teddies all on the bed – I went upstairs and Sam (foster carer's own son) *was asleep on the bed and I lay next to him and fell asleep and there's a photo of me sleeping next to him my first day.* (laughs)

This first image is a very powerful one, all the more so because it was such a touching act of spontaneous trust by this young child and because it was preserved as part of the family's history, to be revisited as the child settled in.

And can you remember what you felt? In those early days and weeks here?

I was very happy – it was a sigh of relief.

Were you at all sad to be away from your parents?
I weren't sad to be away from my parents – I said on my way to this house, 'I don't want to go back to my mum and dad. Don't take me back to my mum and dad.'

The idea that Lorraine was relieved not to be with her parents seems to go against commonly-held views of children reluctantly coming into care. This was the reaction of a particularly traumatised child who discovered a very different experience in foster care and found relief from fear. It is also more likely where children are consistently rejected rather than confused and emotionally entangled by birth family caregivers. To that extent they are free to move on.

Then there was the classic test of family membership – did the foster mother love you *and* treat you like other children of the family?
And she's got a lot of love to give – she has, she's got a lot of love.

And you've always felt that since you came here?
Oh yeah. Yeah . . . she treated me as if I was one of her own.

And that's important?
Oh yes, she's never treated me different from Michael or Michael different from me. She treated us just the same.

Finally, how did the use of the mum and dad words get managed?
So do you call them mum and dad?
No, I don't call them mum and dad.

So you don't . . . ?
I'd love to call them mum and dad – I know people keep saying it's weird but if I hadn't known my mum and dad when I was little, if I'd been adopted from birth and hadn't seen them then probably, then I probably would call them mum and dad. But now . . . I've got the idea that they (foster carers) *are mum and dad . . . I'd love to call them mum and dad. But sometimes . . . it won't come out. I do say to my friends – that's my mum and dad.*

This is an interesting issue in all groups but in this group extreme feelings about birth families might lead to a defence of the foster carers' status as *real* without the words "mum" and "dad", which had negative connotations.

The real family discourse surfaced again in relation to the wish to have the family member status recognised in other areas of terminology. For Wendy, this emerged when she responded angrily to the question, what do you value in a social worker?

Someone who will listen to you and not . . . a lot of the social workers we had they would tell us if we talked about "home" as being where we lived, they say, 'No it's not your home, it's your placement', so in front of the social workers we weren't allowed to call it home.

How old were you when people were saying that?
I can remember it about nine/ten, saying 'It's not your home it's your placement' and they were trying to make it so that it is like normal family but we weren't allowed to call it home.

What about calling your foster carers mum and dad though, was that alright?
Yes that was alright.

It was just calling it "home"?
Yes. It was my home though.

For Wendy, the leaving care process was a connected issue.

So when you got to 15/16 did the social worker start to talk about you leaving care?
Yes, and I said I am not ready to leave. Mum and Dad are quite happy for me to stay and so when I was 18 they said, what are you doing now are you moving out? I said well Mum and Dad are quite happy for me to stay where I am for the time being . . . Because I was in foster care it was our 'placement' it wasn't our 'home'. As far as I am concerned they are my parents. OK not biological parents but they were Mum and Dad.

So is that a message we need to give to social workers then, that it is not just a placement it is your home?
For long-term children it is not a placement. If they are going to be

> *there a long time then it should be called their home and they should be allowed to call it their home.*

There seems to have been a social work practice expectation that these particularly vulnerable young people (though the practice featured in all groups) would be leaving their families and moving into "independence". The practice implications will be discussed in the final section of this book, but in terms of the child's sense of family membership, each misguided offer brought a new affirmation that she was a member of this family and that membership was not dependent on social services procedures or legal status.

Adult life and adult selves

Young unattached adults

The small group of highly anxious, fragile, tentative young people stood out from others in the sample from the chilly, empty atmosphere that was created in the interview itself.

Neil (22) had needed psychiatric treatment through much of his childhood. His behaviour was out of control at school, from when he arrived at age six, and he spent time in a special unit before returning to mainstream school. It was only a little later that he revealed to his carers that he had experienced sexual abuse as well as the physical abuse that was known about. He was very glad of the continuing availability of his foster mother, whom he rang most days, but in adult life he had struggled to find his way. He described himself as a quiet person, but someone who got very angry and had outbursts.

> *I have got a short and bad temper.*
>
> OK.
> *I don't know why that is.*
>
> So what would happen if you got really angry – what would you do?
> *I'd probably really . . . just shout and . . . chuck things about. I wasn't really violent as such . . .*

One of his difficulties, shared by others in this group, was a problem with *thinking straight*, getting his thoughts in order. In the interview itself this came across strongly in his lack of recall, the lack of detail in his responses, and a general lack of coherence. But it had also caused problems when he tried to make a career in the army.

> Did you like the army?
>
> *I did like it. Yeah but I found it a bit difficult in the end because I was getting in a lot of trouble. I sometimes have problems about doing eight things at a time . . . I could only do one thing at a time . . . really . . . and the army didn't really see that . . . And I was getting in quite a lot of trouble and I left really because of that. Yeah that was it. I was just getting in more and more trouble there . . .*

Although Neil showed very little ability generally to reflect on his past and make any connections with his behaviour, later in the interview he did connect this thinking problem with his childhood.

> Do you think you're OK now or do you think you are still being affected by what happened when you were little?
>
> *I think I'm still being affected a little bit . . . Like I can only think of one thing at a time really . . . I don't say always but sometimes I do. I think that way, yeah.*

Neil also felt that his relationships were affected. He had had girlfriends but lacked confidence.

> *Not as confident as I'd want to be really. I do approach people but . . . I still feel a bit eerie inside.*

Although probably the majority of the sample as a whole would describe themselves as having some anxiety in new relationships, with this group there seemed to be something more than just anxiety.

Neil's difficulty with work and relationships was echoed by Gary's experience, although Gary had taken a very different route. He had been encouraged by his foster carers to go to university after a college course. However, he had not been able to get very far in his degree at the time of the interview and was drifting. He was more articulate than Neil, although expressing some of the same lack of memory for events in childhood and describing equivalent problems in thinking and learning. This theme began with the question around his lack of recall of the past.

> *. . . Even these days I can't really remember . . . I don't have a very good memory anyway . . . I don't think . . . I don't remember much – even from five years ago. I don't remember that much. I'm wondering about doing something about it or not. You know people talk about when they were kids, all these things which were on TV and that sort of thing and I don't know any of it. I don't really remember any of it. It's just I haven't got a clue about what they are talking about.*

Of course university work requires organised thinking and Gary described how 'sometimes I have to go back at least 10 times before it sinks in. I don't really take things in that well.' He lost interest very quickly because it took so long to learn or understand things. Even short-term memory was unreliable. It may not be surprising that he could not remember early childhood, but he also could not remember things that had happened quite recently – such as what it was like when he first came to university.

Through his account, there were signs that, unlike Neil, Gary was struggling to make sense of things, including himself. But when he thought about himself, he felt down.

> *. . . I do a lot actually. I think I take things in and dwell on them a bit too much . . .*
>
> And do you feel bad about yourself . . . or bad about being in care . . . or . . . ?
> *Bad about myself really. I sometimes get cheesed off with myself because I am who I am and I wish it could be different. But when it comes down to it . . .*
>
> So it's quite a challenge trying to change. Do you think you will be able to change?
> *I don't know – really – I've never really stuck at anything . . . People . . . a lot of people are always saying . . . I can do this and that . . . you're really good at this and everything . . . but . . . I don't particularly like myself . . . that's what it comes down to really. So whatever people . . . so when boys said things at school or whatever . . .*

and . . . got into . . . I don't really believe what people say . . . It takes a lot . . . I need hard proof . . .

That people like you?
Yeah . . . I think so. When people say stuff – I think, they're just saying that.

The sense of helplessness Phil felt as a child seems to translate into a lack of a sense of focus or meaning in relationships. When faced with the five adjectives question from the AAI he struggled.

If you had to think of five words to describe your relationship with Brenda (foster carer), what would they be?
Phhew . . . I'm not sure really . . . I don't really . . . think about things . . . in that way . . . I don't really have opinions . . . and I've always been like that. Ph . . . like a vote for example – like the polls or whatever – I just say ph . . . whatever. I don't usually vote. Let them get on with it.

How would you describe her – how she was with you?
Mmm . . . I can't really remember . . . just like a normal mum I suppose . . . whatever that is . . . I don't really know what that is!

So how would she react if you told her you'd been bullied at school?
Mmm I think she'd be upset and want to get it sorted out.

So she'd want to do something?
I think so. Yes.

When you were first there when you were little – would she hug you?
I think so . . . at the very beginning . . . I think it took a while for us to get over everything . . .

So you remember that process of separating – you said earlier it was quite traumatic . . .
Well sort of. But I think . . . I'm not sure whether it's from memory or memory of being told about it. Because I was told about it all by Brenda and Simon because we used to talk about it quite a lot. So I'm not sure whether it's my memory or whether it's a memory of her telling me.

Although this carer was, as far as Phil knew about such things, a "normal mum" who looked after him and was concerned about him, he still has this sense of uncertainty about the "truth" of his own experiences. Although there are major gaps for him, or perhaps because there are major gaps, he described himself as preoccupied with the birth family past and was still trying to find out about it and free himself from it.

In adult life, although there was vagueness in this group about foster families, in terms of naming feelings or describing individual carers, there was no doubting the important role that the foster families still had in anchoring these young people.

> So this was an important relationship . . . did that change as you got a bit older?
>
> *Yeah – I'm still close to my family now – I usually ring them . . . if not once a day, every other day still now so . . . still quite . . . close. I don't sit on her lap any more!* (Neil, 24)

This little joke that Neil allowed himself towards the end of the interview was the nearest he came to spontaneity and was quite touching, suggesting somehow that adult life was tougher than those days when a mum's lap was available.

> Gary would also turn to his carers.
>
> So if you got into difficulties would you ring them?
>
> *Oh yes – I regard them as parents. Because they are the only parents that I've had because I don't really know . . .*

The trailing ending of the sentence was not coincidental, but seemed characteristic of his trailing thought processes and his trailing life, both of which he was trying to get in some kind of order.

Parents

Fragility in the parents in this group showed itself in rather different ways. Foster carers had often been tested as these adults had gone through adolescence, especially where teenagers had stolen from them, run away or ended up in prison. Even though it was predictable that these young adults would continue to need to their foster families during adult life, they had their carers' commitment. This was recognised by the adults themselves, who felt particularly grateful to carers for their tolerance and in some cases, forgiveness.

One important theme inevitably in this group was the way in which wide-ranging fears persisted in spite of positive long-term foster care relationships and foster families who were so very much available to support and help out. The most extreme example of this was a woman who was now 28 years old and had arrived in a frightened state in the foster home, aged three. Nicola was now devoted to and dependent on her foster carers, but she was still angry with her birth family and, at some level, still the frightened child. The world around her was a dangerous place and this anger and fear preoccupied her and spilled over, it appeared, in the parenting of her children. Nicola described being obsessed with locking doors and windows to prevent burglaries.

> *I get nervous. I sit here, listening to all the noises. I get up at least 10 times a night to make sure all my doors, all my windows are locked. It's worse now since my brother had his accident. I do get frightened.*
>
> What are you frightened of?
> *I'm frightened that I'm going to get attacked. If I'm on my own I'm frightened that someone's going to break in . . . I always want the lights on, and I had that even when I was little.*

Nicola's fears overwhelmed her and were communicated to her son (age 10), whose own anxiety state led to her request for help from social services.

> *I asked five years ago because Lee had difficulties – after Dunblane. He took it bad. He really took it bad. He was frightened. He wouldn't go to school. He was frightened in case that man came back and killed him and all his friends and I said, 'He's dead, he's not coming back. He killed himself' . . . 'He's got mates – they've got cars, they'll come and get me. They will come and get my friends.'*
>
> Had you been upset by Dunblane?
> *That do upset me. Them little kids were innocent. They didn't deserve this.*

No.
They didn't deserve that. They didn't deserve to die. They didn't ask for a man to come in their school and kill everyone. It was upsetting.

So you were upset and Lee was upset.
I couldn't buy a newspaper, I couldn't have the TV on, the radio on. I couldn't even go outside because people were talking about it.

So you were that upset?
Not me – I was upset because of the children and because of the parents. But Lee took it worse. Because in his head, that bloke was going to come and get him. And I mean this went on for three months and I was asking for help and no one would help.

The fears are associated with her own and thus his own feeling of powerlessness and defencelessness. There is the helplessness of the unresolved adult in parenting (George, 1996), with the added difficulty in seeing boundaries round each self. Any external event could disturb and overwhelm.

Lee howled when Princess Diana died and he didn't know nothing about Diana. I explained to him about it. I mean, even I stood there and howled. I ran downstairs and put the telly on and see here the day she was born and the year she died. Then something else came on and I just stood there. She's not dead. She's not dead. And I stood here until I saw the news again. I said to the kids, if you want breakfast, get it yourselves – I'm not moving. And when it come on and it said she'd died I really howled . . . because she is the best royalty ever.

This sense of being merged with her child in their shared fear and grief was reflected in Nicola's own dependence on her foster mother.

Were you worried about being separated from her at all as a child?
Yes . . . I still do. When she goes on holiday for a week I feel lost. I feel lost . . . that I haven't got my mum there. I know she's on holiday . . . but I do feel lost without her. At least I know that if I pick up the phone she's there. If we need any help she's there. And she's said she'll always be there for us. Doesn't matter what things have happened, this, that

> *and the other . . . and she's said she'll always be there for us . . . she'll always be there to talk things over . . .*

Several adults, not only in this group, said that they imagined depending on their foster carers throughout life, but Nicola went further.

> *I don't want them to grow up, I don't want them to grow old and die. I want them there for life. I want them there till I'm dead.*

This was an unusual example in this sample of someone with what were the characteristics of an enmeshed, entangled, unresolved attachment pattern (Howe *et al*, 1999). Most adults seemed to have survived more by virtue of their defended, dismissing behaviour, even if unresolved, but Nicola was more entangled and preoccupied. She found it hard to let go of her fear of separation or her anger with the birth family or her need for the constant availability of her foster family.

Turning points

The commitment of foster families to these children who had come from backgrounds that held high risks for all forms of emotional and behavioural problems was likely to have been critical in stabilising these children through childhood. The carers had to manage the children's high anxiety levels and even where this had needed psychiatric help, some progress had been made – enough, for example, to ensure that the children could stay in mainstream school and even go on to university. There was little sense of crisis points in childhood, more a sense of ongoing struggles to come to terms with the past, although examples of offending in the teenage years might have led to a breakdown in less committed families. For one young man who stole from his foster carers, their forgiveness was an important turning point. Offering a secure base, emotionally and practically, was neither easy nor always rewarding for carers from these accounts, but it was necessary and had been appreciated.

With this pathway, there was the sense that for carers who had taken on fragile children and offered permanent family membership and a containing relationship in childhood, there was nothing for it but to continue to offer the same in adult life. The consolation for this role must have been that, although all the carers' efforts may not have freed the young men and women from their fears and preoccupations or led to a mutually rewarding relationship in all cases, it all could have been so much worse. This rather sad, but realistic conclusion seemed to have been shared by carers and their adult children. The adults felt that they had been saved from terrible fates. But just getting through the day still seemed such very hard work.

7 Breakdown and rebuilding

Pathway summary: Continuous membership, discontinuous care with placement breakdown/separation occurring in early adolescence following conflict. Relationships/family membership have been rebuilt in adult life.

The previous four pathways provided continuous care and membership, but with different representations of relationships and different outcomes. In Group 5 were placements where the sense of foster family membership continued, even after placements had broken down. These relationships had then been rebuilt in adult life. These are cases involving the placement of infant or toddler children, all girls, from backgrounds of neglect and possible abuse. The foster families in which they were placed were not traditional busy foster families, but had a special reason for the placement of this child, more like Group 2 and more like an adoptive family. Adoption was a possibility but for various reasons did not happen. These were troubled children on arrival, but the placements held until adolescence. The endings were to do with a combination of rows and rebellious behaviour and/or some issues around being in care and the drive towards the birth family. Retrospectively the ending is judged resentfully: 'I was only fostered so the placement was allowed to end' is a criticism made of social workers. Two different routes ensued from this turning point – a move to the birth family at the wishes of the child or a move to different carers. Whichever route was taken, these moves from the initial foster family led to a rapid downward spiral out of the mainstream of family and school and, in more serious cases, into drugs, suicide attempts, mental health hostels and so on. During this period, foster carers remained concerned and in touch. Birth families are seen negatively and as a disappointment and yet are an important part of each story, as identities were thrown into doubt.

Legacy

These young women all had a baby in their late teens. There is no reason why this should be an inevitable part of this pattern, although it was clearly the case that motherhood and the new baby offered a chance to foster carers for mutual reparation and healing, as their child and her child needed support of a kind that was in some ways easier to offer than in the rebellious and stormy days of adolescence. In a sense the worst had happened, the placement breakdown and the teenage motherhood, so the consequences had to be lived with and managed.

The young mothers managed themselves and their babies well enough, in the sense that no outside agencies were involved, but adult life was not straightforward. Depression for one young woman, continuing preoccupation with feelings of being unclean for another, suggested a range of unresolved feelings about the worthiness of the self. The information about the self encoded in their internal working model continued to leave them prey to depression. They were offered and claimed membership of these foster families and needed help from them of different kinds. The foster families were represented as "real families" in a psychological and social sense for the young people in adult life. Carers were at the very least active grandparents to the babies, providing financial support, through prams and baby clothes, and showing partiality for their "grandchildren".

One important legacy which survived the breakup and the downward spiral seemed to have been the learned lifestyle – regular routines, standards of housekeeping, not getting into debt, staying away from offenders, and so on. There was an explicit choice of a lifestyle that matched that of the foster family rather than the birth family. Their view of themselves was moderated through the sense of being a decent member of society, polite, not getting into debt. This was contrasted with the image of a "kid from care" or a "girl from a bad estate", as one young woman put it.

Anger at birth families featured, for letting them down in adolescence as well as in infancy. The adult self is therefore represented problematically as connected with birth family figures who have not found them lovable, but to whom they are nevertheless irrevocably bound through biological, social, legal and, to varying degrees, emotional ties.

A protective factor here appeared to be the acquisition of "extra families" or a supportive partner who could complement or supplement what the foster family offered and increase the general availability of emotional and other resources. Emotional fragility, in spite of the rebuilding of relationships with carers, suggested the need for a great deal of support.

What the children brought with them to these foster placements

There were some powerful descriptions of early experiences, not only stories about neglect in infancy learned from foster carers, *semantic memories*, but some exceptionally early *episodic memories.*

> *There are some things I can remember from before I went into care. One was being in a dark room in a cot, really really stuck in there and nobody would come and pick me up. I just cried and cried and cried all the time.*

The memory is vivid and distressing, told with emphasis by use of repetition. The language is simple and childlike, as if told at intervals since the event. Even in adulthood, the story is told with some of the same resentment and anger that was perhaps experienced at the time, but is certainly experienced in processing the memory. Other odd memories remain to confuse and upset.

> *I can remember sitting on the toilet and eating chips . . . I don't know how hot they were but I was like burning my fingers trying to pick them up.*

This again is a story, a memory, of abandonment and lack of care to add to her mental representations of the self and the world of relationships. These two experiences/episodic memories had direct practical consequences for Melissa during childhood. She had a fear of the dark and needed to have the light on at night. She was also very anxious about any food that might be hot, a sensory memory associated with anxiety. In addition to these direct memories, she had a description of herself as a malnourished infant when she arrived in care.

> *I was described as a little Ethiopian child where I'd been neglected so much that my stomach had swollen through lack of food and that and lack of goodness.*

The image is a particularly powerful one – the Ethiopian child who is literally at risk of starving to death. This would be a significant semantic memory to turn over in the mind and to build into the working model of the self, but also of the birth family who had failed to love and feed the infant. The "lack of goodness" is in the food and the care. Seen alongside the image of the baby lying crying, helpless and unheeded in a cot in a dark room, these are vivid pictures in the memory of a lost child in need of the rescue which her carers provided.

Charlotte gave an account that she herself had been given of the lack of care and the loss of two mothers:

> *My mother developed depression after I was born and my father ran off with another woman. And took the children with him. And this woman liked babies but she didn't like children beyond the age of six months, a year. I was quite badly treated. I was malnutritioned, and eventually they came and took me away.*

It was not unusual, as in previous groups, to hear how these semantic memories, fragments of the story, were felt not to be the whole picture. Subsequent behaviours and fears, for example a reluctance to go to a foster dad, were seen as evidence that there might well be more to know. The possibility of sexual abuse was a big question mark and all the more anxiety-provoking since it was unlikely that the "truth" would ever be confidently known. These children were thus full of anxieties, which they needed to continue to defend themselves against when they arrived in the foster home.

Foster family care

As described in the interviews, the families taking in these young girls were either immediately or within a short space of time aware that this needed to be a long-term commitment – these children could not return home. The imagery of the child *rescued* by these families was generally explicit in this group.

There were links between the child's earlier experiences of neglect and the difficulties then facing the foster carers. For example, Melissa, who had been described as being like an Ethiopian baby, needed encouragement to eat at all.

> *So they obviously had to try bit by bit . . . I wouldn't eat very much at all. Because I'd got into that way of living . . . I hadn't had anything to eat so I didn't eat very much.*

Fears and memories often surfaced at times of vulnerability, especially during sleep. For another child:

> *When I first came into care I used to wake up with bad dreams apparently . . . saying, Len is hitting Marie . . . saying, Dad's hitting Mum, Dad's hitting Mum! It was always, Len is hitting Marie . . . and that . . . and apparently I always used to have the door open a bit . . .*

The experience of nightmares can themselves become memories, though here the word 'apparently', used twice suggests that these are semantic rather than episodic memories. The implication here is that the foster carers told the story as part of the family history and as a way of placing the child's view of herself in this context of a history of domestic violence and of parents who had caused emotional damage.

Charlotte had faced her foster carers with a range of distressing behaviours, many of which continued for some time.

> *I was quite a scared little child from what they've told me. I was very frightened, very thin, and er . . . but very determined. They said I was very determined as to what I was going to do. And mmm . . . Then I began having night terrors – almost immediately and . . . it was every night. My foster parents would have to take turns. Walking me up and down because I couldn't wake up, just had these awful night terrors. And . . . bedwetting went on till quite a late age, which are all classic symptoms.*

The expression "night terrors" suggests possible memories or nightmares about past experiences in the birth family. The expression "classic symptoms" begs the question – symptoms of what? Physical abuse? Sexual abuse? The vagueness associated with the image of the terrified infant leaves the child, now a young adult, with some difficult questions about what really happened in the birth family. However, the contrasting picture of both foster carers patiently walking her up and down to soothe her is a powerful one. It provides an important story of commitment and caring for the child to have in her mind and to tell others. The theme of the "very determined" small child also paints a picture of the wild child who had to survive against the odds but who is then met with a loving environment where this can gradually be relinquished.

One of the very positive themes of these accounts of family care and family life was of the range of activities in which these families encouraged their foster daughters to participate. This was not by any means exclusive to this group, but it was one of the things they were able to reflect on positively even after placements broke down. Horse riding, ballet, music were all expected. Nice clothes and holidays were also part of the picture, with several references made to having been "spoiled". Perhaps associated with these activities were the broader life-style advantages which were generally on offer. These girls were being brought up in "nice families", as they put it, where they were taught how to behave and this was valued in retrospect. The conventional, comfortable, predictable lifestyle that they found in these foster families taught them some important lessons about a way of living that remained with them.

As with previous groups, the question of how similar or different their treatment was to birth children in the foster family was of considerable remembered significance. Here, there were important differences between the families in the extent to which the foster children had felt treated the same as other children in the family. These distinctions were expressed in both of the ways that have become familiar from the language used in earlier groups, that is to say, the quality of parental emotional responsiveness to children of different status and the more subtle ways in which the different statuses were felt to be marked. The clearest positive statement of this was from one young woman in response to the question about her relationship with her foster mother.

If you had to think of five words to describe your relationship with her when you were a little girl?
She didn't treat me like a foster child. She treated me as her own, which not a lot of foster parents will do because it depends what sort of relationship they have with that child, but because I was with them from such an early age I was family.

Before the emotional quality of this relationship could be discussed by this young woman, she felt the need to classify it using the "real family" discourse. This family did have birth children, but the question is addressed here not so much in relation to equal treatment but in relation to a culturally expected sense of being an "own child". This young woman attributes this to some quality of the foster carer, the quality of the relationship, and the age at which she joined the family. The fact that she was the only girl had been an additional factor.

Probably from a lot of ways I was little Miss Favourite from the other three because she liked little girls . . . she'd always wanted a little girl she could do things with, like go shopping . . .

These could have been fortuitous circumstances, although it sounded as if she was and felt specifically chosen. She has detailed memories of the experience of mother–daughter shopping trips.

She (foster mum) *always used to praise me up going shopping – if we did the shopping and she had a lot of shopping obviously with a big family. And I'd help with the bags, put the freezer stuff in the freezer. I'd always say to her, 'Oh you wouldn't have been able to do that without me today' and she'd say, 'No, you've been a very good girl', and she used to praise me up like that. Hopefully I'll do it with her* (daughter) *as well because . . . because they think, 'Oh, Mummy's happy with me now, so I'll do that again next time'. But I always would say, 'I've been really good today, haven't I? I've helped you with the shopping.' And she'd be like, 'Oh yes, you have. I wouldn't be able to do it without you.'*

The importance here of the family ritual is striking and the memory of seeking and getting reassurance is one that she plans to learn from in how she treats her own young daughter. The emphatic need to please is perhaps symptomatic of her neediness. The sense of shared activity, caregiver availability and raised self-efficacy and self-esteem is in contrast to the memories of abandonment and neglect that she had from her birth family.

Other stories were also of shared activities and family outings, but memories were more jumbled up with anxieties and feelings of being treated as different. Jennie, in giving an account of her foster mother, described the following.

> *Well, I don't know how old I was but I was sitting in the kitchen one day, Mum was cooking and I was just like trying to talk to her about like school or something, and my foster brother* (birth son) *came through and she turned round to Paul she grabbed him and goes 'Give us a cuddle' and she mucked about. And then I go, 'Can I have a cuddle?' and she goes, 'Oh, don't be stupid Jennie'. So . . . that puts you in the picture – why I was fairly angry with her.*

A small scene, perhaps, which a birth sibling might have overlooked, but these children were sensitive to any perceived slight or distinction because of their status. For this girl there had also been a sense of being singled out as different at school.

> *I got picked on once or twice – in middle school and high school. Because I've got eczema . . . and I'm fostered. People go – oh, don't your real parents love you? No wonder they want to get rid of you – look at you, you scabby cow. I had to put up with that quite a lot.*

The physical and social difference and stigma at school were a reflection for her of the psychological and physical distance in the foster home. This reinforced a preoccupation with her body and anxiety about physical intimacy, which persisted into adult life.

However, strong positive feelings about the sense of being "family" in a foster family and the contrast with the birth family were often expressed, even when life in the foster home had run into some difficulties. One young woman explained how angry it made her when social workers assumed that her birth family was her real family and called foster carers by their first names.

> *My first social worker used to refer to who I call my mum and dad as Linda and Keith, you know . . . and that wasn't through them saying, call us Mum and Dad, it's because they've mothered and fathered me and as far as I'm concerned you can't be a mother or a father to a child unless you've brought that child up.*
>
> And you called them Mum and Dad when you were little?
> *Oh yes. They always told me they weren't my real mum and dad and the reason I was with them . . . and that . . . but they never treated me any different.*
>
> But you didn't like the social worker calling them by their first name when you thought of them as . . .
> *Mum and Dad, yeah. My first social worker used to call my blood parents Mum and Dad to me, which you can't look at them like that. You can't look at them and say, you're my mum and dad because it isn't that . . .*

The notion of "mothering and fathering" and upbringing as defining a relationship is part of the real families discourse. This account of social worker terminology suggests similar concerns to the account in the previous chapter, where social workers were reported by another young woman to be insisting on calling their "home" their "placement".

Discontinuity of care: the placement breakdowns

Given the continuity of placement since infancy, the mainly positive pictures of family life and the contrasts with the birth family history, it seemed perhaps rather surprising that these placements should break down in early adolescence. Although there was clearly a need for the researcher to make some sense of these disruptions, it was also quite evidently a problem for the young women themselves to understand, particularly given the rapid downward spirals that ensued. The common factor was that there were rows between these girls and their carers that in some senses got out of hand and broke the family apart – with the fostered child leaving the placement primarily at her own request, although the real reason for this move was rather uncertain territory. It is worth looking at these accounts in some detail, as they are important in illustrating the complex interaction between the characteristics of the child, the quality of caregiver – child relationship in each case, and the nature of these long-term foster care placements.

One distinction seemed to be between running away *to* the birth family and breaking away *from* the foster family, although both could be significant factors. Lorna's verdict was that the reason for the breakdown of her placement and return home lay with the fact that she had never been given the truth about her birth family and it was her idealisation of them, assisted by social work accounts, that led to her push to get out of the foster family in her early teens. She had not had regular contact with birth relatives during her early and middle childhood.

> What information did you have about your birth father when you were younger?
> *Oh, everything pretty and sweet as usual . . . Always picking out the best aspects of the person. When I didn't find them at all.*
>
> That's interesting . . . so you'd got the impression he was a nice person or . . . ?
> *Yeah – they're not going to like tell a nine-year-old, your dad's this and he's coming out of jail and they told me he was OK . . . And I wanted to also find out about my real mum and I was told that she was like OK and things like that but not too much about her.*
>
> Right.
> *Which later I found out why because she really didn't like me at all – completely hates me.*

There was the reality of meeting her birth father.

> *My blood dad met me when I was about 12 – about 12 the first time. I don't know how to explain it. He's your typical male tart for a start. Never with the same woman. In and out of jail, promises you the world, tries to buy your love with presents and that doesn't work for me. That never works with me.*

She then had contact with her birth mother, which was also a disappointment.

> *Well – I think when you're telling a child – I think too many things were prettied up with flowers around them, made them out to be these wonderful people but they weren't like that at all they were just so mean, so vicious. My mother is and my father is just a . . . no hoper I suppose, never going to be anything, and mmm . . .*
>
> If you'd seen them when you were little, would you have discovered that?
> *She had been given bus fare money to come and see me but she'd spent it on cigarettes. She didn't bother. They did ask her to put in the effort to come and see me but half the time she couldn't be bothered.*
>
> So you had seen her at intervals but it just wasn't regular?
> *No – I didn't really want to see her when she came round. I used to sit on her lap but I never used to want to sit on her lap. I just didn't like it. She wasn't my mum as far as I was concerned.*

Although these were her memories of contact as a younger child with someone who she did not see as "my mum", as an adolescent in conflict with her carers her hope in her mother revived. She started to tell lies about her foster mother and eventually planned to leave by cycling to her birth mother's house.

> What were you hoping would happen when you got to your mum's – what was in your mind as you set off?
> *Oh just this pretty picture, everyone with open arms . . . how we love our little girl Lorna! and it wasn't like that at all.*
>
> So did you stay with her for a while?
> *I used to visit her – which part wasn't what I would agree with, a 13-year-old isn't the age when they should make such decisions. They need some help. A 13-year-old being in care as well, being very rebellious – I'll do what I want to do. And at the end of the day because I wasn't their* (the foster family's) *real child coming back from running away, I went to this other foster home . . .*
>
> So why didn't you go back to the first foster family?
> *I just didn't want to go back. I was just being difficult. If I'd have been their* real child *it would have been – no, sorry, there's no question about*

it these are your mum and dad. And even though I'd been with them for so many years and they were like my mum and dad when I said no, I'm not going to stay here, the social workers were, well, OK we'll put you in another foster home. The system there was wrong.

Lorna blames the social workers for giving her this "pretty picture" of her mother but also for not seeing that the foster carers were her real parents. From a children's rights perspective this is tricky – she is angry now that her wishes were not over-ruled as they would have been in other "real families".

Somehow lack of "real" family feeling in the next placement reinforced the difference from Lorna's first foster family. Note here how it is the birth mother that is known by her first name and was the source of anxiety.

I was at this new placement and I saw Kathy (birth mother) *on and off, then I was visiting* (foster) *mum and Kathy. I was scared of Kathy more than anything, because she was always quite loud, mouthy, quite bossy and domineering.*

Were you in school at this point?

Oh school went right down the drain. I couldn't focus on anything and that wasn't that I wanted attention I just couldn't focus on anything. Everything was just like – it was like one long film – it wasn't reality. I didn't feel like I was in reality. It was like, I've been asleep and it's one big dream and I'm going to wake up and everything's going to be all right soon. That's how it felt.

So once you stepped out of your foster family, your mum and dad . . .

Well being in care as such I took it for granted they were my mum and dad, they were, they are my family. And I never felt like I was actually in care until I'd left them and gone to another family and then I felt like I was in care. Like I'd then been taken away from my family.

Lorna describes the downward spiral in adolescence as being like "one long film" that was not reality. It was not possible to get on with her life because real family life was what happened in the first foster family that was not now her home. Lorna was now, as she saw it, in care for the first time. Her first foster carers, whom she referred to as mum and dad, were also distraught.

How did your mum and dad feel about you not coming back to them?
They were hurt – they probably understood that it might happen one day. They were hurt though – my mum stopped fostering because she didn't want to get attached again.

For Jackie too, the tensions that emerged in early adolescence seemed to be connected with her involvement with her birth family – but for her, the knowledge that she was "in care" was part of her problem about being in the foster home.

At the age of about 12, I decided I wasn't getting on with my foster parents which no child does at that age do they? I said I wanted to see more of my mum and they took this to mean I wanted to live with her . . .

And you'd lived with your foster family for how long?
Thirteen years. It was very much a case of give her what she wants. Because I believe as a 14-year-old you do not get on with your parents. I don't think anybody does.

Right.
And I had something to use which most others didn't . . . I could say 'You're not my parents I'm going to go home.' And I did.

For Jackie, the "normal" rows of the teenage years were amplified by her emotional vulnerability and her "use", as she describes it, of the fact that they were not her real parents, even though she had felt treated as part of the family.

Always. Always, they treated me as their own. It was . . . We were very close until I began to realise as a teenager I could use things against them . . . So we used to have some quite awful fights. I feel awful about them these days. But . . . at the time it was the only way for me to show what I was going through really . . .

Jackie tended to attribute some of her problems to the fact that she was not adopted at an early age by her foster carers so that she would have had a stronger message about where she belonged. She told the story that she herself at the age of three had not wanted to be adopted and although her mother was also not willing to agree to adoption, in her memory it was her decision at the age of three that had been accepted by social workers.

What difference would adoption have made?

It was very hard to accept that it was a family, because there was the other family, the real family. And there was always pressure that they were the real ones.

It was less clear than for Lorna that the birth family was in itself an attraction, but there was confusion and emotional entanglement during contact. She felt that adoption might have protected her.

I believe I should have been adopted at an early age because I think it would have saved a lot of turmoil. When I was growing up it was a very painful time to . . . it was a case of always being pulled by my real family – they did put a lot of pressure on me. 'These are only foster parents. There's no need to be close to them. You'll be coming home one day.'

This mental turmoil is reflected in her difficulty in remembering details and she talked repeatedly about blocking out the whole period from about age nine to the time she left.

The middle school is very hard for me to remember. I . . . it's blocked. I can't remember it, I really can't. I can remember the place and I can remember the people but I can't remember being there.

As with Lorna, Jackie was painfully aware of the impact that the rowing and her departure had on her foster carers.

I think they liked me as a person then. I think as I got worse it was more love than like . . . She (foster mother) *wouldn't ever give up. When I went back to my family, I think that must have been the worst time for her because she could see what was happening. She could see that I was going to get worse. She could see that it was just teenage rebellion and not what I needed. I think that was the worst for her because she had no power to say, Stop!*

Both blame the social workers for not standing up to a rebellious teenager and not valuing the placement enough. Although both also admit that they made it difficult for everyone.

The series of events that followed like a chain reaction saw a rapid move from Jackie as a child in a settled foster placement attending school to a serious psychiatric breakdown.

And I think it was the biggest mistake of my life, actually. I moved into West Town, which is not one of the best areas to go, mmm . . . and then . . . I got in various bits of trouble and then . . . I think within the year I tried to commit suicide . . . I took an overdose and . . . I was taken to hospital.

The route back to a better relationship with foster carers had not been an easy one, although at no point did her carers abandon her. Jackie, like Lorna, had spent time in a very different foster home after the breakdown where she felt the contrast with her "own" foster carers very strongly.

Oh yes because with them (long-term foster carers) *I was treated as theirs. Whereas in this foster home we were treated as outcasts. We were foster children we were trouble. We were very much labelled . . . because we were fostered they believed we were going to be trouble whatever happened.*

This downward spiral was a very similar pattern to another young woman who ended up turning to drugs, attempting suicide and then being placed in a mental health hostel. Jennie's route had been via another foster home (rather than the birth family) which had initially been successful, but which broke down when she started to steal.

We just didn't get on at all after that. This was when I was 17, it was a very abrupt ending. I went to a place called – (mental health hostel), *when they said good-bye sort of thing, all my bags were packed, everything was bundled in bags, just sitting there. It was a quick kiss and cuddle and like, bye-bye and like nothing. I did feel very unwanted then.*

For her too there was a downward momentum set up by the move from the first foster home that was hard to bring to a halt.

Rebuilding foster family relationships in adult life

In adult life, these young women were in active contact with their foster families, but they had to manage a number of challenges. First, they had to cope with the gap in their histories, the sense of having let those foster families down and caused distress. Secondly, they had ongoing contact with their birth parents, with whom it was even more difficult to negotiate comfortable roles. Thirdly, there was the question of how to manage their adult lives as partners, mothers, friends. Finally, there seemed to be a real sense of anxiety about the worth of the self. This came across as occasional depression, obsessional behaviours and other difficulties.

Managing the two families, birth and foster, in adult life could be hard for a variety of reasons. Jackie's birth family continued to be rather classically entangling – the relationship was described by Jackie as "distant yet compulsory". She felt her mother's lack of genuine concern but also knew that much was expected of her in terms of attentiveness around her mother's birthday, ritual attendance at Christmas family meals and so on. She would prefer to be with her husband and son at Christmas.

> *It's very much wanting to prove that that's your family, that's yours and I have the choice.*

In contrast her foster carers were available, as she described them, but unintrusive in their interest. They were there in a flexible way to take her and her young son to their house for the day or to have the whole family, including her partner, for meals. The early experience as a proper family in that placement had been revived in many senses, although the painful years of separation had left a legacy for both parties.

For Jennie, who had been placed in infancy and met her mother for the first time at the age of 16, the relationship with her birth family was often tense and she was clear in her preference for the kind of person she had become through her foster family and the kind of life that she had come to value. Her birth parents talked of knowing criminals and living in a very different kind of social group, which was not her choice of life-style.

I've been brought up in a smart house, with smart parents. I've been smart, I went to a nice school. Nice high school, nice primary school. Always known nice people and knowing them I just prefer the nicer . . . I'm not . . . I don't hate them (birth parents) *or anything or don't dislike them because of what they look like, it's just . . .'*

Their lifestyle is different from yours?
And they do act very stupid. They are just not the sort of people I . . . I know they're my parents. They're not the sort of people I like to associate with . . . If I move again, I don't want them to know where I am. I want to stay away.

Her birth parents wanted care from her since she was a more competent person. They needed her advice on managing their debt, for example. The roles were reversed but this was not what she wanted for herself. Her verdict on her birth parents was:

Compared to my foster parents, they're just people I know. They're not my parents, not really.

For Lorna the situation was even more tense in some respects, with her birth family continuing to scapegoat her for the family troubles, blaming her even for being in care. She had, however, been able to make very clear links back in to her foster family, in spite of leaving them for her birth family in early adolescence. These links back were cemented by her relationship with her partner and the birth of her baby. The foster carers were providing a secure base. She described how her (foster) mother reinforced the fact that she had not left the family when she met people in the street.

People skip round me and ask about my three brothers if they see her. She'll bring me up to let them know that I'm still seeing her and I'm still a part of her life.

She described how she valued her fostered self and the background she had in comparison with her birth family.

> There are links between you and your dad?
> *Well nothing as far as I can see. I mean if I'd have been brought up with them I'd have probably been quite similar to them but I've been brought up differently and I'm nothing like either of them.*

Memories of contact confirmed this.

> *Usually when he was drunk. I can remember him being at the door once when we lived in – and I was like hiding behind my mum's legs, like in her skirt and that . . . I wouldn't talk to him – which is probably as well now why I don't like people who smell of drink and that. That's like slimy. And he is like a slimy person. The way he cuddles me is a lot different from the person who I class my father hugs me.*

Later in the interview Lorna contrasts her own background and outcome as an adult with that of a sister, Gemma, who remained at home.

> So do you think you would have been different if you'd grown up with Dawn (birth mother)?
> *I'd have been like her – Gemma's just like her. I had a better upbringing living in care than I did with Dawn – I had everything. I had . . . Gemma used to get beat up a lot by Dawn. The only thing that got me was why weren't they* (foster carers) *my real mum and dad – not why can't I go back to my real mum and dad but why aren't they my real mum and dad?*

Even as an adult who insistently defends the definition of her foster carers as her family, the questions remain – but for Lorna they hinge not on wanting the psychological connection with the biological parents but wanting the biological connection with the parents who did bring her up. This is an interesting further variation on the "real families" theme.

Turning points

These adults' accounts stress their survival in spite of being in care and in spite of the placement breakdown. Unlike Group 1 interviews, for example, where adults took their settled lives more for granted, these interviews led on to detailed discussion about troubled adult selves, and both the ongoing problems and the unexpected resources that could be found, if they were lucky. The positive placement followed by the serious downward spiral after breakdown suggested two important turning points in childhood, but these were followed by others.

Carla (18) had particular anxieties about the self. Her three suicide attempts when 14 and 15 had frightened her, as had her difficult relationships with boys, and she felt she had needed more psychiatric help. She defined one key turning point as meeting her present partner at 16, becoming pregnant and setting up home. There appeared suddenly to be a moment of hope and stability.

> *It was the first one ever where he cared more about me than about himself really. He was very caring and if there was a problem, he'd want to talk about it. He wouldn't say, leave it alone it will go away.*

Although there had been much initial concern in the networks around her, the foster family and the social workers, this new family did appear to be working to some extent for her.

> *I'd always wanted a child since I was about 14. It had always been something at the back of my mind. It was very much a case of I wanted to give someone else what I hadn't had . . . I was still very immature when I got pregnant and people thought I wouldn't cope but I sort of grew up overnight really. Very quick.*

Because the baby was premature and Carla wanted to breastfeed, impressive in itself in the circumstances, becoming a mother had been challenging.

> *For the first week because he was premature he wasn't very strong. He didn't suck very well and . . . for the first week he rejected me but I was very determined to breastfeed. I was lent one of the hospital breast pumps and I expressed all my milk. For the first week and a half I think. It became tiring. I'd feed him. Change him. Put him down to bed, have to express – and by the time I'd done that, he was up again. It was a constant battle. It was like feeding twice as much.*

Through this period she felt quite confident of her ability to mother and she felt very close to her baby son, 'I was full of the joys of motherhood'.

But then, as if from nowhere as she saw it, she became depressed.

It was good for a couple of months and then I began to get really bad depression. and I refused point blank to admit that I had it. I had very much a feeling that if I admit I've got depression he might get taken away like I did. I didn't want to admit it because I would automatically be a bad mother for having depression. And eventually it got to the point when I couldn't cope anymore . . . It had built up so much. I couldn't take it anymore. If it hadn't been for Darren (son) *I believe I would have tried to commit suicide again because it was just . . .*

Carla's fear of being like her mother and of the child being removed made it difficult to seek help and taking medication meant the end of breast feeding. Although she had sought help through the GP and the psychiatric services, she remained very vulnerable.

As with others in this group, she was not entirely confident about how to give priority to psychological rather than biological parents as "real family". She also had the idea that, if anything had helped her to achieve her nice home and stable family life, it was her own determination.

It was . . . very much the determination to prove them wrong. It was a determination to prove that it hadn't affected me. It was a complete lie – it had. It was a longing to put it behind me . . .

So what is the "it"? When you say ' "It" hadn't affected me', what do you mean?

The whole lot really. All the upset bits of it. I wanted to prove that however bad things had been, stupid things I'd done, I could logically say I'd done what was right for me.

When it came to mothering she did not have a sense of modelling herself on any mother she had known but on what she did not want to happen, which was for her child to experience what she experienced. This is a very common theme across all the groups. But she did have a very particular definition of what children need.

I've always wanted to bring him up in the best way possible really so that he understands that things do go wrong but you can get through them. I always had the feeling that when things went wrong, I always

> *had the feeling that I didn't want to go on, that there was nothing better. There* was *no future. It was now and now was awful.*
>
> Yes.
> *I think that's a feeling that's terrible. It's something I would prefer Darren to avoid having, that feeling. If something goes wrong then it may go wrong but it's going to get better. Which is a feeling I never had. When things were awful, they were awful.*

Although this positive way of framing the world suggested her view at a cognitive level, Carla still struggled to sustain the belief that 'it will get better' (the "hopefulness" referred to in the resilience literature, Murphy and Moriarty, 1976). The depression and her awareness of her history made it hard for this position to be sustained.

> *When you feel awful it does feel that there's no end. It's going to carry on. It's* never *going to get better. But I've learned to deal with it and I've learned that it's just a one day feeling – you can't snap yourself out of it that day but the next day you can wake up in a good mood.*
>
> So do you see it as something that's happening to you – like an illness?
> *No, no – I see it as something which I'm going to have to deal with. I believe that at the end of it . . . I'm always quite frightened that I've never been able to find my personality as such. I've never found out who I really am. Things have gone so quickly you know. It was child to traumatised teenager, moving around. Then move out and within months I was the family wife as such. And . . . I think the next couple of years are going to be the crucial bit really.*

This touching account showed some healthy capacity to reflect on herself, her experiences and her present state but some big questions remained – what is my personality? who am I? Even though she still described herself as being able to turn to her foster carers for help and to her partner, there is a gap at the heart of her sense of self. For much of the interview she stressed that she had blocks to memory and that this had got worse rather than better. She wanted to look forward rather than back, but then that left her without a secure foundation for building a more positive mental representation of the self. She was able to describe in small ways how she tried to get a grip on things, but her ability to take care of herself was fragile and fleeting – she did not feel able to think about or imagine a future for herself or Darren and lived one day at a time.

> *And I think I manage to control my depression quite a lot through it. If I feel like I'm starting to go down, I pop to bed for half an hour, have a cup of tea and something to eat, watch telly for half and hour and then get on again . . .*
>
> So you have strategies. So when you do go out, do you have people to talk to?
> *Yes, I'll go and see friends usually. All my friends have got children and to be honest it's quite relieving to stick them out in the garden and just sit in the sun.*

She still had regrets that she could not match up to her own high standards.

> *It does get quite hard sometimes. But I've learned to deal with it. I believe that . . . it might sound a bit funny but I believe I'm someone else. I believe that I'm a different person. I believe I'm a lot friendlier, a lot more outgoing and things. But I think to find who I really am, I need to get rid of all the tension . . .*
>
> So you think you could be a different kind of person?
> *I think I could be very outgoing, you know, talkative . . .*
>
> Do you like yourself as you are now?
> *No . . . I don't have a lot of self-confidence. It's more the things I do than the person I am. I don't like the fact that I cannot cope with everything every day. I go to someone's house and it's brilliantly tidy . . . and you know, sometimes I wish I could be different but at the moment I have to accept that I am who I am.*

This moving account of the struggle of a young mother, still only 18 years old, suggested a difficulty for her around how to use other people as resources and some persisting tensions between belonging to her two families. She resolved this by relying on her own "determination", which unfortunately let her down at intervals.

The story of a similar downward spiral in adolescence for another young woman offered a more positive emphasis on available resources in adult life, although the anxieties of both young mothers should not be underestimated. What was striking about Jennie's account of her life to date (age 21) was that it appeared that there were some key turning points and that each experience had given her some resource which she drew on in adult life. Her first foster family had given her an experience of a stable family life where she had a predictable and stimulating environment. They did become her family in a very real sense. Her second foster family had been very emotionally demonstrative and she said she learned to be more open and affectionate. The mental health hostel, where she went in her teens, was a very negative experience for her and she said she ought to be paid compensation for going there, but she also said, 'I learned there that my life is smooth, perfect compared to a lot of people. I've got it well easy.' The carer who offered supported lodgings after she left the hostel was a source of strength, was fond of her, available for her and taught her how to survive practically with cooking and dealing with bills. This carer took in a difficult teenager in crisis and gave her much more than "lodgings". This was a key turning point in Jennie's life. She had lost two foster families, had acquired a mental illness label and was very vulnerable as a young person soon to be beyond the usual systems for looked after children or care leavers.

In adult life, Jennie had a number of resources, both internal and external. Although she had some problems with self-esteem and close relationships with partners, she had a circle of friends. She ran her life with care, she was a planner, and was determined not to get into debt – she was the only one among her circle of friends who had a phone that had not been cut off and she had to limit how much her friends used it. Her original foster family had remained very much in touch since she left at the age of 14. They gave her phone cards when she left, which was both a practical help for keeping in touch and a message of continuity. They had been there at the hospital when she had her baby and provided the new pram. They were grandparents to her child and offered support. Jennie said of them,

> *My real family is my foster parents, no matter what anybody says. They'll always be my mum and dad.*

Her foster brother is very close and regularly comes to see her and they go for walks together. But if she had a problem with money or practical things, she would ring up her supported lodgings carer, who remained very available for her. She said of her:

> *She's excellent. She's open and everything. Like she's very down to earth. If you've got a problem I guarantee she'll sort it out.*

This last carer, who was not expected to provide a family for Jennie, nevertheless provided a family environment and a close relationship which offered her availability, care and protection which had extended into adult life.

Jennie's social worker for about eight years (from when Jennie was seven) remained in touch and had been a constant figure, showing an interest in her welfare, even though she had now moved on to a management role in the agency. This is perhaps the best kind of life story work – to be in touch with a young woman at 21 whom you knew when she was a little girl.

Jennie still had some thoughts from her past that troubled her and which revealed themselves in specific anxieties, for example, about relationships and hygiene. For Jennie, the positive picture of resources available to her and the sense of her resilience have to be considered in the light of her lack of comfort with her physical self. She said little about how she represented herself as a person in terms of her personality characteristics, self-esteem and so on, but has a distressing sense of her body as a source of anxiety. Difficult for her was the fact that she had no information, no memory, episodic or semantic, to explain to herself why she might have these feelings. She did not link them with her infantile experience in her birth family, from which she was removed at six months. Nor did she blame the foster carers. These feelings then are as difficult to manage as preverbal infantile anxieties that appear rooted in sensory experience, in the body of the infant, and where there is no cognitive scaffolding to make sense of them. Like bad dreams, such feelings can inflict themselves when least expected.

In summary, turning points in this group include the positive view of the arrival in this foster family, with serious downward spirals in adolescence following the second major turning point – the discontinuity of care when the placement that had lasted since early childhood ended. It seemed possible that loss and separation in adolescence, not being "held" through crucial teenage years, was very damaging to the sense of self, coming as it inevitably did on top of the stories of loss and neglect in the birth family that hampered their childhood. However, continuity of family membership, with parental concern from carers, left the door open for reconciliation. Having a baby seemed to be an opportunity for renegotiating and healing – as foster carers who had lost their daughters became fond grandparents.

Key for this group is the sense, still, of not being held in adolescence and the resulting fragility in early adult life. Although they were reflecting on a problematic past the problems had not gone away. The mental representations of themselves still had negative overtones and there was a sense of a "missing" real person that still needed to be found. The self was viewed as independent and determined, yet there was also a sense of the self as being at heart still the needy infant described at the outset, with infantile anxieties not having been entirely contained even in stable foster families. Success was apparent in the stability of their lives and their parenting and in some cases in their relationships. But the battle for the sense of the self as lovable and truly effective continued.

8 Rescue, relief and recovery

Pathway summary: Continuous care, continuous membership, rewarding intimate relationships with/gratitude to foster carers as parents FOLLOWING the experience of poor relationships, neglect and/or abuse in a birth family AND in a previous adoptive/foster family.

The key theme here is the sense of relief and rescue experienced by children who had experienced poor care or maltreatment to some degree in both a birth family and a previous substitute family. They went on to experience this third-chance family as a family for life. This pathway tracks stories that include some of the worst and some of the best in substitute family care, some of the worst and some of the best in human nature. If such extremes are challenging to hear about as a researcher, how much more challenging are they to remember and make sense of for the adults who have had these multiple and contradictory experiences of others and of themselves in childhood.

By definition these are later foster placements, with ages ranging from eight to 14 at the time of final placement. The quality of the caregiving and the degree of harm in previous families varied. In birth families the range was from neglect by a step-parent following the death of both parents through to neglect leading to the death of a sibling through to serious emotional, physical, and possible sexual abuse of this child. The caregiving and harm in the previous foster or adoptive family ranged from emotional coldness, emotional neglect or emotional abuse through to regular physical beatings and sexual abuse. These adults tell stories of remarkable recoveries in later childhood, which they attribute to the secure care, emotional availability and often the patience offered in this final placement. Detailed attachment stories are told. It appears that these foster carers took in children whose reluctance to engage in relationships, depression, behaviour problems and anxieties could be lived with and contained within their families. The children also felt they fitted in –

sometimes by being valued as the only girl or because the carers made them feel special and at home in spite of their problems. These, too, were real families.

Some stories seem to suggest that maltreatment by carers *may* be processed by children more effectively in terms of their self-esteem and internal working model (especially with the help of subsequent carers) than maltreatment by birth parents. Betrayal might not seem so complete. Blame could additionally often be laid at the door of social workers. It is also important to note that, although the problematic foster or adoptive family had not offered secure emotional care and had in some cases abused the children, the children had been given a kind of stability, steady attendance at school, adequate food and so on. This point is controversial. It is not intended to minimise the harm in these placements, but may need to be taken into account in explaining the comparative ease with which some children managed to fit in a social sense in their new families, schools and communities.

None had contact or involvement with birth parents in childhood, for reasons that included a closed adoption, the death of both parents and the severity of the abuse by birth parents. Contact with birth siblings occurred – all had previously lived with or been placed with siblings but were separated at some point, by chance, by care plan or by their own choice.

Legacy

All had a (foster) family in adult life to whom they felt close and whom they saw as emotionally and practically available. But, as with the two previous pathways, in adult life there were generally some residual symptoms of emotional difficulty and anger (with the exception of one young woman who had experienced a relatively mild form of neglect in both previous families). There was, for example, anxiety about relationships, eating problems, bad dreams, tempers. These symptoms were not described as causing major problems, but the anxiety was often that the old hurts could resurface at any time. There was a range of emotional strength and vulnerability. One of the more successful young adults had been able to develop a succession of positive relationships with her partner and friends building on the secure base provided by the foster carers with whom she had lived from the age of 14 to 17. However, she too had many partly unresolved feelings and fears about her past. None had any contact or involvement with birth parents in adult life.

For this group there emerged several distinctions to be made in terms of the way in which experiences were described. One distinction was the way in which stories of the successful placements, the third chance families, fell into the "grateful to carers" pattern that characterises Group 1 placements or were in the 'I was difficult but coped with', more conflicted pattern of Group 2. The second distinction lies in the vividness of the memories and seriousness of the harm experienced in the birth family relative to the first foster or adoptive family. Some people had the sense that the major harm was experienced in the birth family, others that it was in the first foster or adoptive placement, and others that harm was caused in *both*. These were confusing pictures with complex multiple sources of information about the self and others to be processed contemporaneously and in adult life.

What the children brought from birth families

Although experiences in the birth family could be very worrying for children in this group, there were some who did not recall being deliberately harmed or being unprotected by birth family attachment figures. Stories here included the account of Amanda, now in her mid-20s, of the death by neglect of a younger sibling. She had some sense of her own responsibility for not getting help quickly enough. This left many questions about the self, but not ones that centred on, 'why did my parents not love me?' In a sense, it left the separation from birth parents less resolved for her because of this. Amanda spoke of this in a strained, childlike voice.

> *Originally I was told that the reason I came into care was that my parents couldn't cope and that my brother had died . . . and that I'd still be able to see Mummy and Daddy but . . . not live with them.*
>
> OK, OK . . .
>
> *Obviously at that age you're upset.*

Christine's story was of the death of her mother at two years of age, followed by the death of her father at the age of five, followed by neglectful care by a disturbed step-mother which resulted in admission to care. Again there was a profound sense of loss and bereavement, but no sense of having been rejected or neglected by birth parents and a consequent diminishing of self-worth. A rather more difficult story to deal with was Anna's account of being one of five children given up for adoption. But even here, her cognitive appraisal of that situation was that of a mother who had been simply overwhelmed.

There were more serious and damaging accounts of fear and abuse in the birth family. For Chloe, the birth family environment had included emotional neglect and physical abuse by both her biological father and her mother's various partners. She had no sense of her mother as a person, but resented the way in which the lack of care led to her loss of a childhood. She had a variable recall of early childhood in the birth family, remembering the facts but not the feelings, not even the fear.

> *Well – I remember all the things like, I remember being hit, you know, my mum having new boyfriends. I can remember the bad side about it but I can't remember . . . but I think there was a lot more bad than there was good.*
>
> So do you remember being frightened?
>
> *Oh no, I don't remember being frightened . . . I suppose I was . . . I remember carrying like knives to bed with me in case we had a lodger come into the room . . . and like me and my brother would be there . . . to protect him . . . but I can't remember myself being frightened . . .*

Her mother's lack of interest in Chloe was perhaps most vividly remembered when she described the day she was taken into care.

> *My mum must have known for ages they were taking us but she hadn't prepared us. She sat there . . . she had a glass of whiskey in one hand, a fag in the other . . . she didn't kiss us good-bye . . . give us a hug or nothing like that . . . Don't get me wrong . . . my mother was never somebody who would shout at me or smack me . . . she just would rather not get involved . . . she was just drugged up all the time.*

Her mother's neglect is explained and excused to some extent in terms of her addiction to drugs. Chloe had stronger feelings of anger towards her father, because of his active rejection and violence.

> *He was very old school . . . he always made it clear that he never wanted me . . . he wanted my brother, he wanted a boy, he never wanted me . . . he had children from two other marriages . . . and he never wanted a girl . . . so much of that was physical. I remember my brother breaking a key in the lock of his car . . . and literally that was a wet belt not just a smack and I can remember my brother asleep on the settee and I was hiding behind the settee. I really hate the man . . . he's really frightening . . . he's not very tall and I know now he's got an artificial hip but if I met him today I'd still be scared of him.*

It is unclear whether feelings of fear are more strongly associated with her violent birth father than with her mother's violent partners because of the increased sense of betrayal and emotional rejection or whether the quality of the violence was itself more frightening.

Her memory of who she was and what she was like as a little child was limited.

> So what kind of little girl were you before you were taken into care . . . ?
>
> *I don't know . . . No . . . I don't know nothing about myself, what I was like, I don't know about the toys I played with . . . all I can ever remember is being a nursemaid to my brother . . . I used to cook for him, feed him . . . I was like a little mum . . . I've just been talking to my brother about this . . . and I remember when he had chicken pox, I was the one looking after him . . . that's all I can really remember.*

Although she resents at some level the fact that she had to look after her brother, it does leave her with a positive image of herself to hold onto in the face of adult caregiving that was both neglectful and abusive.

The first long-term placements

Many of the adults in this group were able to remember the day they were taken into care. For one young woman, the process was marked by the social worker's pretence that they were going on holiday and the fact that she and her brother were taken to separate placements and then not allowed contact for several months. She said, 'They split me and my brother up . . . and I'll never forgive them for that'. Here there is explicit anger against social workers, a theme which will be more widely explored later.

Others, however, entered these first long-term placements with their siblings and had a strong sense of shared fate, both in the loss of birth family and in coping with the poor care they then faced. Poor care was defined either in terms of being treated differently from birth children or in absolute terms. Where there was a memory that the foster carers treated them as different from birth children and, in some senses, as unworthy of care, this was bitterly resented. As Kate described it:

> *I was there for nearly five years and it was the worst five years of my life . . . We got . . . They had two children of their own. They were the family and we were just the lodgers. We were just the foster kids. We were nothing basically. They used to – obviously young children, you get them to go to the toilet before they go to bed but half-way through the night they'd wake you up to go again. We had to have a . . . I know it sounds funny, but I can still remember it now, we had to have four squares of toilet roll and if we didn't have it we had to lay awake all night trying to find it. I mean it was silly things like that. They used to close the door and put like the old tobacco tins at the door so if we opened the door and got out they'd know . . . mmm . . . I mean sometimes I mean we weren't well fed with my mum anyway so we needed building up in a sense. We were basically skinny I mean at seven I was only three stone.*
>
> Yes . . .
>
> *So sometimes meals was just a bowl of soup. And we was . . . our dinners was separate from theirs. We weren't allowed in the front room when they were in there. Me and my brother used to do the washing up you know, they never done anything. Silly things. They used to say 'Right your chores' . . . I know you have to do chores anyway . . . but I had to clean the whole front room.*

This account was prefaced with the statement that these carers were not allowed to foster again after this placement.

From Kate's description, her role as big sister in the birth family continued, as she tried to make things less distressing for her younger siblings.

I was even looking after them when I was in that foster home.

That time must have been very difficult.
They did come before me in my sense. I did help them . . . there was the occasional – 'go away, I don't want to know . . .'

So if they had kindness would it be kindness from you?
Yes . . . (became upset and tearful)

And where would you go for kindness?
From myself. I got pleasure out of them being happy. That made me happy.

School, in this context, was a relief.

It was as though I was allowed to be let loose for the day. I was good at school, I done my work – I mean I've always done my school work before anything else. It was just like a release. It was so nice. It was like coming out of prison.

This account of such lack of care in a foster home was not, unfortunately, unique. A very similar story came from Emily, this time the youngest in her sibling group.

They were a very posh family and she had one daughter. I think she must have done it purely for the money. We had to stay in one room and it was all like – she had favourites. And me and my oldest brother we're quite academic and because the other two weren't up to it, if they couldn't do what we could do, they were told they were thick.

Similar to Kate's experience, the foster children were not allowed in most parts of the house.

Well we were only allowed in one room and that only in the evening. We couldn't be in the house when she wasn't there – we had to wait outside for up to an hour after school so that they'd pick up their daughter.

One vivid example of this exclusion from normal family life, or even consideration, was the fact that the extended foster family get-together for Sunday lunch could not include the foster children, so they were sent out for the day.

We were out all day Sunday on the buses. Mike, the foster dad, used to take us down the corner shop and get us four bus passes and then we'd go out for the day. He'd give us a packed lunch. And then we would get back about 6 o'clock.

But you were quite young then – 6?
Yes. 6.

So you were expected to stay out together all day?
Yes, we had no particular place to go, just out of the house. So . . .

For both these girls, these placements had been preceded by residential placements that had offered them more care and more freedom. They commented:

That foster home was worse than children's homes really. Because at least the children's home felt like home. You could go anywhere you wanted to. You could go in the front room, in the dining room you could do what you wanted.

I quite liked the children's home. It was home, one big happy family.

Kirsty had a similar feeling of being singled out in her substitute family, but this time singled out for emotional rejection in an adoptive family. Kirsty and her more lively but also more demanding and difficult younger sister, Sian, were placed for adoption, aged seven and five.

I used to get . . . basically – because I was the oldest . . . I used to get it . . . Sian used to get really bad tantrums – she used to scare me so much – me being the oldest one but I was scared . . . I was a person who didn't show my emotions but she would – if we got sent to our rooms . . . she used to lay on the floor and kick her legs it used to scare me . . . I used to be grounded most of the time . . .

Right – and what would grounding involve?
Being up in my room. Sian hardly ever used to be . . . I used to get

blamed for everything but towards the end they used to say, 'we don't care where you're going, just go wherever you want . . .' I never used to sit down with them in the end . . . I used to have meals in my room . . . just because basically I had no interest in common with them.

So the adoptive mother, can you think of five words to describe your relationship with her, what would they be?
Non-existent really. We weren't close at all. Hardly at all.

Can you think back to that relationship, can you think of words to describe it?
Cold, it was very cold . . . on her side . . . she liked order . . . She liked kids who were there to be seen and not heard, that type of thing . . . She just wanted perfect children and you don't get perfect children.

It is not possible to know the extent to which the children themselves had brought problems into this adoptive family from the birth family which the adopters simply could not cope with or whether the adoptive parents had problems of their own or some combination. But the pattern that established itself left this child feeling unloved and isolated.

These were often complex relationships, in which foster carers and adopters were floundering and the question of control, for both carers and child, led to the family home becoming a battleground. Melanie found her foster carers' behaviour hard to understand.

Why do you think they fostered?
Well they had no children of their own and they'd get money for doing it . . . that's the only thing I can think of . . . they're so money obsessed . . . that's the only reason I can think because they didn't show me no love, no compassion, anything . . . they're just . . . I just couldn't explain . . . unless you knew them . . . they're just absolutely mad . . .

Although some of the rows she described, such as over her truanting, seemed unsurprising, there were other incidents that confused and upset her because the foster carers' reactions seemed irrational, disproportionate, or both.

To start off with that was really nice and then there were little things . . . like I lost my pencil case at school one day . . . and she literally hit the

> *roof. You know the little china pots you make at school, and clay masks, she smashed everything, every single piece of pottery I ever made . . . you know she went ballistic because I lost this pencil case. And the next day I went to school and the headmaster had my pencil case and at the end of the day they were calculating what had been stolen out of it, obviously someone had nicked the pencil case. And I went home and she didn't apologise to me or anything. They were so warped I can't understand it.*

Tania described how the carers' control of her included endless preoccupation with her showering and bathing. They would smack her and lock her in her room if she disobeyed. Discipline verged on the bizarre and disturbing because of their membership of a spiritualist church.

> *They used to go to spiritualist church and that started getting frightening. I mean I'd never experienced anything like that. Things like we had to sit there and it was, 'Someone's going to come after you, if you don't start behaving yourself'. And I hadn't done anything . . . That does send you doolally, you start cracking up . . . I don't know whether it was the teenage bit they couldn't put up with, they . . . they got a medium in, a spiritualist medium, to see what was going on in my head . . .*

She felt powerless to change things, another reason for distrusting social workers.

> *I can always remember saying, 'I don't want to be here, I don't like it'. I kept saying, 'They're mad, they're mad', but nobody took any notice of me.*

Tania had had the experience of fear, physical, emotional and possible sexual abuse in her birth family followed by what could be described as emotional or psychological abuse and some physical ill-treatment in her foster family. She herself used the words, "physical and mental cruelty" to describe this experience. Although these experiences were clearly distressing, she seems to have tried to hang on to her sense that she was OK and it was they who had the problem. She described feeling that at school she was a "normal teenager" and said 'even the headmaster said, "she's no different from any other child we've got in the school" ', when the foster carers complained about her behaviour. She was clearly an angry teenager at this stage (in her early teens) but in terms of her self-esteem she clung on to the fact that she was "normal". Nevertheless, her mental representation of herself as a "daughter" and these carers as "parents" was confused.

> *I thought . . . you don't know if Derek and Irene are supposed to be your parents . . . because I went to this couple and they had no children, are they my parents?*

When the placement finally ended, it was on a Christmas Eve and the ending was initiated by the carers, who said that they could not cope any more. Even then she remembers feeling anxious and lost at the ending of her life in this family that had become all she knew.

Beth, the child who was placed youngest in this group in an unsuccessful foster home (at 18 months), had the most difficulty in settling comfortably into the subsequent "rescuing" family. This could have been a consequence of a number of features of this earlier experience. The emotional abuse in the first foster home was severe and singled her out for rejection, leaving more of a legacy of anger and bitterness than negative experiences shared with siblings. It was the foster mother whom she found to be both rejecting and psychologically distorting. As with Tania's experience of spiritualist foster carers, induced fear of supernatural forces were a part of this placement.

> *She was the abusive one, things like she used to say she was a witch and things, like she used to hit me a lot. It was like she had had some sort of personality problem you know. I would be made to eat in the kitchen, I was sort of still eating with a spoon until I was eight, you know she would sort of deliberately serve me up the food which she knew I didn't like and my sandwiches for school every day were just bread and butter sandwiches and a flask of milk. My breakfast every day was porridge. No she just had like this huge . . . it was like she had to have control and she had to, whatever it was she had to control it and if she couldn't control it then she would just flip out and you know just get rid of it you know.*

> Can you think of five words to describe your relationship with her? What would they be?
> *I am going to try and think of nice words.*
>
> Choose the words that first come into your head when you think of your relationship with her as a child.
> *Evil, psychopathic bitch* (giggles) . . . *No, something along those lines.*
>
> So evil, give me an example of her being evil.
> *Things like she used to take some sort of joy out of the treatment she would give. She had 13 dogs and the dogs, it was written quite a lot in the files and I also felt a hell of a lot that the dogs were more important to her than her children were and particularly than what I was to her. I suppose I was always like the black sheep you know. Things like she used to lock my bedroom door with a dog lead tied to the banister. My earliest childhood memory was being made to eat a spider, it was like being locked in my bedroom and not being allowed out to the toilet and so having to go to the toilet in toys. Eating wallpaper because I was so hungry at night, spitting in my hands and drinking spit because I was so thirsty, yes things like that.*

Beth recalled Christmas lunches.

> *Yes, I mean even at Christmas time like my foster mother and father and my foster sister and then like my nanny and grand-dad they all sat in the lounge and I sat in the kitchen and I remember hearing like, there used to be like the hatch in the kitchen through to the lounge, I can remember like hearing like all the crackers being pulled and all the rest of it and sort of thinking 'oh' but you know . . .*

There are unfortunate echoes here of other placements described above where children were treated as less than birth children, fed separately and differently, not supposed to go to the toilet at night. Basic physical needs that should be met in the context of a developing secure emotional relationship were not met, but were experienced as putting them at further risk of rejection and hurt within relationships with caregivers. The fact that such children go on to experience disturbed relationships with their own bodies is perhaps not surprising when bodily signals have a history of leading to distress.

The accounts of cool and controlling relationships in foster care and adoption were told with some feeling, but more extreme was the experience of physical and sexual abuse suffered by one girl and her siblings in an adoptive family. They were placed as a sibling group, at some distance from where they were born, through a social services newspaper advertisement. All went well, Louise said, until the adoption orders were made and the social workers stopped visiting.

> *They would . . . they first checked on us till the adoption . . . and then . . . they stopped coming. They thought . . . OK everything's going to be fine . . . and then it started. He thought – you're mine now. They can't do anything.*

Then there came the "telling off" on Sundays when, having taken the family to church in the morning, the father would later beat them with a belt or a cane. The sexual abuse of her older sister started first, followed by the sexual abuse of herself. The cruelty is graphically described, with her sister being beaten for wetting the bed and then taking sheets to a neighbour before school to be washed in the hope of evading detection. The role of the adoptive mother was described as one of complicity rather than protection.

> *She said that she didn't know anything that was going on but I reckon she did because I remember one time, my brother told me, he was in the kitchen with my mum and my sister and I were getting told off and he heard everything . . . like slapping and everything and there was my mum just washing up . . . But she was pretending she couldn't hear anything. I remember one time she came into our room and I had my hands on a chest of drawers waiting to get hit by the cane . . .*
>
> Yes . . .
>
> *Yes . . . and I was getting hit by the cane and like I was moving my hands because I didn't want to get hit . . . moving like . . . and she came in and said, 'What are you doing?' and he said, 'I'm telling her off' and he told her what I was doing, like moving away, so she held my hands so I couldn't move . . . So I think she knew what was going on. So he*

hit me like twice as hard like and twice as many times as I was supposed to get hit . . . so she didn't really care.

Here the use of the term "telling off" must have normalised the punishment within the family, even though such an assault had a Dickensian sense of being cold-blooded, planned and with the number of times for being hit somehow laid down to a formula. The contrast with the highly respectable public face of this family was very hard for the children to deal with, as was the question, why me? This psychological confusion was added to by the "special" treatment associated with the sexual abuse, which this young woman said she only made sense of in later counselling.

The emotional support in these placements came from siblings, even in these extreme situations. 'Why me?' became 'Why us?'

So what would you do when you were upset when you were with this family?

What we did was, if I got abused I'd tell my sister and my brother, and my sister would tell me and my brother and if my brother got abused he'd tell me and my sister. So we were all close then . . . We turned to each other . . . and went ohhh then but like . . . hit him . . . Look at him and look at her and then . . . oi . . . I can't do it . . .

This account of sibling support breaks down, with the language becoming incoherent, as if the attempt to capture what it was like to share this experience of abuse together defeats her powers of expression. The sense of confusion continues, but Louise is then able to articulate the gap between the public and private faces of this family.

So was he quite frightening?

What . . . my dad? . . . Yes, he was. Like ever so . . . like . . . you know. He had a split personality really – if you'd like to call it that. Because on Sundays we used to go to church and then shopping . . . by the afternoon or evening we'd get smacked or hit. When you think . . . woh . . . he's supposed to be good as gold . . .

Eventually, she said, her teenage brother could no longer tolerate the abuse of his sisters and disclosed to teachers at school. They were immediately removed and the adoptive father was tried, convicted and imprisoned.

In summary, this catalogue of negative foster and adoptive family experiences followed on from negative birth family experiences. Often there had to be other moves, attempts at placement for adoption and so on, before children reached the foster family which was still their family at the time of interview. The children had multiple problems with the sense of self and the ability to trust in adults at the point of this final placement.

Foster family care in their final placement

These children found themselves finally in foster families that offered a healing relationship, that allowed them to recover from their distress, and that enabled them to let go of some of their anger and need to control. There is a mass of detail about these families in the interview data, but for the purpose of this section it seems appropriate to focus on the stories/memories that most accurately capture the parenting qualities in these carers that appear to have made the difference. In a theoretical context, these are stories of the building of attachments for older children (aged 8 to 14) in the context of sensitive and available parenting.

Often, it could be the very moment of meeting the new family that provided the striking contrast with what had gone before. This account is from Chloe who was 14 years old at the time of this placement. She burst into tears as she started to describe this scene with her new foster father.

> *When I first went there . . . I was . . . sorry . . . I'm going to get emotional here . . . They're the only people who've . . . ever . . . done anything for me. The first time I met them and David sat and talked to me as if I was something, I was somebody . . . he weren't talking to social workers, what does she like? But talking to ME about it. And I just remember . . . I just couldn't stop crying . . . I didn't understand what was going on . . . I'd just been moved 25 miles from my friends at school . . . I didn't know how I'd cope with all that . . . a new family . . . but he was . . . they were just brilliant, they turned me right round. If it hadn't have been for them I wouldn't have got any GCSEs, I wouldn't have been able to read and write, I wouldn't have the life I have now. I don't know any other way I can explain them . . . they're just*

wonderful people . . . brilliant they're just really . . . they are so brilliant . . . I could go on about them all day . . . they are just such nice people.

Where children had been in neglectful, controlling or unkind foster families and had felt powerless and unlovable, the fact that new carers treated them with respect and concern was overwhelming. This further account given by Chloe, now in her 20s, was able to provide clarification of what she means by the kind of parenting that "turned her around".

So if you think about that time with Anne and David, can you think about five words to describe your relationship with Anne?
With Anne . . . very caring, understanding, sensitive, there's just so many things . . . I could go on all day . . .

Could you give me an example of her being caring . . . ?
Mmm, it's just . . . I can phone her up now and if I have a problem she'll say, I'll come round and talk to you or . . . when I was living there and said, this is upsetting me or something like that I knew that I could sit down and we'd have a conversation about it. She's the only person in my life who would sit down and tell me what she honestly thinks I should do . . . and she'll give me honest and true.

It was the physical and emotional availability that counted, plus openness and honesty. When previous foster carers had been unavailable and even harsh emotionally, the value placed on availability is not surprising. But the importance of carers who were straight with you was especially significant where previous carers had been irrational and confusing. As in infancy, these children needed straight information about the minds of the carers and help to reflect on their own minds in order to begin, rather late in the day, to discover their own capacity to think (Fonagy, 2001).

What was significant for this young woman, as for other young men and women across the sample, was the very important role that emotionally available foster fathers could play.

And David . . . five words to describe your relationship with him?
Oh, he's just brilliant. They've done a hell of a lot for me . . . they're just wonderful people . . . if I had to chosen five words I'd say the same

> *about him . . . he's . . . he's caring, kind, sensitive . . . I can't think of the words to use . . .*
>
> Can you give me an example of him being caring . . . ?
> *I suppose one thing that springs to mind isn't the kind of thing you think about but I went to Spain with them, and I took my friend Lisa, and David because he didn't want us walking to the disco, which was over the other side . . . he took us and he stayed there all night just to make sure we kept safe. He stayed all that time even though that must have been as boring as hell for him . . . you know, a teenage disco, but he stayed there . . . you know . . . I'm sorry . . . but that's the one that springs to mind . . .*

For Chloe, the fact that fear of her birth father was still a major issue for her meant that a kind foster father was especially important in thinking through what "fathers" or even men are about. This episodic memory is a classic attachment story of how a caregiver was sensitive and protective and put his own needs secondary to his wish to protect her. Other teenagers might not find such protectiveness so welcome or memorable, but for a child who described her own birth parents as simply not caring what happened to her, this story has a particular poignancy. Also striking is the sense she has of how it felt to him to get bored waiting for his foster daughter and the gratitude is proportionate to her capacity to think about the content of his mind. Important also is the fact that in spite of her sense that the incident was minor, she does remember the experience as meaningful and symbolic of the concern he felt and of the relationship.

For others, the discovery that this new foster family was the family for them took much longer. One young woman had experienced, in addition to four years in a less than happy foster home with her siblings, an unsuccessful adoption separated from them. At the age of eleven, Amanda had been seen as 'the one with problems'. In that adoptive family she admits, 'I shut them out . . . I don't think they could cope with my bad moods'. At that point she felt isolated, 'I was alone. If it's possible to feel like that. I felt alone. Because I'd always been with them (siblings)'.

After the adoption broke down, Amanda was placed in a foster home, which she was told would be for six months only. But during that time she began to feel not only that she did not want to move again but that this family was special for her. Even when she first went there it seemed different.

I wasn't treated with kid gloves, the boys had a go at me . . . I used to give it all back to them . . . I wasn't treated no different. It was as though I'd been there all my life. It wasn't – 'she's a new girl', it was 'she's part of the family now – get on with it'.

But you'd been told that you were only there for six months.

Yes. After a couple of months I had settled in, I was in a routine. I got to like . . . I was calling them Jane and Gordon in the house but when I went out . . . I called them mum and dad. I thought if I call them that indoors they're going to say something. So . . . come the point where they said, you either call us mum and dad or you call us Jane and Gordon, the choice is yours – so from that day it was mum and dad. And then when six months got closer I thought, I don't want to leave here. I thought I can't talk to them I was too embarrassed, so what I did was write them a letter, which my mum's still got.

There are several key points in this story. First, the sense of the ordinary and the normal in family life, as Amanda defines it, was important, in particular the robust but matter-of-fact way in which this whole family responded to what had been seen as difficult to manage behaviours before. The point at which she asserted herself to write the letter for the review, saying that she wanted to stay, was important in terms of self-efficacy – she had made the choice in a way which had not occurred in previous placements. In addition, her mother valuing that moment enough to preserve the letter affected how that moment in time is mentally represented and makes it symbolic of the magical nature of the family connection. The day of the review then becomes equivalent to the day of coming into care or the making of an adoption order, marking a transition or turning point. It was hard to wait for the "verdict".

It went on quite a long time actually . . . I even remember it now and mention it to me mum now, and just laugh. And my social worker Frank

> *came out and said 'Well, we've made a decision but you won't know it till half past four'. Well, that was three-and-a-half hours away, then he said, 'but I can tell you now that if you'd like her to stay she can stay'. Well, that was one of the happiest days of my life. Apart from my son being born, that was. I thought, 'Now I belong somewhere', because I knew them and I could get on with them.*

She mentions this day to her mum, even now, as a rite of passage into the family.

Amanda emphasised her closeness to her foster mother, but the most detailed attachment story came in the discussion of her relationship with her foster father.

> *He was just involved. A proper dad. He was interested in all of us equally. Even the older ones who weren't at school. He cared. About what* we *were doing. Even when he went away on courses, he would phone us up everyday – are you behaving yourself? Everyday he wanted to speak to us. He could ask your mum how the kids are, how are you and not speak to us, but he would actually speak to us. He went on two courses and would say, 'Are you behaving yourself?' 'Yes, Dad!' Obviously we weren't* (laughs) *– Mum wouldn't even tell him.*

Here we have the sense of the father's involvement and interest in Amanda and also the sense of this being special yet shared with both birth and other long-term foster children. This is very similar to the accounts of real families in Group 1. Like Group 1, this foster family was a busy foster family, but the children mattered as individuals. The question and answer were ritualised, ending with 'Yes, Dad!'. The mother's conspiracy of silence is part of the ritual joke. Family ritual is an important marker for belonging, for the predictability of the carer and for the sharing and preservation of family history.

Telling here also is the sense of the father as keeping the children "in mind" when away from them. This classic parenting trait of accessibility as defined by Ainsworth *et al* (1971) is valued and selectively remembered by the adults as they look back. Amanda's account of both foster parents is that whenever they were out shopping in town they would think to bring something back for her. This sense of being "thought about" is containing (Winnicott, 1965) and offers a powerful benefit for children who are learning to value their own individuality and minds and to think about others' minds rather late in childhood. This builds then into her definition of her role in the family.

Even though I'm not theirs, you know . . . I was part of a family. I wasn't separated, as I was in that other placement as a foster kid. I was just there, I was their sister, basically. I couldn't do without them now, not at all. I haven't been there for seven years and I'm still there.

The immediacy of this description of family feeling in childhood is at least in part because it has continued into the present intensity of her involvement. She is "still there" within the family boundaries even though she moved out seven years ago when she had her son.

Although this early sense of being part of the family and the joint commitment at a review was a turning point, the process of change in Amanda's sense of self was slow. The containing power of this foster family, carers and brothers, was vividly described as she remembered, pictured herself in her early teens. Being treated as a family member going through a difficult phase rather than as an outsider that cannot be coped with and might be sent back was the hallmark of this family experience.

I did have bad moods then but they weren't as bad. At one stage I grew all my hair, all my fringe, so no one could see me. And I used to sit in one chair. And they put this thingy on it saying, Amanda's chair, don't sit! It was sort of thing . . . but that made me laugh. It brought me out of it more likely.

These moods – did you feel sad, depressed . . . what sort of feelings did you have?

I mean I'd get bouts of where I'd just sit and think of everything. That's why my mum took my life book away because I'd just sit there and brood over it.

Yes.

That's why she took that away. And I'd just think and as before . . . Why is this happening to me? Even though I was in the place where I wanted to be. Why is this happening to me? Why doesn't nobody want *me? Why can't I be with my mum and dad? But now it's all different.*

These moods lasted quite a while and she offered an explanation of why she came out of them. She realised that she had to move on and let go of her grief at the loss of her younger siblings.

You said it took two years for your moods to clear?

Mmm. I still have moods but it must have been better when I started doing GCSEs. My mind was being more occupied. And I was – I can say I forgot about my brother and sister, I mean I didn't but I had, if you know what I mean, I had to get on with my *life now.*

This turning point was only made possible by the stimulus to achieve at school and the continuing patience and containing availability of the carers. As she put it, even when moods led to rows, she never feared separation or placement breakdown.

No . . . I knew that they could cope with it. I knew that it would blow over in a day and we'd go back to normal. It would all be forgotten. It wouldn't hang over my head.

The turning point at GCSE stage was later reinforced by other turning points, particularly the birth of her own son, Jamie, and the reading of the Inquiry report into the death of her infant brother. This report answered some of her questions, in particular allowing her to let go of her sense of her own guilt and to face the painful fact that it was her parents who were responsible for her brother's death.

The year after Jamie was born, I was 19. It hit me so much. The reason . . . as I got older I felt more guilty because it was me who rang for the ambulance. If you read the book . . . a young girl – I can't remember exactly which words . . . that was me. The phone box was just opposite where we lived and I thought, it's my fault it didn't get here in time. And all through my life I felt guilty until that book. And I thought after I read that book – it's not me, it's them. Even though I'd been told by my mum and dad and by social workers, it's not your fault . . . Yes, it is, Don't you tell me it's not. It is. And I think that contributed to my moods as well.

The link between the anxiety about the survival of her own son and the death of her infant brother needed to be broken in order for Amanda to move on.

This is a particularly extraordinary story but so many of these themes of moving on are reflected in other stories, particularly the theme of making the commitment to the new family and the quality of parental emotional availability and family membership. This is Caroline's account of her anxieties about loving relationships and the moment of sealing the new relationship in the foster family.

> *You've got find a new route, on your way. There's no point, because I thought there's no point loving too much because as soon as you start loving someone you're going to move on again. It was always . . . like, oh, you love your mum and dad and then you move on . . . and then . . .*
>
> So did it take you a while to believe that you were going to stay in this new family or did you trust that you would stay?
>
> *Mmm – I trusted my instincts really. And Naomi* (foster carer's birth daughter) *told me as well. She said, 'I heard Mum and Dad talking that you were going to stay.' 'What do you mean stay?' 'We are going to see if we can have you full time', because it was full time anyway and I said, 'Ooh!' and she said, 'What do you think?' And I said, 'YEAH!' so she went and told Mum and Dad, 'I've just told Caroline what you've been talking about' and they said, 'What does she want to do?' And she goes, 'She was over the moon and she wants to stay'. And I went downstairs and gave them a big hug. 'Ohh I want to stay!'*

Two further brief examples of parental availability will reinforce the similarity in the language and concepts across different cases. Louise, who had been physically and sexually abused by her adoptive father, nevertheless felt close to her foster father.

> *Ray was doing a course like on child abuse anyway and he asked for my support about it so it was helpful and he understood what I needed. He didn't pressure me into talking about it, saying like the first three years he didn't know what was going on in my head, what happened. He said, 'You don't have to tell me if you don't want to, but if you want to tell me I'm listening. I'm all ears.' Like he said, 'You don't have to*

> *tell me. I'm not pushing you.' And I told little bits at a time . . . little bits I told him, he was like, oh, like shocked. He wasn't aware what was happening and he said, 'I'm surprised you get on with me so much. Most people are . . .' And I said, 'I suppose it's the love you give me', and he said, 'Oh', and gave me a massive big hug. He gave me everything I wanted in a father figure.*

This is an account that begins with the foster father's respect for Louise and her feeling that she has something to give him. It moves on to further examples of sensitivity in allowing her to take her time, up to three years, to tell her story to him, and concludes with the example of spontaneous physical affection and her definition of him as a "father figure". She gave a further vivid example of his sensitivity and availability.

> Can you think of five words to describe your relationship with your foster father?
> *Ooh! I think all positive words actually, caring, loving, supportive, he gives good guidance. I suppose a good dad.*
>
> Can you give me an example of him being caring?
> *He always showed me affection. Whether he was tired or not . . . He's a teacher . . . even if he was on the computer at two o'clock in the morning . . . 'Ray, could I have a word?' 'Yeah, yeah.' And he'd stop* everything – *'Now what do you want?' If I needed something, he'd get it for me, he'd try his best to get it. He'd discuss what I wanted and try his best to get it . . . everything. If I wanted to bring someone round . . . 'Yeah fine'.*

This night-time picture of the troubled teenage girl who cannot sleep and the tired teacher who still had time for her is movingly described here. His relaxed approach to her friendships may seem a small thing, but several children, including Louise, had experienced the neglectful or abusive former foster or adoptive family as closed and exclusive, with hostility expressed to children meeting others or bringing them home. The "real family" idea featured in various respects in her story. She noted that unlike foster families who left children in respite placements when they went on holiday, "her family" did not do this. As she put it, 'Yes . . . I was always part of the family. I still am really'.

But in spite of her gratitude expressed towards this foster carer as a "dad", Louise found the use of the word rather threatening. She was not alone in needing to distinguish between different meanings and usage of the words "mum" and "dad", but she had particular difficulties because of the previous abusive adoption.

> So did you call them (foster carers) mum and dad at home?
> *No because "mum" and "dad" was like swearing in someone else's dictionary if they never swore in their life. Mum and Dad was like difficult for me to say.*
>
> So who was the mum and dad in your life?
> *Ray and Joan* (carers) *because they were always there.*
>
> Why was it difficult to say those words? . . . Was it to do with your original birth mum and dad or the adoptive mum and dad?
> *It was . . . both really. Because – when I was adopted I called them mum and dad and my real mum and dad, mum and dad, I'd come to the stage when I was adopted . . . I thought if I call them* (foster carers) *mum and dad things are going to go wrong, I'm going to get moved again because I said something wrong said mum and . . . I've tried saying it and it's like . . .*
>
> So you talk about her as mum but wouldn't say mum to her face?
> *It's like on letters to my foster parents now I put, Dearest Mum and Dad or whatever and it makes them happy or to nan and grand-dad and it makes them happy because they are Dean's grandparents which is like* they are *my family.*

This confusing picture, and the confusing language in which it is expressed, suggests that mum and dad are both special terms of endearment and yet like swear words in the sense of dangerous and forbidden words and ideas. Even where the foster family was successfully meeting their needs, the idea of family, as defined psychologically, socially or linguistically, continued to be perplexing.

New placements/children feeling in conflict and coped with

Although the legacy of different kinds of poor care, neglect or abuse was resolved in some respects in subsequent foster families through sensitivity and emotional availability, the alternative version, as in Group 2 cases, could still apply whereby the child brought so much anger and distress into the new placement that it was made very difficult for the carers to parent co-operatively, and conflicts or anxieties of various kinds still troubled the new relationship. This was not surprising where a child, as in Emma's case, had experienced a sense of threat to her survival. Perhaps more surprising, and indeed encouraging for Emma's mental health, is the fact that, as an adult, she has the kind of reflectiveness and insight that allow her to understand the basis of the conflict with her foster mother in her last, more satisfactory placement.

> *She was, I suppose, trying to be like this loving mother kind of, you know, sort of comfort me for all the things that had happened in the past and everything and that would have been brilliant if I had been younger. But because I was older and because of the previous placement like I had to grow up very quickly. It was basically like you either grow up or you don't survive kind of thing and so in that aspect I was quite sort of grown up for my age and so you know, if I had sort of been like eight or nine when I had gone there then I think I would have been able to take to the sort of treatment that she was trying to give me a lot better than what I actually did. Instead it sort of turned to a lot of resentment and I had a lot of anger inside me because of what had happened because finding out so much that you know the person who I always thought I was I actually wasn't, you know, and that you know my birthday wasn't this day, my birthday was this day and . . .*

This last sentence is a reference to the fact that part of what had to be undone was the false history that had been created for her by her first foster carers, including pretending to be her birth parents, changing her name and giving her a different birthday. This, in addition to a range of emotionally abusive parenting behaviours, comprehensively distorted her identity and sense of self. It left her with a legacy of survival tactics, including physical aggression, getting into fights with girls and boys at school.

However, although the new foster home was tense at times, Emma's behaviour shifted towards more ordinary 'typical teenage arguments'. As an adult, she was able to make connections between her early experiences and her difficult and aggressive behaviour in this foster home and at school.

> What's the connection do you think between what had happened to you and getting into fights?
> *I think in a way it was sort of the kind of I had to be in control now you know. It was sort of in a way even now my natural reaction is if someone comes towards me too fast then I automatically strike back first and so the attitude there is kind of you know to get in there first before they hit you kind of thing and so I suppose in a way it was like I had had all this sort of abuse for so many years and now it was like my turn.*

> So when you were in that first foster home, how would you have handled being upset?
> *I just used to sort of like be crying at night in my bed or I think after a while it just got to the point of what's the point of crying because there is no one exactly to sort of hear you or comfort you or anything and so I suppose I, like things used to upset me but I had never sort of realised that they had upset me or you know never sort of made the connection that it had upset me and so where I was kind of given the chance to be my own person, all the things that had ever upset me you know, like now I have had time to realise I was upset you know so it was like nine years or so of upset, anger, disappointment you know every day of my life there was . . .*

> So, you couldn't take that upset to your new foster carer and say 'give me a cuddle?'
> *No. It was too late, I never liked the idea of sort of asking for a cuddle, I would never do that, no. It was never a question, a statement that I was ever brought up with, you know and so instead I used to have, instead it would just come out in a huge argument and like I would*

take out a lot of it on my foster mother, particularly my foster mother because I was closer to her and so I would take more out on her.

This is a remarkable account of the process of moving to a survival position of attacking and being in control when upset and then moving defensively to the denial, even to herself, that she was upset – but later the explosion coming when care was offered and all the feelings welled up. She even has the insight to understand that taking out her anger on her foster mother was not because her mother most deserved it. It was because of the usual (apparent) paradox that she was actually closer to her foster mother.

There were, however, still some opportunities to learn about childhood, mothering and sensitive loving relationships in this final placement and with this foster mother.

I suppose because she used to give like cuddles, she used to give me a bath and she would like read me the bedtime story and tuck me into bed and things like that, just things like mother things, you know but because no one had ever done them before, so it was just like completely like 'wow' you know.

The process of trying to recapture early childhood experiences and enjoy 'mother things', while also being in many ways more sophisticated than other ten-year-olds, was a problem for Emma.

I was trying to relive the baby things, you know, trying to do all the baby things you do but at the same time I was like this ten-year-old. But on top of that was sort of, I wasn't I suppose like the typical ten-year-old, you know and so it was quite highly confusing as to quite what I was.

This confusion as to who or what she was led to fears that she was unsafe in a close relationship. This led to some challenging behaviour.

So did you make it quite difficult for her to look after you?

I suppose I sort of did. I didn't like the feeling that she was getting too close to me sort of emotionally and I suppose in a way it was because I felt that I would be taken away from there or you know something like that because it was like the last two foster homes that I had been in,

> *they were OK but at times this woman* (former long-term foster carer) *was really nasty to me but in some way I suppose I must have loved her because I was always brought up with her and so I, you know, it's like people always say, particularly children in care, you know like they sit there and realise how horrible their mother is and everything and then they turn round and say 'oh but I do love her' you know and you are like 'well why do you love her?' Well maybe I did, because she* (carer) *was my mother you know and it was like however horrible she was you felt as if you must love her because she is your mother and you could never dare turn round and so 'oh I don't love my mum' you know and so.*

What is striking here is that she uses her capacity to reflect on how family relationships work to trace the connections between her early experience of foster care and this new family. Because she was placed young and was told that these first carers were her parents, she is left with the confusion that this person who she had expected to love her because she was a mother was "horrible" to her. This case raises the question as to whether if you are maltreated by a foster carer (or adoptive parent) who you *believe at the time* to be your mother then this may be more difficult to resolve and has more impact on self-esteem and behaviour than the experience of the others in this group, who were old enough to know that the caregivers were "only" foster carers or adopters. Alternatively, it could be that, if the negative experience comes earlier and to a preverbal child, it may simply be harder to resist or process. The cognitive appraisal of any situation, and particularly the meaning of parental behaviours in the child's mind, will inevitably affect how that information about others and the self is processed and becomes incorporated as mental representations into the internal working model.

Anger with social workers

Through the stories offered by this group ran one common thread – blame and anger towards social workers. This is not surprising given the fact that they had all had unfortunate experiences in substitute families provided by the local authority. It is also consistent that the anger against social workers was least apparent for the young woman who had been severely abused in an adoptive family but did not have the experience, described by others, of social workers visiting and apparently ignoring their plight.

The descriptions were of social workers changing frequently and therefore not being someone the children could trust or, and this was the most fiercely resented, social workers who were involved for so long that they became a "friend" of the foster carers and did not spend time with or listen to the child.

> *There was one social worker around but he was never introduced to me as a social worker. I always believed that he was a friend of the family's and he never sort of spoke to me on your own, he never sort of made any clear contact as to 'Oh Ruth, let's come and have a chat now' you know and whenever he did come I was always told to go and play in the garden with my sister, so it was kind of 'Let's play happy families while he is around'.*

Where the move into care was badly handled, this fuelled the sense of grievance at not being listened to.

> *You see it's one thing I'd say about social workers, they don't tell you nothing . . . you know you are always left in the dark . . . like I said about going to school . . . you're like at school and they say you're going on holiday . . . why didn't social services prepare you? People underestimate the power of a child. You know a lot more about what's going on. We're not stupid at the end of the day.*

As described above, some resented the separation from siblings very bitterly and blamed social workers. On the other hand, others either asked to be separated from siblings and were glad their wishes were respected or feel in retrospect that they would have done better through having had the chance for a completely fresh start. These decisions were recognised as not simple, but feeling consulted was valued.

Resentment of social workers and being in care continued to feature for several people as they described being in their successful subsequent foster families. Here the picture was more complex. There was a sense that it was the "rescuing" foster family who ought to take the credit, rather than social workers who were thought to know about the other family and did nothing.

I think they must have known. They (first foster carers) *put on a good show for them, a good front. Even on my son's life I'd swear that they put on a front just for that hour . . . It was Mum, Mum and Dad, what helped me not social workers. I call them Mum and Dad because I've been with them longer than my real parents.*

Even in this short extract we can see another element that also seemed quite common and reflects themes in other groups; if this rescuing family that made them so welcome and gave them love and healing experiences were to be defined as a real family, then it was important cognitively to dissociate them from the care system. Reviews, for example, were unfortunate reminders that you were just "in care" like other foster children. This is Christine, an 18-year-old.

So they had to see you and then have reviews . . . I go to reviews now. I've been to the last three reviews. So I can just stand there and say, I'm not answering your questions.

Do you still feel quite angry?
I still get angry at reviews, yes. We don't cover anything at those reviews that it's worth covering. They say things like, your health? I say yes. Everything they ask is on a form – like the social worker would come and see me and then I'd fill out the form and that would be the review.

You've been in this family nine years, stable, no problems of any kind?
Yes – and 18 reviews!

Being in care generally could produce feelings of stigma, if only in the form of unwarranted and unwanted "sympathy".

And one social worker came to the school and told the head teacher that I was in foster care and I didn't have anywhere to do my homework. And then all the teachers were all, "Oh dear do you want extra help? You're in foster care and you haven't got anywhere to do your homework." But we had plenty of room and I was really angry. I put in a complaint about that social worker.

Although angry with social workers, some people were able to reflect on the demands they made of social workers and the way in which at times this was their way of coping with anger about their situation.

So how did you get on with social workers?
Well, I used to be horrible to them. I used to give social workers a hard time. I used to manipulate social workers. I used to put them to the test.

Can you give me an example?
I told a social worker when I was nine that I wanted to leave the foster home (where she now is) *and she wanted to go straight away and tell Lesley and Stan* (carers). *I didn't have no respect for her.*

What should she have done?
She should have asked me more, she should have asked me why. You can't have respect for someone who just takes a nine-year-old's word. All my social workers are so soft – like the present one – the more horrible you are the more they go all soft. I only had two that I liked.

Why did you like those?
They just tell you. Straight.

Is that like Lesley and Stan?
(Laughs) *Oh yes they tell you straight. They don't put up with any crap.*

Why do you think you found social workers so difficult?
You've got to be angry with someone, haven't you? Shelley (sister) *was angry with Lesley and loved the social workers. I got angry with the social workers.*

This is a neat analysis of the way in which splitting, with in Christine's case a fierce allegiance to foster carers, reinforced the sense for her of belonging to the foster family rather than the care system.

Another feature of the real family discourse in relation to social work interventions, which occurred in other groups but came out in this group very strongly, was the criticism of the way in which social workers, and leaving care teams in particular, did not treat them as family members but made the assumption that they would want to move out as soon as possible. This was especially galling in late placements, where they were still "catching up" and felt very much at home for the first time. For some young people, enthusiastic workers had arrived in the home when they were 16 or so and offered them a flat and independence.

> *Why offer me a flat when I'm living in a family environment? No one would offer Jeff* (foster carer's own son) *a flat. It's just because you are in care.*

In this case the family had moved a long way from the original care authority, but the offer to her at 16 was a flat back in that authority, far from the family and life she had established. This insult, as she saw it, to her identity as a family member contrasted with her own view of her future, said only half-jokingly, that she would still be there when she was 30.

These criticisms of social work practice do not lead to any easy answers. These adults recall that when they were in bad placements they wished social workers would intervene more. When they later felt at home in their last foster placement, even a six-month review was intrusive. Their wish to be both safe *and* in a normal family is one of the biggest challenges in working with looked after children (or indeed children in birth or adoptive families).

Reflections on the adult self

As these young adults talked about their rollercoaster lows and highs and then described their current lives, it was possible to see how strengths of various kinds had been built up. It is not possible to know exactly where those strengths came from, but there seemed to be some very profound emotional shift that had occurred in the second long-term placement that had made a difference. What is harder still to separate out was whether the most important strength – the capacity to use carers as a secure base in adult life – worked well because that secure base did not need to be entirely internalised since it was very much available at the end of a telephone or in the form of regular visits.

The sense of relief and belonging after the placement in these safe families was being reinforced on an ongoing basis as these young adults moved into careers or parenthood. Motherhood, in particular, was a testing time and the grandparental support was crucial for women in this group, as in the previous group.

It is helpful to consider two ends of the spectrum in understanding the extent of the autonomy that had been achieved. Zara, coming to her family at 12 and now in her mid-20s, was still in need of very frequent contact with her foster family. She described her weekly routine.

> *I go home for every weekend. It's for Ricky* (son) *mainly and I help Mum out. Ricky does what he wants to do.*
>
> So you're here Monday to Friday?
> *I go to my mum's Wednesday to break up my week. Monday's my town day. Tuesday I work at the shop, Wednesday's Mum's. Thursday's housework, Friday's get ready for the weekend! Busy but I could do other things.*
>
> So you're still very involved in your family?
> *Oh yeah. Drive me up the wall sometimes! They can't get rid of me! No, it's actually 12 years since I came here on the 3rd November, two days before Fireworks Night, that's how I know.*

Although Zara does have some friends and her own life to an extent, she is still closely involved with her foster family, never liking to have more than two days apart, judging from this schedule. When she anticipates the future she sees this role continuing, not seeking a partner for herself but looking after son and her foster carers.

> *Oh 10 years on – I'll have a 17-year-old son. I'll still be hanging on to Mum and Dad, probably living with them by then, pushing them in their wheelchair! I've always said that – in joke. I suppose Ricky will be here, hopefully with a decent job. As long as Ricky's happy and my family's happy, that's OK.*

In contrast to this comfortable but rather dependent picture, another young mother seemed to have been able to build on her secure base in the foster family and develop a range of outside resources. Chloe had a marriage that had already lasted several years, a supportive mother-in-law and a group of friends – in addition to the ongoing interest and concern of the foster family. This left her more in the driving seat, more autonomous, since she could flexibly avail herself of these various relationships, using them at different points in time and for different kinds of companionship and support.

Anxiety was never far away for most in this group, even when individuals were more autonomous and resources were available. Kirsty, living at home with her foster family, was not sure where to go in work terms and struggled with her self-esteem and her relationships. She felt that she was always testing her boyfriend's commitment.

> *I just won't talk. If he tries to be close to me I just turn away . . . and then there are other times when I need to be close to him . . . so . . . it's weird. But he just puts up with so much, but see that's another thing. Why would he put up with it if he didn't like you? That's when I try to be realistic . . . I test him like I test everybody. I test people. I get in moods just to push them a little bit further then they'll say, right I've had enough now and I'd have proved myself right wouldn't I? They would have given up on me like everyone else . . . I just have that feeling . . .*

Kirsty sees herself as needing to take control and effectively provoke rejection. One of her defining childhood experiences was of being singled out for rejection in adoption. The damaging consequence of this kind of rejection is to leave her with this constant doubt. Even though she is now 20 years old and her new foster parents adopted her, she has a fear, that she knows is irrational, that they might "send her back".

Although these are complex tales of serial families, the need to come to terms with difficult childhood memories continued to place a burden on children into early adult life and left a range of symptoms in its wake. This was true despite subsequent compensatory experiences. For some there was simply a question of reluctance to be close emotionally to specific individuals, with preference expressed for a big circle of friends rather than having best friends.

There were a number of adults across several groups for whom the legacy of problems of emotional intimacy were associated with problems of physical intimacy. This was remembered from childhood but still caused some stress. Cuddles had never been easy for one young woman. Her relationship with the father of her child was short-lived, but even in long-term relationships with the carers, in whom she had love and trust, there was some awkwardness.

> *Even if I was upset and I was crying and got a cuddle, I would never put my arms around that person. To comfort myself as well. I just couldn't do it.*

For those who had experienced serious physical or sexual abuse, whether in birth or previous substitute families, adult symptoms could be more worrying and were in some senses similar to Group 4. The surfacing of doubts about the self focused on the body in the form of eating problems, obsessional concerns about cleanliness in the home, and in the form of additional sensitivities of various kinds.

One young woman described how certain social situations, like big family lunches with her in-laws, were very difficult for her, 'I get suffocated . . . I just have to go'. The image of suffocation is a very powerful one, but sums up for her some need, perhaps a residue from a childhood that included physical and severe emotional abuse, to be in control. But she recognised that in her role as mother she had to allow a continuous intimacy. Her marriage appeared to have worked well in spite of this question about control and distance, but it perhaps suited her that her husband worked away during the week and this left her space in the relationship to process these feelings and make choices about whom she wished to spend time with. At this point in the interview, discussion of the adult present, it was clear that the upbeat account of her rescuing family had to be understood in the context of a not surprising degree of ongoing personal vulnerability.

> Do you ever feel down about things?
>
> *Oh God, yes. Sometimes I'll sit there and have a good cry . . . a lot of the past affects me a hell of a lot now . . . If I'm watching something on telly, it'll wind me up and I'll take it out on my daughter or my husband, Jack. Little things. I could be watching . . . East Enders and something could come up . . . I dream a lot as well . . . like Jack's going to die*

> *because . . . I love him so much . . . I don't want anything to happen to him I'm afraid of losing him . . . afraid of losing what I've got . . .*
>
> Do you have dreams based on the past . . . ?
> *Sometimes I do . . . Jack might wake me up because I'm crying about something . . . sometimes I might start lashing out at him . . .*
>
> What are the most powerful memories when you think about your past?
> *I think that's more my dad I dream about than anything else . . .*

The fear of losing what she now had troubled her, alongside recurrent images of a father whom she had not seen for at least 16 years. Bad dreams, not unique to this group by any means, were a particularly forceful reminder that the difficulties and early traumas would probably never entirely go away, in spite of the benefit of the new family. The nature of dreams is to cast memories and fears in potentially fantastical and alarming forms that are beyond the mental control which can be established when awake. This reflected residual feelings of profound powerlessness, as if the hurtful birth father, adoptive father or foster mother might still have power over the adult as they did the child.

Turning points

This chapter has tracked the key turning points: the move from the birth family was viewed as necessary but the move to another family that did not offer love or security put the young people's development at risk. Their memories of the subsequent move to a caring family not only gave them a different experience that put them back on track but also gave them support in viewing previous care as abusive rather than their fault. Anger (with previous carers or social workers who let it happen) replaced self-blame.

The overall feeling in these lives is that awful things can happen and did happen to them – even when benign organisations intervene. This was balanced to some extent by the subsequent good care. But insecurity in several areas of their lives needed to be constantly managed, even in adult life, with the help of their foster carers. Long-term foster care in this group, as in others, could not stop at the point of "leaving care".

9 Hurt, angry and disappointed

Pathway summary: Some continuous/some discontinuous foster family care and membership, but the lack of an emotionally secure base in childhood and no "real family" for adult life provided by the care system.

Although others in the sample may have had ups and downs within and between families, this final group moved from childhood to adulthood without the knowledge that there was a family provided by the local authority that they could fully rely on to be available to them in adult life. They were angry and disappointed in their hope of finding a family to provide a secure base.

The placement histories were very diverse in this group. They might have been placed at a few weeks old, placed following an extended period in residential care, or have the experience of a succession of unsatisfactory foster families. They may have experienced continuous foster family care and membership in childhood, but still not have had the kind of caregiving experiences that led to the family feelings described by other groups. One young woman, who had been placed at a few weeks old, remained and was adopted in her teens in a family where random violence and disciplinary beatings were commonplace. In such cases, a sense of family membership might persist, even though it was not a family that was loved or loving.

Disturbed behaviours started in childhood for most but not all, then intensified for some in adolescence. This included elective mutism, aggression, stealing, drug taking and self-harm. The two people in this group who most clearly had no family to turn to (one man and one woman) both ended up in prison.

Anger at not being listened to was common. Those who had been actively mistreated stressed the difficulty for them as children in telling and for social workers in seeing or believing that apparently successful, if not exemplary, carers were harming or frightening children. The stories are similar to the difficult placement experiences described in the previous chapter – the difference here though was that these adults had not then gone on to other foster families who were able to retrieve the situation to some extent and set them back on to a healthier pathway.

This pathway does not necessarily mean that adults in this group did not have any good relationship experiences in childhood. One of the themes for this group was that some adults had developed the capacity to draw on others, perhaps through previous relationships in residential care or a subsequent relationship with a boyfriend's parents or with a social worker to sustain belief in the self. For one woman, some support was coming from a police officer who had once arrested her. The fact that referrals of these adults in their 20s came from social workers was in itself a testimony to the existence of some continuing contact or relationship that was being sustained.

Legacy

Although this absence of success in a permanent substitute family had negative consequences, at the point of interview some progress was being made. One young woman who had gone on a binge of drink, drugs and promiscuity after leaving her foster/adoptive home had settled with the help of what she described as a "family of women friends". One young man had spent time in prison but had since got his university degree and still had some contact with a social worker. A young woman who had also spent time in prison lived in a stable home with her three children and was building bridges with her birth mother. This group of adults had been forced to seek out alternative sources of continuity and security. Tensions as a partner or parent and continuing problems with anxiety cast a shadow over most lives. Anger at the fact that they had been placed with carers who they felt had not cared for them, or had actively harmed them, was also hard to come to terms with, even in adult life.

Placement in and, for some, escape from unsuccessful foster/adoptive family environments had been critical downward and upward turning points. Reaching rock bottom, for example, prison or drugs, or being totally humiliated by a partner, seemed to provoke a fight back. For several women, having their own child was a critical turning point. One woman who had been aggressive and out of control and another woman who had been immersed in drugs both said that pregnancy meant a complete full stop and a determination to lead a different kind of life.

Even the dire experiences which some described in foster care were accompanied by the sense of having learned about ordinary lifestyle things: conforming to school expectations; self-presentation; how to live a respectable lifestyle; how to play the piano; what a home should look like and the etiquette of socially acceptable daily life. This may have proved protective, for some, in establishing settled adult lives.

What these children brought to their placements

The possibility that these might have been more difficult children from the outset than in other groups was not borne out by their histories. These young people did not have the more extreme stories to tell of physical, sexual or emotional abuse in their birth families. They were not necessarily the children in the sample with the apparently most worrying early years, although some had had difficult experiences prior to their long-term placement and may have been difficult to care for.

Two adults in this group were placed in foster families at a few weeks old. Although pre-natal damage and poor care in the early weeks are a possibility, they were young infants placed in foster families earlier than infants are often placed for adoption. The birth family background was still part of how these adults tried to judge their childhood. One young man explained how his "biker" parents' lifestyle could not accommodate a child – a story he had been told – although he did have occasional contact with his mother. This story stopped short of a more blameworthy rejection, but he remembered struggling with this story of a mum who did not or could not keep him.

> *But this is something I've only got in reflection . . . at the time I wasn't aware of her lifestyle and who she was at all . . . I mean as a younger person . . . as a young child . . . I think my awareness of her was completely unreal sort of thing. I pictured . . . for various reasons . . . maybe we'll get into this, whenever I'd be disciplined it was always, oh, where's me mum? I always yearned for this perfect situation that I didn't feel that I was in. I felt like I was being shut out from being with*

> *my mum like. I realise now that I was probably better off in care . . . because they* (birth parents) *were like unconventional people . . . you know it's just . . .*

This account of "yearning" typified this young man's preoccupation with the feeling of loss at not being brought up in a "normal" family. The loss is more of lost opportunities than loss of identifiable people that he knew, since no caregiver, birth or foster, had appeared to him able to offer love or a "real family" experience.

Another person placed at a few weeks, Lena, was less drawn towards her birth family, with whom she had no contact. As an older child in her teens, she learned that it was her birth mother's mental illness that had led to a decision being taken by her extended family that she should be given up. It is important to note, as we look for protective factors in these difficult histories, that this woman's story for herself is of a mother's tragic loss of her baby through no fault of her own rather than a tale of rejection. She can set this story against the view of her foster carers, who were called mum and dad throughout childhood, who went on to adopt her, but who, in her view, had been unsuitable to be parents.

Other accounts painted a picture of going to and fro between the birth mother and foster care, again with maternal mental illness being the problem.

> *My mum had mental health problems. She wasn't able to take care of me but thought she was. And a whole load of kind of babyhood being in and out of care . . . when I was in voluntary care, which didn't really make sense, because she felt that she was well enough and she'd take me back kind of thing. So I'd be comfortably somewhere and . . . that just went on till I was four-and-a-half.*

> So quite a long time . . .
> *Yeah . . . too long really.*

Again, the mother's mental health is the cause of the separation, which minimises blame. Blame attaches to the social services department, but this time not because of separating the child from the mother but the opposite – they kept returning her to her mother. She had a clear sense that the uncertainty and the delayed admission to care had contributed to the problems that she had, which in turn made it difficult for her to settle in a family.

Any memories of when you were with her (birth mother) at all?
I don't know if they are memories or what people have told me. It's difficult to know . . . Beryl (social worker) *said that she* (mother) *left me . . .* she (social worker) *had to break into the house and I was on my own in the house . . . and they don't know how long I was there for . . . and that kind of horrifies me. I remember eating beans from the tin with my hands sort of thing . . . so I must have been about four . . . something like that. I remember quite . . . some things but not much. I think she just . . . kind of forgot . . . had periods when she just forgot that she had a child . . . and was looking after a child . . . do you see what I mean? And she'd leave me with people who weren't . . . like she'd drop me at nursery and then forget to pick me up, things like that. That's what I've been told.*

The story and the memory of being just left or even forgotten is not imbued with strong emotion and yet 'that kind of horrifies me' captures her own feelings, as an adult and a mother herself, about what she had faced as an abandoned child.

A rather different and even more complex picture emerged when the source of harm was one step removed from birth parents, for example, a stepmother and stepsiblings, but a birth parent appeared to let it happen. A powerful example of this came from Fay, who experienced physical, sexual and emotional abuse from her stepfamily. The context here was that she and her sister were singled out for rejection by her stepmother and this ill-treatment was reinforced by the older stepsiblings. These incidents are threaded through with a commentary on the role that her father did or did not play.

He wouldn't give us cuddles because like she'd turn round and make some comment or other. . : and he basically was in the shed most of the time building motor-bikes . . .

So he'd be doing something else . . .
Oh yes, me and my sister were the ones who had to clean the house. I

remember I had to carry the dining chairs from upstairs to downstairs and I must only have been six at the time . . .

These memories stay with you . . . ?
They do . . . I think he . . . he never got involved . . . The only time he did stick up for me was when Helen (stepmother) *slung me across the kitchen and I banged my arm on the radiator to like break my fall . . . And only then was the one time he stuck up for me and that time she'd hit my sister with a colander . . . you know to drain vegetables . . . across the hand and all four fingers were bleeding quite badly but that was the only time he stuck up for me.*

So it was quite extreme what happened?
Oh yes. And I know now that the brother always locked my sister in the bedroom and there was obviously abuse going on there . . . And also the stepsister was . . . making . . . me do things with her friends . . . boys . . . and then she'd make them pay for it, and she would say, if you don't do things, she'd tell her mum and me and my sister were so scared of her . . .

There was a sense of shared fate with her sister, which may well have been protective, but her feelings about her father remained mixed as Fay struggled to rescue something for herself from this history. When asked for words to describe her relationship in childhood with her father, she said:

We haven't got a relationship . . . to describe him . . . there is no relationship . . . I do think he could be a kind gentle man . . . if it wasn't for her and he would be quite a loving dad I'm sure he would be, loving, kind, you know, and just basically want to care for his daughters, but he's not allowed to.

Here she slipped into the present, as she did elsewhere in the interview, with her preoccupying anger with her stepmother dominating the interview, alongside her continuing wish to believe the best of her father, in the past and now.

Adults often tried to capture in the interviews a sense of their childhood selves. For adults whose childhoods proved troubled, whether in birth families, stepfamilies, and/or, as in these cases, in foster and adoptive families, it was not surprising to learn of various kind of coping strategies. As with other groups, there were examples of children who appeared to have shut down, defended themselves in attachment terms against distress. Sometimes this was remembered as a conscious decision, not only as a way of staying safe but also as a way of staying in control.

So what kind of little girl were you, Heather?
I was very quiet – apparently I was very good, I was never naughty – I was very kind of goodie unless someone got in my face if you know what I mean . . .

And then what would happen?
I'd just kind of run off, just run away from it.

So you'd leave rather than retaliate or be angry . . . ?
Yes – completely shut up . . . I had a . . . I think it's called frozen child syndrome where you refuse to talk to anybody . . . for a little while. (Yes) *I think that's why I went to* (children's home) *to try and get me out of myself.*

So people were worried about you?
Yes – I completely went in on myself. But I don't really remember that as a bad time . . . I remember the adults saying – she won't talk, she won't talk and I remember in myself being . . . oh . . . I remember feeling quite happy with myself because no one could approach me . . .

So were you in control really?
Yes – I felt in control.

It's interesting that you can remember that feeling . . .
I can remember really clearly adults saying she won't talk . . . you know what I mean . . . and I thought . . . I can if I want to . . . you know.

Yes. So keeping adults at a bit of a distance at that point?
Yes – I think by that point I'd had enough really!

So when are we talking about – transition to (children's home) between six and eight?
And there I came out of myself.

So why do you think you didn't want people to know about your feelings?
Because I'd been like a yo-yo – you know what I mean . . . been everywhere. There was no consistency . . . nothing that was the same. You would never know – the next day, am I going with somebody else, you know what I mean?

This is a revealing account of a child's experience, but it also suggests the way in which Heather appears to have access to the memories of thoughts and feelings. There is no way of knowing if she did or did not experience being that silent child in quite that way, but the "memory", or the story now told to the self and others, is of a powerful rather than a helpless child.

Foster family care

Although none of these adults had been placed in a foster family in childhood that they could rely on in adult life, the pattern of events was very varied, with one young person placed in infancy remaining their entire childhood in the same family while others had a succession of unsuccessful or unsatisfactory caregiving environments. What was lacking was the sense of at least one set of close, rewarding family relationships described by other groups. In its place was the sense of disappointment and of being let down by the system as well as the families.

Hannah had had a succession of placements, including an adoption placement for 18 months that had failed. She tended to minimise the importance of these moves, while offering a ready explanation of why they happened.
I think they were expecting like a sweet little girl and I was a mixed up little girl basically.

There were several memories of children feeling powerless about moves. Alice (aged 10) had been moved to a placement, which was fostering with a view to adoption, with carers for whom religion played a major role in their lives. At the introductory visit she was taken to mass.
It was just like – I didn't even know what God was or anything. I hadn't

> *even been introduced to the idea of God or nothing. When we got back, they pulled me by my clothes and said, why didn't you genuflect? Genuflect? What are you talking about? It was like what?!* (laughed) *They showed me – they made me kneel down on one leg and said, that's how you genuflect and I was just like, what? What are you talking about? They got me confused completely – that's one thing I mainly remember. And we had a few trial weekends and I hated them . . . and I still had to go and live with them.*
>
> Did you tell the social worker what you felt?
> *I said I didn't like it but it was deemed that it was best for me.*

Her sense that she would fail to match up to their expectations was confirmed in numerous ways in subsequent years.

> *At home if I got a good school report they would pick on one thing that was bad. They would go through it and try to find the one thing that was bad in it. They would never say – oh, you did really well in English. They never complimented me ever. Never had one compliment.*

For Alice, there had been some uncertainty as to whether this family life was what families were supposed to be like. These carers had been obsessional about cleaning.

> *I didn't dare not to clean. I just like thought, OK I'll go with this. And as well I thought – maybe this is what families are like . . . this is how families work, I don't know. I want to fit in. I want it to work. I don't particularly like them but maybe if I do what they say they might love me or they might care about me.*

For others the move into foster care had been welcomed, but this then turned to disappointment and hurt. Anita described how excited she and her sister had been at leaving the abuse in her birth family.

> *It was quite late in the evening when we got to this foster home. Eight or nine o'clock, and me and my sister stayed up all night talking because for us it was exciting and for the next couple of weeks we were terrified we'd be sent back . . .*

After a six-month placement, in which Anita had felt treated differently to the birth children, they were moved.

> *That was bleeding awful as well. I mean the woman – couldn't walk very far but she managed to chase us round the front room with her walking stick.*

Cruelty from carers could come in the form of spontaneous or routine physical assaults as part of "discipline", as Elaine described:

> *I couldn't wait to get out. My brother used to bang his head when he was little to get to sleep and our foster dad used to cane us to shut him up . . .*
>
> Caned both of you?
> *Yes . . . I got caned as well.*
>
> And you were little then.
> *Yes – I remember it very well because we were both in the same bedroom. Lee slept on that bed and I slept on this . . .*

The addition in this memory of a sense of the room in which it happened and the role of big sister to a vulnerable younger brother, whom she was unable to protect, added to the vivid sense of bitterness. She described how she and her brother fared in their next placement which was just as harsh, 'If you passed wind or ate a biscuit you'd get beaten or slippered or caned'.

Arguments in the teenage years, particularly between teenage girls and foster fathers, led in several cases to physical fights.

> *And we'd have fights and he'd shake me and he's ripped the top off my T-shirts and that, thrown me across the room and I'd throw something at his head and he'd throw me fully clothed into a bath of cold water . . . all sorts of things . . .*

Alison, who had been placed in early childhood, described how she felt that these carers were her parents, but had contrasting experiences of the foster mother and foster father. Her foster mother seemed to do all the right things in promoting her abilities.

> *. . . I suppose I was in her mind the perfect daughter because I . . . liked*

> *music very much, played the flute, liked singing . . . artistic and she was very happy . . . she was very proud of me.*

Yet the foster father was, as she put it, a bully.

> *What you have to realise, this is what I was just saying, because I didn't know any different . . . my dad is known for being a big bully, a really big bully, mmm . . . he can be very aggressive . . . and I don't know how he . . . certainly today I don't think he'd get away with being able to foster children.*
>
> Tell me about how he was a bully when you were a child?
> *Mmm . . . he would have tempers, temper rages really, and he would shout, shout and punish, punish us . . . for very little things . . .*
>
> Physically?
> *If he got into a rage . . . he would pick up anything, a bit of wood, or something like this . . . or in the house, shoes or belts . . .* (laughs) *these things and . . . teach us a lesson . . . but it was over really silly things . . .*

Although Alison said that she had not suffered as much as other foster children in the family, she still had examples from her own experience.

> *He . . . it's funny because as you're growing up it seems such silly things . . . but I can remember . . . This is my first memory of my dad . . . that . . . one of the other children had put something . . . some lime seeds . . . white stuff . . . like on tennis courts but they'd put this in the chicken feedstuff . . . and he'd asked everybody who'd done it and the last person to be asked was me . . . So he assumed it must be up to me . . . He got it in his head . . . that I was the one who had done it and he . . . wouldn't . . . take . . . no . . . for an answer that I hadn't done it . . . and I know I was only about five something like that . . . and here he was dragging me up the stairs, kicking me . . . and I had to stay up there for that night and the rest of the next day . . . without having any meals or anything like that . . . that's just an example . . . quite a trivial thing.*

This experience of random violence, recounted in a tentative manner, made her watchful and fearful. However, she described, again haltingly, the same mixed emotions as children abused in a birth family often feel towards their parents.

> Can you give me five words to describe your relationship with him (foster father) as a child?
> *I was very fearful of him . . . and I loved him as my dad . . . I can't think of anything else to say . . .*
>
> So if we take fearful, what would be an example of fearful?
> *. . . Well just his . . . . . . face . . . . . . just brush it aside, it doesn't matter, and the next . . . you could do the same thing and he could get so angry and you never knew where you stood with him because he was chopping and changing . . . his moods . . .*
>
> So do you remember watching his moods as a child?
> *I knew when to keep out of his way, I remember keeping out of his way . . . That's one of the things I wanted to say to you, you know the five words . . .*

Long pauses of this kind that occurred when she talked of her foster father are often associated with unresolved loss or trauma in the AAI scoring system (Main and Goldwyn, 1984–94).

Among these stories, there were differences between those children who clearly felt confusing emotional ties to a parent figure who was also a figure of fear and uncertainty, as in the case just quoted, and those who were with a frightening foster carer with whom they had a less significant relationship – as Carrie, another young woman under attack from an unpredictable carer, put it:

> *On a good day I did feel I could get on with him but I was still dubious because he could turn at any minute . . .*
>
> So tell me what happened when he turned?
> *He used to drink a little bit. Sometimes . . . it would just be a weird thing like breathing too loudly . . . he'd say – you're breathing too loudly. I remember just looking and he'd say what are you looking at?! And he'd completely provoke an argument . . . And he'd pull me downstairs by my hand and he'd just shout at me over nothing. Like for an hour.*

What would he be saying when he shouted?
Just like – you're a waste of time, you're this . . . don't breathe too loudly . . . dldldldl-er-just losing it – not the way an adult should talk to a child.

So the message was – you're a waste of time?
And a thing he often used to say was 'You're as mad as your mother' – which looking back it was a completely outrageous thing to say. And he used to poke me in the chest . . . just like this – until I had a red mark. That was when I was growing up and developing breasts and all that. A man poking you, particularly in the chest . . . to get his point over – which wasn't even a point, it was just nonsense.

So if you had to think of five words to describe your relationship with him?
I was frightened of him, he was volatile.

In a number of the stories, the anger of foster carers seemed to be fuelled by a sense that the child might be out of control, might have "bad blood" drawing her towards mental illness or promiscuity. However, such accusations reinforced the child's own fear of this occurring. There were clearly cycles of difficulty within these relationships and the children were almost certainly difficult to parent. But the detailed accounts of physical assaults and emotional rejection seem indicative of harmful caregiving.

In their adult life, as they looked back, there remained the fundamental question of whether the conflicts and the 'punishments' were indeed the child's fault after all. As with troubled adults in other groups, where did good/bad, normal/abnormal, me/them begin and end? This was put poignantly by Andrew, who struggled with this question many years after his placement broke down. He had felt very emotionally rejected by his foster mother, but the placement with her in infancy meant that she had effectively been his mother. He recalled a fear of losing her and concluded that there must therefore have been something called love.

Mmm . . . I remember thinking when I was a young child, when you first think what it would be like without your parents? And you lie in bed crying because you don't want them to die in the future sort of thing? So I mean there was obviously love there from . . . her . . . and I don't know, I just got this impression that . . . I mean I know I'm not focusing enough on your questions . . . but it's difficult . . . because I'm trying to think about the relationship between me and Sandra (foster carer) *all the time . . . because the relationship broke down when I was 12, right, I went somewhere else which was her decision? I'm not sure whether or not she was a bit of a crazy case, to be honest with you . . .*

OK . . .
I've had this frame . . . this framework in my head for a long time until I was 17/18 . . . that she was really normal . . . that the whole situation was there for me to take but I screwed it up because I was . . . not a bad person . . . maybe a bad person . . . and that her morals and her view on life was an alright way to go sort of thing and if only I had played the game then it would have been alright, you know. But . . . looking back . . . in hindsight . . .

This is a man struggling to make sense of the failed family experience, the complexity of an intimate relationship that he came to resent and a lingering doubt as to whether it was his foster mother or himself that was to blame. Andrew's answer tails away – hindsight is not helping him solve this essentially insoluble dilemma.

Some, after much deliberation over many years, finally came to reject this kind of self-blame and doubt.

I was still confused – I thought that maybe they were in the right, they were the adults . . . I felt like I was doing wrong, maybe breathing too loudly was wrong. And maybe I am a naughty girl . . . Maybe I am bad. I was still kind of thinking . . . Looking back I can see that I was completely normal . . . you know – that what I did was right.

Where children were placed very young into these families, the sense of the carers as social and psychological parents was very strong and made it difficult to turn to the birth family for an alternative identity. One young woman who had described discipline in the foster family in terms of physical assaults went on to say,

They are the only mum and dad I know . . . I mean I've got close to my (birth) *mother since but I'd find it difficult to call her mum or mother . . . although she gets disappointed . . . I call her Sheila . . . because I didn't grow up with her . . . I mean my childhood . . . They* (the carers) *are all I know as parents . . .*

There were more stories of harsh treatment by carers, with certain themes recurring. Unlikely though it might seem, more than one child had experienced being forced to eat mustard as a punishment. Several described canings and being beaten with other implements. What was particularly difficult for the children (as in the previous group) was that these carers were often seen as model foster carers and the children might be doing various other admirable things, such as playing musical instruments or having ballet lessons. Although these are a small minority of the 40 stories in the sample, they are an important reminder of the distorted family experiences that some fostered young people, and even some later adopted by their carers, were dealing with as they entered adulthood. This was particularly confusing, in terms of incoherent multiple models (Main, 1991), when this had felt like a real family.

All I can say is some children suffer tremendously . . . at their father's hands and . . . still . . . they love their fathers . . . You can't really explain it . . . You can't put your finger on it . . . I hate him (foster/adoptive father), *I hate him. I say that deep down . . . I love him as well.*

Telling and not telling

In the context of these stories of unsatisfactory or harmful care, the young adults were asked whether they had tried to tell anyone and to assert their own "truth". Very similar themes emerged here, with children fearing the consequences of telling, seeing the closeness between the carers and the social workers and knowing that everyone appeared to think that they were lucky to have such a good placement. They simply felt they would not be believed.

It went on for about five years. But you can't say nothing at the time because they don't believe you . . .

Do you remember trying to tell someone . . . ?
No – too scared . . .

Did you have marks on you going to school?
Yes, but they were always on my back or my backside.

Social work visits?
No, because no one came to see us. One social worker I had, he was really nice – I didn't dare say anything because I knew what would happen afterwards.

So the carers – how did they both behave?
She never caned me but she'd get the slipper out. It was more him.

So what kind of family were they?
Well if social services came around, they were as nice as pie. You couldn't wish for two nicer people – you know, but as soon as they went it was all, get away. There was no love there – no cuddles at bedtime, no goodnight kiss . . . One good thing about it, when I was seven I learned music, I learned to dance, I got grade 6 violin – so I can thank them for that . . . which I do.

So they arranged all those things for you?
It wasn't that I wanted to do them – I had to . . .

Here we have all the reasons for not telling represented, resulting in confusion for the child and a memory as an adult of childhood powerlessness.

Some adults could remember trying to tell the social worker, but not getting the message straight.

I didn't think I could get it across without an explosion. Do you see what I mean? I felt that it would have beaten me – it felt like . . . if I said I hate this and I want to go he (foster carer) *would have jumped up and smacked me in the face or something. Do you know what I mean?*

So was it a fear of their reaction that stopped you saying too much?
Yes.

> Even though you'd known your social worker, Joyce, since you were very young?
> *But she was still their social worker – the establishment. It felt like she was in league with them.*
>
> When she visited she would chat with them?
> *It was really weird – a week before she came it would get all nice again. They would be nice to me and it would be like happy families. Then she'd come . . . and they'd say – it's going well, it's been going well for ages bladibla . . . and I had to sit there thinking – it hasn't been good for ages . . . !*
>
> So they knew that what they was doing was not right and . . .
> *Yes – it felt like it was all show . . . they'd go – I was supposed to have time alone with Joyce, but they'd go into the kitchen and there was a hatch – and they'd leave it open. They'd be standing like – just there – in the small kitchen, quiet. They'd be just there and Joyce would be talking. There was no way I could say – get me out of here . . . let's go . . . you know yet that's exactly what I wanted to say. I remember saying it over and over again in my head but just not being able to get it out.*

This section is quoted in detail because it captures important themes with implications for social work practice. As in other accounts, the difficulty of telling was associated with fear of a retaliation and fear of not being believed.

There could also be disappointment after "telling", particularly when children had felt unsupported by a non-abusing carer.

> *She* (foster/adoptive mother) *kind of turned a blind eye . . . I can remember when I'd really had enough, I really did . . . and I knew this wasn't . . . normal . . . or the norm . . . mmm . . . and I spoke to a social worker and I said that Dad has . . . attacked me as I say . . . and there was a recent happening and I said, 'Mum, you were there, when he did this to me . . . mmm . . . weren't you . . . you saw what he did' . . . and the social worker said to her . . . 'What did he do?' . . . and she said, 'I . . . I witnessed nothing . . . I wasn't there' . . . and she was . . . she was . . .*

This story was told in a very flat voice with little emotion, yet the repetition at the end, 'she was . . . she was . . .', seemed like a real cry from the heart.

"Extra" families

Given the absence of successful foster family care, adults recalled seeking out and in some cases finding alternative sources of emotional support. In one of these families where the tensions between teenage foster daughter and foster father had been growing and residential care was on the cards, it was the parents of a friend that stepped in. This special offer of care for her was valued all the more because it was spontaneous.

> *Well . . . when Brian and Margot said they were going to keep me whatever happens, at the time, to make that sort of . . . I can't think of the word . . . commitment to someone they hardly knew and they weren't even foster parents – and they'd got their own kids . . . something like that, that someone wanted to do for* me. *That meant a lot obviously . . .*

For one young woman it was residential care that offered the sense of relief, although this was rapidly followed by problems.

> *Stayed in the children's home till I was 15. The first year and a half was the best year of my life. It was brilliant. Got to work with horses, which I wanted to do . . . And then I don't know what happened to me. I must have started rebelling. At the time I wouldn't have thought I was rebelling but I rebelled a lot . . . I started getting into trouble. I was an alcoholic, I rejected home and for a year I was a down and out, I was really bad. And then they moved me from that home when I was 15 . . . the police came. They took everyone else out and moved me, handcuffed me and everything . . . I hadn't done nothing. Then I went to another kids home – that's where all the trouble was . . . it was brilliant there though. The first night I did a runner with my boyfriend. For the weekend. Got found again. Got brought back again. Within three months of being there I was in prison, then I got six months in prison.*

Although the residential care experience did not produce stability at that point, it did give her the first taste of rewarding activities and sensitive care from key staff members, whom she described in detail and who she contrasted with a succession of previous emotionally and physically abusive carers. This gave her something to build on when she left prison.

Barry (25) had had the support of a social worker whom he described as being like a friend. After also being in prison in his late teens he determined never to return and set off on a route through education which led to the successful completion of a degree. It was not easy at first to see where the motivation or support for this came from. He had no family of any kind to turn to and his friends were not people who shared his interest in education. The one significant relationship he described was with a social worker who had not been officially his social worker since his early teens but kept in touch over the years and visited him in prison. This is how he described the process of changing direction in his adult life, in an interview conducted a few weeks after his graduation.

> *And someone like Pete* (social worker) *has been a great inspiration to me . . . because he's been a caring character . . . you know, without him . . . I don't know . . .*
>
> That's important? . . .
> *I'm not saying he's like a father figure all the time, but I know he's there sort of thing . . . whereas my dad's a wayward character you know . . . he's been in prison probably more recently than I have for some thing or other . . .*
>
> So after prison you got your GCSEs . . . ?
> *Then I decided I didn't want to get my hands dirty anymore and I wanted to be driving a nice car . . . rather than working on it and decided to do an Access to Higher Education course for over 21s and spent a year doing that . . . by the time that happened . . . I applied for a place at university and it all went from there . . . And it still ain't sunk in yet . . .*

This ongoing availability of his former social worker offered some kind of secure base to a young man who had been very much at risk of a life of crime. It also offered "inspiration" and a role model. He still struggled emotionally, but had this achievement and continuity to fall back on. Social workers who stay in touch with child clients after they have left care are probably at risk of criticism about boundaries, but this was one of a number of cases across the sample where the availability and concern of someone who knew you when you were young and stood by you through adolescence was felt to be very valuable.

Transition to adult life

The consequence of the more distressing caregiving experiences was often some kind of downward spiral in the teenage years, as adolescent boys and girls moved from low self-esteem, as a result of emotional rejection or physical abuse, through to acting out, drugs and so on. Troubled feelings were sometimes enacted as self-harm. That was described as a release.

> *When I was at Mark and Carol's* (foster carers) *I did. I remember rubbing my face up and down on concrete when I was . . . hiding from them outside somewhere so they couldn't find me . . .*
>
> So what was going on in your mind when you did that . . . ? Can you remember? What would you have been thinking?
> *What at Mark and Carol's?* (Yes) *I can't remember . . . I think I'd get so frustrated and if I . . . because I never used to be one for throwing things really . . . or breaking things . . . I suppose . . . in a way, I did realise . . . thinking back over the last couple of years, it's a release . . . I feel so much better when I have done it . . . something like that . . . because . . . Yeah . . . it's like taking drugs I suppose . . .*

This slip from the past to the present is because she has continued to self-harm in adult life. Explaining why it continued, she says that even when she left the foster home where she had become unhappy, she still felt out of place.

> *I think what it was . . . is . . . emotionally before I got depressed, my body had just had enough, it couldn't honestly take it . . . That's the hardest thing really, being placed with a new family with them all looking at you, I hated all that . . . in the end I'd had enough . . . I'm supposed to be getting some sort of intense therapy, so I can*

> *find somewhere to put the past . . . so I can begin living my life again.*

A number of young people spoke of their need for therapy to 'find somewhere to put the past' and to stop self-destructive behaviours. Where the struggle with depression and addiction did not get resolved in new adult relationships with partners or children, therapy was attempted. But here the experience described was often that therapy made things worse (as mentioned in other groups) and that weekly sessions could not contain the powerful feelings that flooded these adults when they were invited to reflect on their past.

> *Therapy did help in the beginning but all these new memories came back which I'd forgotten about and because then I'd be left for a week thinking about it . . . then I couldn't deal with what was happening so I'd get drunk. I wouldn't get up for the next few days, because I'd be depressed about what we'd been talking about . . . and once a week wasn't really enough, because I'd have these new problems, things I remembered, to deal with, and that had a lot to do with the big breakdown last year . . . I was hoping that I could have therapy so that I can just find somewhere to store it and to be able to live with what's happened. All the time I sit there and try to think of ways to not think about it . . . you know . . . keep myself busy by cleaning the house God knows how many times . . . and all sorts of things . . .*

This young woman was in a stable relationship, but was not finding it easy to get on to an even keel, given the recurrence of memories which she was not able to come to terms with or integrate into her sense of self. There were a range of metaphors for dealing with the past such as 'storing it', 'putting it to the back of the mind' and so on. The hope was that therapy would help with this, but for most, therapy seemed to bring material into consciousness which they plainly felt unable to face. Compulsive cleaning or bathing, self-harm, drugs and alcohol were attempts to banish those memories and feelings rather than being able to face and resolve them.

Parenthood

Becoming a parent might have been a risky proposition given these histories and yet here, as in earlier groups, it could also be an opportunity for growth and a move back to normality. Jenna, who had been in prison, described how becoming a mother had been the major turning point and helped her to move towards a more 'normal' life. She was determined to give her children a better experience than she had and although she struggled in some respects, she appeared to be settled with her three children. Although she had neither had a secure family nor gained extra families as a child, she had tried to find herself resources of different kinds. Her experience in residential care in her teens had provided her with some good relationship experiences. A police officer she met when she was arrested had befriended the family and given her some material help and support. She was still in touch with her fostering officer. She had built bridges with her birth mother, partly on the basis that it was her father rather than her mother who had "put her into care" at 18 months. Thus she had a sense of herself as being part of a family even if this was rather at a distance, 'She's not really a mum – it's not a mother–daughter thing – more like friends'.

Deanne, who had become very involved in drugs, stopped as soon as she knew she was pregnant.

> So was there a crunch point where you sorted your life out?
> *Getting pregnant. I suddenly realised. The second I was pregnant I stopped everything and became single minded . . .*
>
> So was there anyone around to help you at that point?
> *Mmm – I volunteered at a charity shop and made some amazing friends . . . wonderful group of women in their late 20s early 30s and they just became my family really . . . Completely turned my life round.*

As with other accounts of turning points in other groups, this is a story of being able to locate resources and make use of them. This young woman, who had been adopted by her foster carers as a teenager, had nevertheless had her best experiences of relationships in residential care prior to that placement. So it is perhaps not surprising that her resource is a group. But the decision to settle down and commit herself to her child proved decisive. Four years on she was living in a comfortable flat and, as she put it, felt like her own person. Her description of being a parent sums up a number of themes of what parenthood meant to adults from care – not only in this group, but it is particularly poignant for Deanne because the experience is not shared with any family that she can call her own.

What about those first feelings when Martin was born?

When I was pregnant I was really worried I wouldn't love him. That I wouldn't be able to care for him and I was completely petrified I would reject him . . .

That's interesting.

Never having known real love. And the second he was born I was completely filled up with love – I was just like a well. I was just completely besotted with him – luckily from the second he was born.

And how has that developed?

It's just completely transformed my life. It has enabled me to love. Which I wasn't able to do before – I just wasn't a loving person. It wasn't turned on. My mind, my mechanics weren't working like that.

So that loving relationship with Martin made you change your idea about yourself?

It did – it made me love myself . . . which I didn't do before . . .

Some people need support with that but you said you use your own resources?

I don't need others to rely on – I rely on myself.

This is a complex picture, in which strengths and anxieties mix. It is often seen as a negative when care leavers talk of finding themselves through their children and yet for any parent, the motivation and the experience is inevitably bound up with fulfilling and developing a sense of the self. The contrast for Deanne between her loved child and her memory of herself at the same age reinforced her pleasure in her child.

So what kind of little boy is he?

He's a complete chatterbox, very loving, very cuddly, he's good at drawing. Very bright – as bright as a button . . . good with his reading. Boisterous.

Is he very different from how you would have been at his age?
Yes – because he's very vocal. He says his feelings completely. One minute he's happy – the next he's oooh – he's very emotional which I wasn't. I was completely turned off.

Adult relationships

As with parenthood, relationships with partners might present risks to these vulnerable young people, but could also represent opportunities. Several young women first had relationships with very controlling men, where they were expected to conform to a set of expectations that left them feeling as powerless as they had in childhood. This led to sense of turmoil and depression.

Me and Jim (partner) *didn't get on . . . And I think what had happened was that through all the years of carrying everything round on my shoulders . . . and everything that happened, I was taking in and in the end I just fell through the ice and hit the depression then . . . and I fell right to the bottom really.*

The role of drink and drugs in blotting out pain was a feature of her life, as in a number of other lives. Although in the sample as a whole using drugs and alcohol was more likely to be a teenage phase that had been overcome, there were clearly some for whom the struggle with addiction continued into adult life.

It was possible for some people to learn from damaging partner relationships and move into a more rewarding partnership. Another young woman who had described a series of similarly difficult and controlling relationships had hit lucky, as she described it.

And then I met Ivan and he's totally changed my life, my perspective and since the time I've been with him I've completely changed I suppose.

How long have you been with him?
About four years . . . mmm . . . and we had Gemma fairly soon after we

got together but I've been to college and done different courses, computers, doing business A level and I'm very happy being a mother, very happy.

This experience of a relationship in which she was treated with love and respect enabled her to look back on the foster family where she had been physically ill-treated and unhappy and resolve some of the feelings of doubt about who was to blame.

I blamed myself for things . . . but now being older and going back there, staying with my (foster/adoptive) *dad . . . and . . . I can see that it's not my fault . . . it's never been my fault . . . it's just the way my dad is. He's got a very narrow-minded outlook on things . . . very strict . . . and you know, I can put that behind me now, I know that I'm not a bad or wrong person, and . . . I . . . these last few weeks actually . . . I've been able to put everything behind me . . . and I feel really happy, for the first time . . .*

Notice that although this was an unhappy family experience, in her mid-20s she was still visiting the family with her child. This too was not unusual, even in this group. In another similar interview in which the foster family was described with great anger and bitterness, the young woman mentioned that the foster carers had recently come round for dinner and they get on much better now. Although families had not provided an emotionally secure base in childhood or adulthood, the continuing contact with the family allowed the young adults to continue to work through very difficult memories and to feel empowered to manage and resolve them to some extent. As with other aspects of this study, it shows how similar these experiences are to birth families, where resolution of family conflict in adult life might also be important.

Angry or sad preoccupation with the past, in contrast, always made it more difficult to settle in the present and make relationships, as Andrew described.

I think that a lot of feelings and emotions and thoughts I have every day . . . every minute of every day maybe even . . . are all tied up in my upbringing . . . I smoke puff all *the time but I think to myself if I sat down and tried to say that to someone . . . maybe like yourself or someone who doesn't come from your field . . . it's like 'Huh . . . We all have those problems mate!' Sort of thing. 'You've got to get on with things, boy!' You know what I mean. 'You've got to get yourself together. Stop making excuses . . .'*

The anger with the self at being so preoccupied makes the task of moving on even more difficult. Andrew's fear that he might seem weak and self-pitying to others was an added pressure. The preoccupation with the past came across not only in the content of the interview, and the reliance on drugs, for example, but also in the confused tone and language.

I lived with this family, the . . . it's very difficult . . . to try and assess . . . what my life's about . . . who I am . . . and how I feel about my past . . . how it affected me and that. On the one hand you get this Oprah Winfrey type thing, deserves and needs counselling and this sort of stuff, and as soon as you're an adult you've got to get your act together. What I'm . . . er . . . trying to say there is . . . I don't know . . . because my situ . . . I mean I know . . . other peoples' situation . . . through school . . . for example . . . I told you I waffle . . . at school for example . . . you assume that everyone's got a normal life and you haven't. And I know that the normal life doesn't exist to some extent but I know . . . it's difficult to . . . to know how I've been shaped by my experiences . . . and it's difficult to work out sometimes whether or not I was a normal kid in terms of my behaviour or whether or not I was an irritable kid and whether or not that's a natural attribute of mine, a sort of genetic thing . . . or whatever goes on in my brain . . . or whether that's a behavioural thing developed through that environment . . .

Although this man has acquired the ideas, language and concepts to debate the big questions of his life, it has not helped him to find all the answers.

Turning points

It was not easy for these young men and women to make sense of complicated and often unhappy childhoods, as this chapter and this last quotation in particular suggest. Allocating blame and the implications for the internal working model of self and others were a persistent problem. The turning point that each placement move represented added risk factors for these young people in terms of problematic caregiving. Young people were moving into adulthood hurt, disappointed and without a secure family base.

Protective factors for some seemed to have surfaced in relationships outside the foster or adoptive families, in particular, relationships that provided support in pregnancy, promoted education or helped mitigate the worst effects of addictive behaviours. Such relationships could be with a ballet teacher, a friend's parents, a social worker, residential workers, a "family of friends", a partner or a child in adult life. These relationships were not planned by professionals, but were chance occurrences that shored up flagging self-esteem, restored some faith in human nature, and assisted troubled children and adults to find some stability.

Inevitably in this chapter there has been a tension between how much certain foster carers should be seen either as "not coping" with difficult children or as being actively neglectful or abusive, on the basis of the accounts provided by these adults. It has been a premise throughout this study that the quality of the foster family relationships will depend on the characteristics of both child and carer. Nevertheless, it does appear that some foster carers, including some that later adopted the children, acted in ways that were actively damaging to the foster children. The fact that even some of these children remained in touch with their carers is a reminder of how strong family membership can become, even where carers are not experienced as an emotionally secure base. Remaining "part of the family" in adult life, it appears, can be a powerful force for non-biologically related families, as it is for biologically related families.

At this important message, central to the study as a whole, we move now to consider how the analysis of these seven pathways can lead us towards a theoretical model for understanding long-term foster care and provide ideas for practice.

Part III

Conclusions and implications for practice

10 **The significance of a secure base:** towards a psychosocial model of long-term foster care

The question that launched this research study was how foster families, provided by the local authority, could meet a child's need for a family for life. The approach chosen was to analyse the reflections of adults who were building their lives on foundations laid down, for better or worse, in foster families. From a review of the foster care research, the meaning of foster care as a family form and a source of "permanence" were seen to be key issues, while stability of placement and well-being of the child were identified as key outcomes of successful foster family care. From developmental psychology, security of attachment and resilience features, such as self-esteem and self-efficacy, were identified as likely to be generated in effective families and to lead to healthy and successful adult outcomes. The adult interviews were conducted and analysed with a view to exploring these factors as represented in life stories of foster care. However, other factors that also emerged from the data shed rather different kinds of light on the foster family experience. Having started with a clear focus on the centrality of attachment as a way of explaining family relationships, the voices of the young adults in the study introduced a more varied view of foster families. The analysis needed to draw on a rather different discourse to highlight the strongest message from the interviews – the centrality and meaning of foster families as "real families". In this chapter, such different family discourses will be brought together with the adults' experiences, as reflected in the previous seven pathway chapters, before moving to consider the implications for social work practice.

The seven pathways demonstrate the importance of some key factors: the continuity of placement; the quality of caregiving; the importance of family membership; the level of children's emotional damage; and the role of factors outside the foster family, such as school, friendships, social workers. However, it was clear across the seven pathways that no single factor could explain the route which was taken through childhood into adult life. Even stability and continuity from infancy to adulthood, rightly valued in current policy and practice, could occur in a foster family that offered nurturing and a secure base or in a foster family that over time became emotionally and physically abusive. Similarly against expectations, very late placements in foster families after severe abuse in the birth family and a number of moves could nevertheless provide a family for life. The quality of caregiving in families appears to have played an important role but it was also interacting with a number of other factors. Children's development and sense of a secure family base are contingent on a number of diverse aspects of their histories, their families and their current environments which have an impact into adulthood. However, the patterns are not random. Stability, continuity, secure caregiving and a sense that this was a "real family" to belong to appear to have increased the likelihood of stable, fulfilled adult lives and adults with those experiences were less likely to suffer from problems with depression and low self-esteem than those who had had poor or unstable family environments.

However, another important theme which has been highlighted throughout was the way in which in all pathways, and even among those who experienced more than one abusive family environment or who did not find a family for life through foster care, there were young adults who had gone on to personal, academic and career success. The resilience literature suggests that, out of any group of adults who have experienced adversity in childhood, there will be a number who surprise us and confound expectation by doing well. As the conceptualisation of resilience has developed in recent years (Rutter, 1999) it has been possible to understand this process of survival against the odds in increasingly subtle terms. The data from this study has illustrated some of those subtleties across the pathways. As the theory would suggest, resilience is not a fixed trait across time and sources of stress. Even those adults who were apparently functioning well could have bad dreams or find themselves overwhelmed by a particularly moving drama on the television or find it difficult to cope with specific challenges, such as becoming a parent. Similarly, even some of those who entered on downward spirals in adolescence into drugs or prison later discovered that they had academic aptitude, personal qualities or the ability to sustain social networks that stood them in good stead as they matured into adults. But the process of managing the past in the present would almost certainly continue to represent a challenge for all of these adults throughout their lives – it was simply a challenge that some were better equipped to deal with than others.

What became apparent from the pathways data was that the rather different conceptual frameworks could be interwoven in ways that offered the possibility of an integrated and dynamic psychosocial model of long-term foster care (see Figure 10.1). The model draws on the core theoretical considerations reflected in the attachment and resilience frameworks while capturing the key messages from across the different pathways, detailed in the previous chapters, about what children need and can get from foster care that will offer them the best chance of a stable and fulfilling adult life. Inevitably, therefore, it also identifies what may be missing in foster family placements that do not meet all these needs.

The model is dynamic, suggesting that there are lines of influence between, for example, security and love and the capacity to act and think. The influence is likely to be two-way, with the capacity to think, for example, in terms of resolving losses from the past, facilitating the child's acceptance of loving care and increasing the likelihood of the development of a secure base. The desired outcome of the foster care experience as modeled here is the capacity to cope with the many demands and challenges of adult life, to look forward with hope.

To love

Learning to love arises in the context of being loved by others and, through that process, of experiencing the self as lovable. Loving another in a relationship requires the taking of risks, risks that are made tolerable by the belief, based on experience, that other people can be trusted not to hurt and abandon. Thus loving relationships are built on the experience of predictable, sensitive care leading to the core attachment concept of *felt security* (Bowlby, 1969, 1988; George, 1996; Howe *et al*, 1999). This sensitive care must address physical, social, intellectual and identity needs as well as emotional needs, in order for the child to feel valued for all aspects of the self, to feel loved unconditionally. Adults who have had the

Figure 10.1
A psychosocial model of long-term foster care

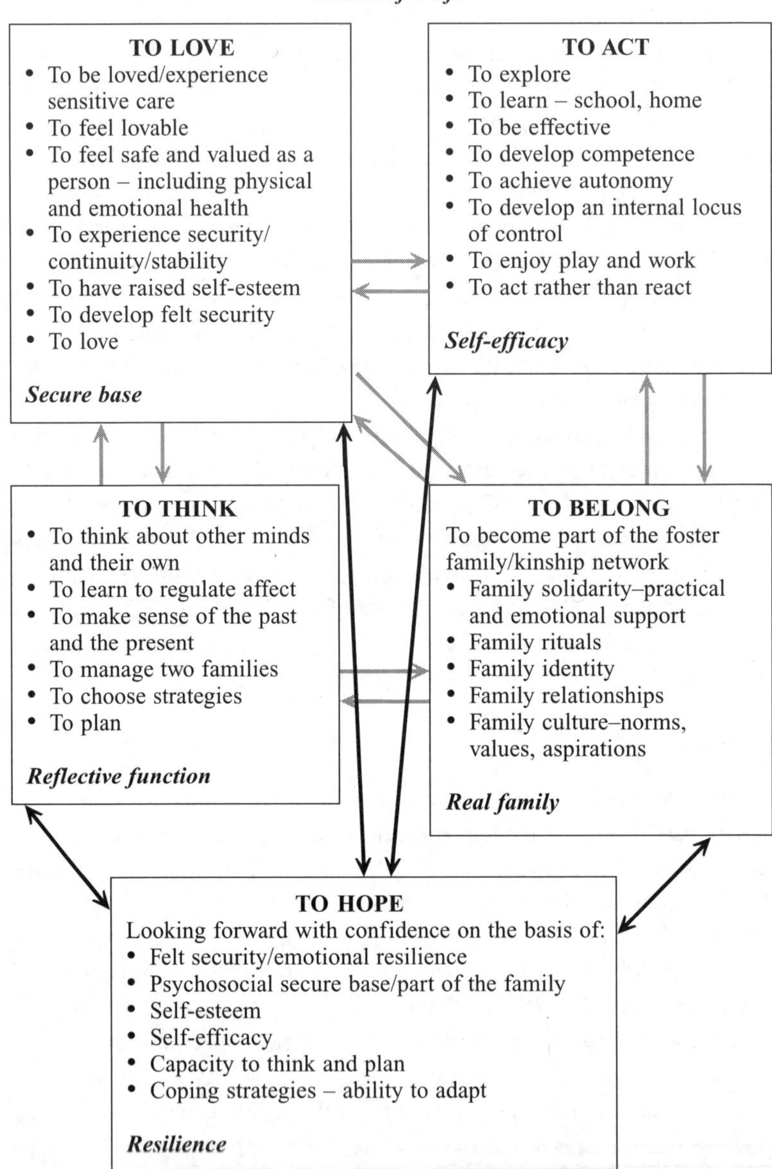

experience of secure, loving care are more likely to approach new relationships with friends, partners, and children with some confidence that, within these relationships, they can love and be loved.

For almost all of the adults in this study, felt security had not been the experience in their birth families. The majority birth family experience across all seven pathways was one of inadequate care, neglect, abuse or abandonment. For a minority in this group, this had also been the experience in previous foster or adoptive families. The lesson the child had to learn in those environments had been a very fundamental one – to adapt in order to survive (Crittenden and Ainsworth, 1989; George, 1996; Howe *et al*, 1999; Mrazek and Mrazek, 1987). Children who learned to be quiet and compliant or who learned to use emotions to attract attention may have been able to construct an organised avoidant or ambivalent defence. But the presence of fear in most histories, whether fear of abuse or existential fear in the presence of severe neglect and abandonment, would have had a disorganising effect. Those children who were fearful, chaotic, helpless or controlling demonstrated in their behaviours their struggle with anxiety, low self-esteem and low self-efficacy. These children had not had access to a secure base. Internal working models were predominantly negative, with adults describing vividly their childhood anxieties about self and others. As Bee (1999) puts it: 'the concept of self serves as a sort of filter for experience, shaping our choices and affecting our responses to others'. Our evaluation of the self, the self-esteem that is most powerfully generated within close relationships, plays a major part in dictating how we evaluate and respond to experience. This was the challenge that the foster carers took on, when attempting to offer a secure base to children whose caregiving experiences had led to a breakdown in their capacity to trust.

In the few cases where there had been good or "good enough" care in previous caregiving environments, this had both psychological and social benefits. Some who had been orphaned had experienced previous secure, stable care from birth parents. Others had received good care from previous short-term foster families or from residential workers, often those who were the first to offer concern and affection as a child was moved out from frightening or neglectful birth family situations. There were also cases where, although the overall care from birth parents had not been good, for example, in the context of parental mental health problems, children had nevertheless experienced some affection or had experienced high expectations in terms of academic achievement.

As children entered their foster homes, they were mostly quiet and suspicious, though there were some stories of aggression or randomly seeking affection from strangers. The task of adapting to and accepting good care did not necessarily mean the giving up of existing defensive strategies, but it did mean becoming more flexible, better able to use reason *and* emotion, to think *and* to feel, to give as well as to accept love. Disorganised controlling strategies in older children needed to shift into more organised defences, often defended and avoidant, before children could begin to use carers fully as a secure base that could be trusted. But even the more distant children in Group 3 or the more anxious children in Group 4 gradually saw their foster parents as being available, emotionally and practically. The process of relationship development was presented in rather a diffuse way in some interviews and, being retrospective, may have glossed over or indeed exaggerated difficulties. However, the core experience of feeling loved unconditionally by a sensitive and available carer was described vividly over and over again. The resulting feeling of increased self-esteem, learning to love oneself, was nevertheless slow to develop.

Not unlike the process of attachment formation in infancy (Bowlby, 1969), older children in foster placement seem to have relied on the new parent to make the first overtures and dictate the pace at which the two started to join together in a mutual relationship dance, tuning into each other as synchrony developed. In infancy, the need for the parent to make the first move is largely a result of the limited behavioural repertoire of the infant. Although programmed to seek proximity and with a range of attachment-relevant behaviours in place, such as scanning the face of the caregiver, the infant does not know how to direct their attachment behaviours in a purposeful and patterned way until they have learned the interactive skills of smiling, taking full advantage of the parent's conversational pauses, and so on. For older children coming into placements, as described in this study, with a repertoire of avoidant and controlling behaviours, such as being silent and withdrawn, lying, stealing, manipulating or alternatively approaching any stranger for attention, it was necessary for them to receive some emotional and behavioural education before attachment relationships could be formed. These children needed to learn how to communicate their needs directly, how to trust the availability of caregivers and how to regulate affect without retreating back behind their defences. A secure attachment may not have been fully achieved. But a more useful and realistic standard is the capacity, shown by many of these young men and women, to feel *more* secure in their families, to *begin* to accept the secure emotional base offered by the foster carers and to build on it in terms of the *increased* ability to accept love, to feel lovable, and to give love in relationships.

As adults, it was possible to see a wide range in terms of how successful, in respect of achieving felt security, foster family placements had been. As described in the different pathway chapters, relaxed adults in stable, rewarding relationships with stable, rewarding jobs contrasted with a number of adults, some of whom described equally vivid experiences of available sensitive care and others who had less satisfactory care, who were still anxious about the self and rather wary of intimate relationships. The sources of these different outcomes were inevitably a complex interaction between the child and the environment into which they came.

Continuity of placement or at least continuity of relationship had offered security and predictability of a most basic but nevertheless important kind. As one young woman said of her first days in the family, 'I remember snuggling into a nice, warm bed and knowing that my clothes were at the end of my bed . . . I just sort of let myself go as such and I just enjoyed what I was seeing and what I was doing. I just became happy I suppose.' But, the quality of relationship experiences for those children in those families depended on the interaction between the level of disturbance in the child and the quality of caregiving. Other factors, such as age at placement, expectations of foster carers, and attitudes of social workers had some part to play. But cases where late placed children in their teens were turned around emotionally by warm, patient and sensitive caregiving were testament to the fact that the drive towards proximity in relationships is so fundamental to our being that it can be activated well beyond infancy. In contrast, two adults in Group 7 were placed in infancy but recorded experiences of rejection and abuse that troubled and perplexed them into adult life, as they struggled with possible explanations for not being loved or seen as lovable – Was it me? Did they just do it for the money? And so on.

Attachment theory would suggest that the centrality to development of the experience of an emotional and psychological secure base arises not only because of the raised self-esteem that accompanies feeling loved and lovable, but also because it frees the mind from attachment preoccupations. Felt security liberates the self to act – to explore, to learn, to develop self-efficacy and to achieve autonomy in ways that are critical for foster children, as for all children.

To act

Attachment theory proposes the existence of two behavioural systems in infancy – the attachment or careseeking system and the exploratory system. The attachment system generates attachment behaviour, which is focused on achieving the proximity of the caregiver and receiving care and protection. The predictable availability of the caregiver releases the infant from persisting in the crying or the calling and allows the infant to pursue what they are also biologically programmed to do, to learn and to explore. Although attachment theory might appear to suggest that attachment needs must be satisfied before exploratory systems are activated, the model is more one of cycles of interaction – with tentative moves to explore alternating with checks back with the caregiver to ensure that the secure base is still accessible.

Just as in infancy, when the experience of predictable sensitive care frees the infant to be interested in and learn from the environment, so the secure base offered in foster families can free older children to be interested in, learn from and enjoy activities, school and all aspects of the world around them. With older children, as with infants, there is an interaction here between being *active* and being *loved*, since the promotion of activity is part of sensitive care and the experience of success in activity in turn feeds back into the sense of self-esteem that is developing in the context of the caregiver–child relationship. This feedback loop involving activity works not only in relation to school, ballet classes and so on, but also in the simpler process of shared activities in the home.

The previous family experiences of the children in this study, prior to this long-term foster home, had left them with a range of emotional preoccupations and behaviours that limited their interest and the energy available for exploration. Their experience was most commonly of unavailable, rejecting or insensitive care, whether through abuse and neglect or through severe parental mental health and substance dependency problems. Although some had previously found comfort in experiences outside the home, such as at school, others recalled clinging to the dinner ladies but not engaging with school work, not "exploring" but still being preoccupied with attachment considerations.

Once in foster care, quiet, well-behaved but secretive children still nursed their anxieties and fears about the past and the future, often shutting themselves off from the major source of stimulation and learning – their carers. Others more energetically engaged in demanding the attention of other people, but in ways that most often led to a turning away and disappointment. Pleasure and success in their own endeavours were not part of their experience in their birth families nor, for some, in the early months and even years of placement.

In their foster homes, the importance of activities, of being active in a constructive way, was a feature of many of the interviews. As well as emphasising the importance of school to the children and campaigning on their behalf to overcome difficulties such as dyslexia, many foster families engaged their children in a range of other activities. For some families this would be dancing, ballet, music, horse riding, while for others there was a shared enjoyment of sport. Sometimes this followed traditional gender divides, with girls involved in cooking and shopping with foster mothers, while boys accompanied their fathers to their places of work or made things in the workshop at the bottom of the garden. But high expectations of constructive activity applied to both genders.

For most adults, the memory of being encouraged to get involved and take pleasure from activities merged with their general sense of reliable, sensitive care. It was part of the shared pleasure in the relationship with carers. But for some, their memories were of a more unsettling combination of harsh treatment alongside high expectations to perform. Although less satisfactory as a family experience, it was clear that even these adults had drawn on some of those activities in shaping their sense of themselves as academically successful or musical or talented at dance or good with horses. One young woman who had been physically assaulted by her foster father and coolly treated by her foster mother but had reached advanced grades on the violin said, 'I can thank them for that . . . which I do'. Where harsh treatment was linked to belittling and undermining the child's confidence in their ability, this was recalled with particular bitterness.

The experience of being active can generate not only self-esteem, but also a sense of *competence* and *effectiveness* that contributes to increasing autonomy. Being helped but encouraged as a child to fix your own bike, as described by one man, increased confidence but also promoted independence. Being consulted when new foster children are to join the family gave the message that children could contribute to family decision-making, as well as treating them with respect as people with feelings and ideas of their own that needed to be taken into account. This is developmentally significant for all children, but particularly for formerly maltreated children in the care system, for whom feelings of helplessness and powerlessness often militate against the development of an internal locus of control.

Being *active* in the sense of undertaking activities is therefore important, but only tells part of the story in terms of its protective value. In the resilience literature (Rutter, 1985) we find the rather different, though linked, perspective on the concept of activity which rests on the importance of *acting rather than reacting*, seen as significant to the ability to cope with stress and challenge. The link lies in those core notions of competence or effectiveness. Acting rather than reacting as a concept is most closely related within attachment theory to the broad notion of autonomy and is central to the adult outcome of secure attachment, being *free to evaluate*. It is important to make explicit the connections between these concepts and the process that facilitates their development in the child in foster care. We need to use the stories that adults told of this process, or its absence, to demonstrate the role that being active in this sense played in childhood and went on to play in their adult lives.

Perhaps the simplest way of approaching this is through the twin concepts of power and choice. In their birth families, where children from this study had often felt powerless because of feeling trapped by fear of caregivers or because of the generally chaotic and unpredictable nature of home life, their freedom or power to make choices was limited by the need to survive. Choices were undoubtedly made, even at the level of developing strategies in the light of whatever threat presented itself, but survival choices are not the same as those geared to maximising happiness or personal fulfilment. Behaviours that children in this sample had been driven to, such as stealing food from other children when hungry, can be understood as effective strategies to some extent and promote more of a sense of self-efficacy than hiding in a bedroom. But, as Fahlberg (1994) points out in her model of attachment formation, if the satisfaction of need is not rooted within a relationship, the child is not learning the lesson of trusting other people and being able to use them as a resource. Children are reacting to circumstances of threat rather than being in the position to make active choices, for example, about what to eat, when to eat, who to eat with, and so on.

In foster families, as these adults described, many had felt respected and given choices by foster carers from the start. Even being allowed to take their time to get used to the new family was experienced as respectful and empowering, as encouraging the child to find their own way forward in their own time. In the teenage years, support for their autonomy by carers was indicated by statements such as 'they supported me whatever I wanted to do'. In contrast, when children continued to feel powerless in foster families where, for example, they felt singled out for rejection or found foster carers to be intrusive or bullying, it was apparent that this had left them angry and uncertain.

Although strengths in promoting autonomy in the foster families were important, other factors in their specific situation as foster children had some impact on their ability to develop a sense of autonomy. The general sense of powerlessness in the birth family that many reported was exacerbated in many cases by experiences in the care system. Adults reported being moved from the birth family to foster care or moved between foster homes with little notice and little choice in the matter. Separation from siblings was a key area where consultation was valued, when it occurred, but where no consultation occurred or they had been deceived, for example, being told they were going to separate places for a holiday, the sense of loss and anger still rankled. Most carers helped children to experience self-efficacy in ways that counteracted these past experiences. Where children had experienced harsh treatment in the foster family, but had felt unable to speak about it, they felt further disempowered and helpless.

In adult life, being active and autonomous showed itself in areas of functioning varying from further education to employment to parenting. The drive and determination to succeed in a career, the drive and determination to stay out of debt, the drive and determination to give their children a good upbringing were all examples of ways in which these young adults drew on strengths developed in childhood and declared their intention of making choices and taking responsibility for bringing about successful outcomes. The fact that these were free choices, sometimes encouraged by carers but often in the face of negative expectations by outsiders, was itself impressive. The more obvious success of the university graduates was matched by other equally significant kinds of achievement – the teenage mother who was determined to breastfeed even though her baby had been in special care after birth; the young man of 30 who had only been out of work for eight days since leaving school; the single mother of three who had come off drugs after leaving prison and was settled in her own home.

In adult life as in infancy, the attachment system and exploratory system interact in all our lives, as most men and women act independently but negotiate a comfortable distance from their secure base. For adults in this study, that secure base had often continued to be within the foster family or was shared with or to some extent replaced by adult partner relationships. The mechanism of the secure base remains the same as in infancy, however, in that the need to check back with the attachment figure will intensify at moments of stress and anxiety. For some adults in this study, the use of the carers as a secure base was simply an occasional phone call, with perhaps additional calls at times of stress, financial or emotional. This more intermittent contact could be either because they felt sufficiently secure, stable and/or self-sufficient not to need more frequent contact or because some degree of distance during childhood simply carried on into the adult relationship patterns. Other adults had very frequent contact, sometimes daily, even into their late 20s. In some of these cases this seemed to be simply a cultural pattern, in which family members lived close to each other and close involvement in each other's homes and lives was a family tradition. In other cases, though, it seemed much more clearly the case that there was a powerful emotional need to keep in touch and a sense that this contact was necessary to their very existence. This was most strongly expressed by several who talked of their anxiety about separation in terms of the fear of their foster parents dying before them. One young woman feared for her sanity if her foster father were to die. Although some (but not all) of these adults functioned well at work, in relationships and as parents, their sense of autonomy and their confidence in their ability to act on their own behalf was in some senses more fragile and was dependent on the continuous availability of the parental attachment figure – the foster carer.

Where security had freed adults from attachment concerns and led to the capacity to act autonomously in childhood and then in adult life, this had a positive impact on their sense of themselves and their relationships. Although in the first few months of life the capacity to explore can be simply liberated by emotional security, from infancy onwards children who are growing towards autonomous adulthood will need to acquire another important ability – the ability to think. In order to be successfully active or free to evaluate and make choices, the individual needs to be able to anticipate, to plan ahead, to understand the options. The mind must be free to review the situation, not dominated or driven by anxiety or fear arising from earlier experiences or current uncertainties. This is a cognitive development. Emotional security in itself does not make it happen, but the capacity to think, especially about others' minds and one's own mind, to "mentalise" as Fonagy (1996) terms it, flowers in the context of security in an attachment relationship and can be seen as inseparable from it. Foster children need to learn to be effective thinkers if they are to move forwards in all aspects of their lives.

To think

All children have a great deal to think about. From the cot to the classroom to the club, growing up requires the child to reflect on and make sense of their world. To summarise the significance of the reflective function, it is helpful to turn to Fonagy (2001).

Reflective function enables children to conceive of others' beliefs,

> *feelings, attitudes, desires, hopes, knowledge, imagination, pretence, plans and so on. At the same time as making others' behaviour meaningful and predictable, they are also able flexibly to activate from multiple sets of self–other representations the one most appropriate in a particular interpersonal context. Exploring the meaning of the actions of others is crucially linked to the child's ability to label and find meaningful his or her own experience. This may make a critical contribution to affect regulation, impulse control, self-monitoring, and the experience of self-agency.* (Fonagy and Target, 1997; cited in Fonagy, 2001, p. 165)

This emphasises the importance of thinking in enabling foster children to find meaning in their own and others' experience and to manage feelings in a constructive fashion.

As the model suggests (Figure 10.1), the foster family experience of sensitive care that offers love and a secure base, and contributes to self-esteem, liberates the mind to think and reflect as well as to act. Within that relationship experience a number of shifts occur. First, as anxiety is reduced and confidence in the self and relationships increases, the internal working model can move towards a more secure, more positive set of beliefs and expectations of self and others. Secondly, within a more stable, predictable environment where feelings can be named, thought about and discussed, less destructive strategies can be learned to manage those feelings. Defensive, controlling strategies can move towards more balanced and flexible strategies that include turning to others for comfort. This is a difficult process and it takes time, as the adults in this study reported. But primarily it requires a cognitive shift in ideas and beliefs based on the experience of caregivers who can offer direct assistance with thinking.

The cognitive scaffolding normally provided from infancy by sensitive parents had to be provided for older children in this study by foster carers who themselves had the capacity to think about the foster child, think with the foster child, and enable the child to think for him or herself. Foster carers who were available to talk things through with children helped them give a shape to experience and make sense of their own and other minds.

> *If you said something to her, she'd sit down and have a good conversation with you, ask your decision on things. So that if she asked you something and you didn't think that was right and said no, she coped with it, she tried to understand.*

When carers consistently tried to understand, kept the children in mind and contained their anxieties, they made those anxieties manageable and reflected back to the child their confidence in their joint ability to cope. This gradually enabled the children to begin to keep the carers in their mind as an internalised secure base and to develop coping strategies of their own. For some more vulnerable minds, who found it particularly difficult to achieve an internalised secure base, this process needed to be reinforced by caregiver availability into adult life.

Maltreated children who come into foster care are likely to have been exposed to threatening and unpredictable care, which makes it less likely that they will have developed an understanding of others' beliefs, feelings and so on – a developmental process that is well-established in the majority of children by the age of three or four (Dunn, 1988), but which maltreated children may struggle with all their lives. Neglectful or abusive parents are less likely to assist children in this process by giving them comfortable access to their minds, and children may not want to look into the eyes and the minds of frightening or frightened parents and see themselves reflected there. Children will struggle to manage affect because distracted, troubled or angry parents will not find it easy to put their own feelings into words or to help children put their feelings into words. Understanding the meaning of the actions of others is also a challenge for children whose experience is of actions that may be unpredictable or appear to make no sense.

When children find themselves in foster families they may experience for the first time a more predictable world in which they can be enabled to start the process of learning to think. This subtle process could be tracked in the interview material. Even the predictability of clothes at the end of the bed and clear boundaries allowed children to see the world in a different light. Some adults were able to describe how carers actively took time to think through with the children their thoughts and fears. As the young man who described his carer consulting him about new foster children put it, she knew what he might feel, she was 'a very understanding lady'.

Some of the more obvious lessons in thinking that were well described in the study came about through the foster carers helping the children to think through their past and manage their feelings and their current relationships with birth family members. This kind of thinking has always been valued in the social work literature and in family placement practice. More specific and concrete than the broader lessons in understanding other minds, it nevertheless provided children with a sense that the way to "come to terms" with difficult feelings and memories was to think them through. It is in this area that normal developmental tasks and the specific tasks of the foster child overlap. As with other kinds of learning, the motivation to think in order to get past stories and feelings of upset, guilt and responsibility and move on with their lives was a strong one. But equally, the wish to avoid the pain of thinking required sensitive, subtle and, above all, patient carers.

Thinking about the experience of separation and loss

For each child, an intrinsic part of managing the move into the foster placement was thinking through, managing and adapting to the experience of loss. This is widely identified in the literature on foster care and on attachment as a source of risk in itself. Psychologically, the experience of loss is likely to lead to feelings of grief and bereavement for the foster child in ways that are similar to the experience of adults. But because children are still actively learning about themselves and the world around them as part of their development, loss and separation need to be understood and made sense of or they can lead to cognitive confusion and uncertainty. As Fahlberg (1994) and others (Jewett, 1994; Schofield, 1996) have pointed out, the process of adapting to the loss of attachment figures will depend on the meaning attached to the experience, for example, abandonment, abduction or, as in some cases in this study, rescue. Different cognitive appraisals seemed to relate, not surprisingly, to a combination of what was being left in the birth family, what greeted them in the foster family and, in some cases, how the transition was managed by social workers.

In most cases, loss will lead to an immediate increase in anxiety, if only in the short term, which will in turn increase the use of defensive strategies and reduce the capacity to think. The cognitive task is to find some way of accounting for the loss that protects the self-esteem and the sense of self-efficacy, while providing some realistic hope for the future. Hopefulness, a belief that bad things can turn into good things (Masten *et al*, 1990), is an important resilience characteristic but needs to be based on some cognitive appraisal that offers a resolution. Adapting to loss in this study was often associated with managing the birth family story in the context of the caregiving in the new family. The ability to move on seemed to have been associated with a balanced and realistic appraisal of the birth family and a gradual understanding that the foster family was offering a happier and safer experience than would have been possible in the birth family. Where care in the new foster family was not good, resolving the loss was more of a challenge.

Contact with birth family members could be helpful in achieving this cognitive and emotional resolution, sometimes by showing *both* that the birth family cared enough to see them (that is to say, the birth family was not entirely unloving and nor were they as children entirely unworthy of their love) *and* that the birth family could not parent them properly. Even where the contact experience was of birth families who let them down, this allowed them to contrast the reliability of foster carers with the more risky option that remaining in the birth family would have been. There were some cases where the loss of the birth family was managed in a fairly balanced way in the absence of contact, but foster carers took the same active role of letting children talk through feelings. More than one adult remembered talking through contact issues with their foster carers and being helped to understand and accept why birth parents might repeatedly mention wanting the child to return home. The foster carers' capacity to assist children in thinking things through in relation to the birth family, whatever the history or the level of contact, was an important and frequently mentioned parenting virtue. At best, it could help children to grow up relating comfortably to both families.

Loss or separation from *siblings* was thought about in very varied ways by the young men and women in the study. For a number of maltreated children, protecting younger siblings had offered a source of self-esteem and a role, as well as providing at least some kind of rewarding intimate relationship. Separation from a younger sibling was viewed by them as a defining moment in their childhood, when they lost faith in social workers and felt truly alone. But for others, and this was one of the perhaps more surprising features of the stories, complex sibling relationships with more disturbed older or younger siblings meant that liberation came when they went to a placement on their own or their sibling left the placement. Several even requested such moves. One young woman said that she had envied her brothers going to placements on their own while she was left sharing an otherwise happy placement with an angry sister who never settled. Another young woman said that once she had been moved away from her sister, at her own request, 'at last I could make a fresh start and be myself'. As with the loss of birth parents, the quality of relationship experiences made all the difference. Shared experience of maltreatment could be a shared trauma which might seal or sour sibling relationships. But the needs of children could change over time. One young woman gave an account of valuing and relying on the sibling support while in an abusive adoptive family, but later wanting to move on to a placement on her own and leave some of that behind her. "Moving on" meant different things to different children and needed to be managed differently. Again, though, thinking this through with the help of carers could liberate the child's coping capacity.

Although the loss of an attachment figure presented psychological challenges, it was apparent that children had also lost the possibility of a normal childhood, as culturally defined. The birth family may have been dysfunctional, but at least it was recognisably a family like other people's, a "real" family to whom one was biologically connected and which was therefore socially legitimate. Most children had been well aware of that sense of being different. The alternative story or status, the current situation of being a foster child, not only required explanation of its origin, but also required explanation as a kind of family identity in order for conversations to proceed. Why are your parents not looking after you? What is foster care? Who are foster carers? Are they paid to look after you? Does that mean you are "in care"? The loss is of social legitimacy, since whichever way the situation is approached, via the flaws in the birth family or the flaws in this "second best" family status, the upshot is that the child is different and at risk of being seen as somehow of less value than other children.

The loss needed to be managed intrapsychically and interpersonally. The child had to cognitively process the losses and the gains. The task of managing the loss and moving on was often hampered, even for those in the sample with a clear sense of overall gains from foster care, by a haunting sense of something missing. As in Sroufe's description (Sroufe, 1997) of different pathways leading sometimes to similar outcomes, it did seem that depression and low self-esteem could follow from a range of different kinds of placement, some continuous, some discontinuous. There was a risk of depression setting in, when an often ill-defined black hole appeared before them. The 'why me?' question that haunted them had within it the sense that life was unfair and that out there were children with normal families whose parents did not die, disappear, neglect or abuse them. Here the task of thinking through and coping with their specific losses was compounded by the awareness that other people, normal people, did not need to go through this process. Going to school, starting college, meeting people at discos, they knew they were different and that life was unfair not to have allowed them to go from birth to adulthood in connection with a birth parent. Although many were able to say to themselves, 'I've been so lucky in finding a family to love me', one young person simply added, 'but I can't help wishing that my parents hadn't died'.

Thinking through and managing memories and/or stories about the birth family

Where children had adverse experiences in the birth family, they were left with disturbing memories or were later given stories of early harm that were disturbing, or both. They may have had contradictory experiences in relationships with maltreating caregivers leaving them with what Main (1991) described as 'multiple (incoherent) models' but this kind of confusion was then exacerbated by conflicting information from multiple sources about parents and the self. Most common of all, and perhaps inevitable, was the fact that the stories were always partial and offered incomplete pictures. Where memory provides an incomplete picture, the mind tries to fill in the gaps, to find some story that makes sense (Howe, 1998; Mollon, 2000).

This process is further complicated for fostered children and previously fostered adults when negative or positive spin is put on stories in subtle and often unconscious ways by foster carers, social workers, birth parents, grandparents, siblings, peers, life story books and files. However, some stories were, regardless of the completeness or the manner of the telling, more difficult to manage than others. But it was apparent from the early interviews onwards that it was not only the severity of maltreatment or poor care as an *experience*, as a procedural or episodic memory, that mattered, it was also the degree of awfulness in the *story that then had to be told to the self*, the narrative that was partly based on episodic but often more powerfully rooted in semantic memory, the stories told to the child, that the child had to incorporate into their sense of self and that affected their sense of their own worth. Although the unhappy "truth" about the past could be worrying, it was equally important not to have the story "all prettied up", as one young woman put it, since that led to confusion about why they were in care, fed fantasy, and indeed might contribute to ill-fated reunions in adolescence.

Socially, publicly, these stories were stories that had to be told not only to the self but also to others every time someone needed to know who they were – since it was hard for this not to lead to questions about why they were in care or who their "real" parents were. In our society, we identify ourselves constantly in new relationships with friends and partners by our family stories. We are placed socially, but also conclusions may be drawn about the kind of people we are. Even being an only child or a twin or the child of divorce can lead to certain (unspoken) assumptions. The foster child's story, that my mum and dad hurt me or did not love me or did not want me or was mad or bad or killed my brother, could not easily be shared. As children from the study moved into peer group settings in primary school and learned about what families were supposed to be like, the fact that they had been hurt or abandoned rather than loved and protected by biological parents left a sense of betrayal of the natural and cultural order of things. The discovery that children were expected to be like their parents led to further anxieties, about bad blood and the heritability of everything from schizophrenia to child abandonment. This could in turn be exacerbated by other children and adults, including in some cases angry or exasperated foster carers, also picking up on the 'you'll end up just like your parents' theme. There is an inevitable feedback loop here, as social commentary on the foster child's status as the child of unloving or just absent parents added to the child's doubts and anxieties about the connections between this family history and the self.

Although this negative picture was quite a common experience, most children had been enabled by carers from a very early age to think through and deal constructively with the birth family story and the experience of being challenged to explain themselves at school. Stories that parents had not been able to cope or had mental health problems were quite comfortably managed, even where the consequences of those problems had been quite severe. Contact could also help in some but not all cases. Regular contact with birth parents where there had been neglect could be unnerving where mentally ill parents still behaved bizarrely, but generally dealt with any possibility of idealising or demonising the birth parent. Those who remained insecure and fragile emotionally, even in adult life, had almost all been left with either a memory of fear or a story of something fearful, such as physical assault in infancy or sexual assault, which appeared to have no other explanation than that the parent meant them harm and that they, as children, had not attracted or perhaps been worthy of love and protection. But it was not the case that all those who had such stories were fragile – the age at leaving the birth family and the capacity to think through that experience with the help of carers seemed to make some difference.

Managing and thinking through the story of poor or abusive care by previous foster or adoptive caregivers also required the assistance of the foster carers, although social workers had often been called on to validate the child's experience. Several young people reported that social workers felt bad and apologised about placements where they later discovered the child had been ill-treated. The fact that an adoptive parent or foster carer had faced criminal charges or was not allowed to foster subsequently was firmly incorporated into the story. As described in Groups 6 and 7, it was possible to divert feelings of personal hurt and self-doubt into anger at social workers and at the previous carers themselves. These then became easier stories to tell.

Foster carers, therefore, were valued for helping specifically with the challenging mental task for foster children of making sense of the complex past and the sometimes uncertain present. Difficult histories of neglect and abandonment, and sometimes difficult experiences of contact with the birth family since, could be managed emotionally if cognitively there was a framework that allowed the child to take a balanced and realistic view. But this process could only happen in the context of the broader task of thinking through that is going on in the close and containing relationship with the carer.

As part of the general thinking through of the story of the past that needed to be done, there was an additional task of dealing with the *care identity* and managing *stigma*. The child's position *as* a foster child remained to some extent anomalous and negatively constructed. It is what Goffman called "a spoiled identity", which can reduce a person 'from a whole and usual person to a tainted, discounted one' (Goffman, 1964). One problem for fostered children is that, in partaking of the same set of cultural norms as the rest of society, they may come to incorporate this negative view into their beliefs about the self.

> *The stigmatised individual tends to hold the same beliefs about identity that we do; this is a pivotal fact . . . The standards he has incorporated from the wider society equip him to be intimately alive to what others see as his failing, inevitably causing him, if only for moments, to agree that he does indeed fall short of what he really ought to be. Shame becomes a central possibility . . .'* (Goffman, 1964, p. 62).

From this study it appears that, where foster families had the capacity to help the child think this through, reinforced very significantly by providing positive alternative identities, they offered a cognitive framework for dealing with or helping the child manage the risk of harm to the self-esteem caused by the threat of stigma.

Feelings such as grief, loss and guilt could also be managed once stories were shared and thought through in the safe context of the foster family. The need to revisit and rework some of these issues in adult life, in order not to lapse into being controlled by the past, was another important part of the continuing and containing availability of the foster carer's mind. Touching base emotionally was accompanied by touching base mentally, with foster carers helping to shape experience more constructively when challenges, such as the loss of a partner or the birth of a child, brought on bad dreams and threatened to reduce fragile stability to chaos.

Although the loving, acting, thinking parts of long-term foster care experience help to explain how children move on developmentally, the secure base found in foster families appeared to be closely connected for many fostered children with the idea of the foster families as a "real family" of which they were and are a part. Since *belonging* and *being part of the family* dominated many of the interviews across all pathways, it is an aspect of the model that requires some expansion here.

To belong

The meaning of belonging, being part of a foster family, is multi-dimensional. From the accounts given by the adults in the study 'family relationship' seemed to comprise at least five separate, though connected, features: family solidarity; family identity; family rituals; family relationships; family culture (Figure 10.2). Although the origins of this family membership lay in childhood, what was most striking and distinctive in this study was the account that was being given of the ongoing family membership experienced after the child had left care and the family had no official role in their lives. Such tests of being a "real family" were part of an elaborate structure of ties that provided its own kind of scaffolding for adulthood.

Family solidarity

Long-term foster families and often their extended families were able to offer family membership in the form of practical and emotional support, as of right, to children with whom they had no biological or legal connection. This commitment can be understood as a characteristic of any kinship network (Allan, 1996; Allan and Crow, 2001; Young and Willmott, 1962). Including foster children in the family can therefore be usefully conceptualised as the foster family's recognition of foster children as "kin". Allan (1996, p. 53) suggests that kinship, even where there are legal or biological ties, is a very complex and fluid concept.

Figure 10.2
Part of the family

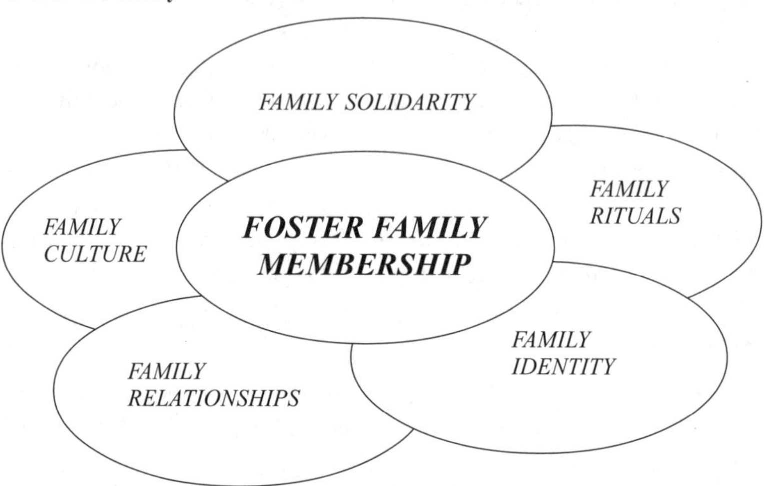

> *Kinship, though apparently based on simple principles of biological and legal relationships, actually entails a complex of social and personal considerations as well as legal and biological ones. Who counts as a relative, who is accepted as being part of the kin group, and what obligations, rights, privileges and responsibilities flow from that vary very widely and depend on numerous factors . . . The details of the relationship certainly vary, but there is an over-riding moral view that, other things being equal, primary kin should share a commitment to and solidarity with one another.*

Allan (1996, p. 55) goes on to suggest that a useful way of understanding kinship ties in families is to think in terms of "diffuse enduring solidarity". This expression captures the persistence of these "obligations, rights, privileges and responsibilities", as reflected in the study, but also reflects the "diffuse" and variable levels of intensity in shows of solidarity across the lifespan, depending on need, resources and many other factors.

The *activation* of this solidarity could occur in a number of ways across different foster placements and even after placement endings. It might occur automatically at culturally expected moments, such as the birth of a child, or on demand from any member of the network. Though a powerful mechanism, it could be demonstrated in very simple acts, such as an adult foster son asking for and getting help with an electricity bill or a carer keeping a teenage foster daughter who was moving to another placement supplied with phone cards, to maintain the links, give messages of continuing concern and make herself available if needed. The key element here is the *expectation* of unconditional interest, concern, help and, above all, continuity of involvement over space and time.

Helpful also to this aspect of our model of long-term foster care is a comparison with the analysis which Allan (1996, p. 64) offers of another family pattern that lacks a clearly defined script – families after divorce.

> *Like other kinship ties, these relationships do not follow a simple social script. They are normative in the sense that there are strong expectations of continuing commitment, but they are not built upon easily specified, agreed social norms.*

In foster care, one could argue, there is an agency expectation of *professional role commitment,* but this may not be the same as the normative expectation of *kinship commitment,* which offers solidarity and a sense of belonging. Social workers who talked about "placements" not "homes", or did not accept the fact that children called foster carers "mum and dad" and referred to birth parents by their first names, reinforced this distinction. Leaving care systems which promoted independence rather than "enduring solidarity" confirmed this, by making it clear that this was just a placement from which any sensible child would be planning to leave as soon as a flat could be found – foster carers were not parents, ergo this was not a family. "Foster care as family" was often quite simply taken for granted by foster families and foster children, but the move towards family membership and solidarity described in this study has always to be understood in the context of all the forces that militated against the "real family" being accepted as such by outsiders.

Family ritual

Any society can be understood in part through its rituals and family rituals are a major part of our cultural life. Belonging to a foster family in this study meant that their family rituals extended to embrace the foster child. Family photographs on the wall included the foster child. Christmas and birthdays became special in family specific ways, in childhood and also in adult life. Whether you were a student away at university or a sailor back from sea or a mother with three young children, the ritual family gatherings mattered. For major lifetime events where *parents* were required, foster carers stepped in. Being part of the family meant that foster fathers gave foster daughters away at their weddings and foster carers attended their foster children's graduation ceremonies. These seemed to be the points at which foster children and their carers were able to say to each other in effect, 'This is our free choice. We have no biological, legal or social obligation to offer this public proof of family membership – but we do.'

Family relationships

Some rituals, such as the sending of Mother's Day cards, brought the definition of the relationship and the right to give and receive such cards into sharp relief. Although not all adults referred to their foster carers as mother and father when face-to-face, many nevertheless saw family relationships in terms of the usual family labels and/or talked to other people about their brothers and sisters, uncles and aunts. These labels, whether put into words or simply operating at the level of the cultural meaning of the relationship for the individual, acted in complex ways as evidence of belonging, but also as *placing* foster children in terms of a family identity.

Family identity

The struggle with stigma and difference arising from difficult birth family experiences, sometimes reinforced by the foster or in-care status, could be counteracted, to some extent at least, by the sense that this family was offering not just emotional healing but a place in society. This helped young people to answer the question posed in the introduction to this book – 'How are we supposed to live a normal life?' (foster child in Parker, 1980, p. 146). Belonging to the family helped them to have a place in the community in which they lived. They became known in the local shops and pubs and among their foster parents' friends as part of that particular family. The depth and significance of family feeling and identity in adulthood varied, as they do for all adults who reflect on the relative significance of their family membership. But for foster children who had suffered early damage in families, there could be a special pride in the membership of this particular family and gratitude for the gift of it. The self is psychosocially constructed and therefore it is not surprising that the task in foster care of developing an identity, often revising the self-concept, is likely to draw on both the quality of the caregiving in attachment terms *and* the extent to which the foster family restores the child's sense of belonging to a family and therefore gives them a family identity in what is very much a family-focused society.

For some, this process of identification with the foster family replaced the birth family identity, most usually where placements were made in infancy, where birth parents had died or where there were specific reasons, such as fear or a history of abuse, for wishing to discount the birth family identity and choose the foster family identity. But for many others in childhood and even later in adulthood, there was also a strong sense of connection with the birth family. This may have been based on an active relationship or, more commonly in long-term foster care, may have arisen from the simple sense that a birth family was always your family and that kinship rules applied. As regards family rituals, therefore, in some cases both foster parents and birth parents expected and received birthday and Christmas cards to "mum and dad" from a person who regarded themselves as a son or daughter in both families.

It seemed common for family identity in transracial placements to follow a similar varied pattern. Although this was a small sub-sample in this study, Thoburn *et al* (2000) also found a rich variety of family memberships and identities in their much larger study of placements of children of minority ethnic origin, some of which were transracial placements. It seemed possible that, for some transracially placed children in this study, there was a particularly active curiosity about birth families, where there had not been contact during childhood, and a more active sense of dual family membership, where contact had continued. The awareness of ethnic roots outside of the foster family was dealt with in several cases by choice of area to live in adulthood and so on, although family rituals and other aspects of family membership could continue in both families.

Shared family culture

Almost all adults' lives bear the hallmark to a greater or lesser extent of their families' way of doing things – their values, norms and aspirations. Being part of a foster family means that foster children, looking for guidance on "how to do things" as they grow up, are likely to take their direction from the foster family. This was certainly the case in this study. Each family had its own particular norms and values and belonging to that family meant paying close attention to their particular family culture. At one level, this may have been simple lifestyle choices, such as being interested in football, fishing, classical music or foreign holidays. At another level, it could be matters of moral principle, such as consideration for others, a determination to stay out of debt or a horror of dishonesty and crime. Family culture was likely to include matters of domestic standards, such as ensuring that a house is clean and tidy or, in contrast, not minding if the living room was strewn with toys. Subscribing to this family culture and following its direction successfully seemed to lead to feelings of self-esteem and competence. This is not surprising given that self-esteem is largely determined by the sense of living up to one's expectations for oneself (Harter, 1987) and those expectations are likely to draw on the foster family culture. Provided that the foster family was offering expectations that were pro-social and aided fitting into society, as was the case in these families, the wish to conform to the family's norms and values increased the likelihood of stability of work, accommodation and relationships.

Aspirations in childhood and adult life will be specific to the foster family and there are some inevitable differences, particularly in respect of occupational aspirations. There were aspirations to leave school and get a trade in one family and aspirations to go to university in another. Children who felt part of the foster family were most likely to follow the pattern of their foster carers, but some made different choices if they had different role models or had known different aspirations, such as in their birth families or previous foster families, which could be accommodated within the foster family. Where, for example, children arrived in care with high academic expectations from their birth family and were placed in a family with very different family employment traditions, then academic aspiration and achievement could still be a matter of shared family pride.

Taking on the family culture in addition to the various other components of family membership provided a more broadly defined "secure base" that increased the likelihood that foster children would be able to face up to the stresses and strains of adult life. As the model demonstrates (Figure 10.1), family membership thus combines with other psychosocial factors to offer the foster child a basis for some degree of optimism about their own capacity to manage their adult lives successfully.

To hope

To enter adult life with hope and some confidence requires the individual to experience themselves as having the resources to deal with such challenges as getting training or further education, finding work, living away from home, managing adult friendships and partnerships, and coping with parenthood. The experience of loving and being loved, of acting and being effective, of thinking more flexibly and coming to terms with the past and the present, of belonging to a family, all had their part to play in making it more likely that such challenges would be managed. Where coping mechanisms developed as a result of raised self-esteem, self-efficacy and improved reflective function, this contributed to the adults' capacity for hope for the future. But in most cases that hopefulness needed to be shored up by the confidence that, if internal resources were to fail, they then had access to external resources in the form of significant support from other people – most usually the foster families of which they were a part. This is the importance of *interdependence* rather than *independence* (Stein and Carey, 1986). That combination of internalised resources and the capacity to trust in and use available external resources has the power to reduce anxiety and promote competence and confidence.

These qualities that contribute to hopefulness are characteristic factors in resilience. In adulthood as in childhood there are a series of challenges as each life stage is reached, such as coping with parenthood or the death of a foster parent. In these situations the adults described how they managed to retain a faith in their own ability to parent a child or to survive without the support of the person who had provided a secure base in childhood. It seemed important to have a balanced view, to know your strengths and to accept that it is normal, for example, to experience grief. This kind of emotional literacy is a mark of maturity that not all had achieved, but where it had been developed, it was in the context of a family where carers were described as having been emotionally available and having taken the time to listen and to help them put feelings into words.

Where there were negative reactions to these adult stresses they most usually took the form of depression. Although post-natal depression and depression after the loss of a parent are not unusual in the general population, adults in this study who experienced depression after such events linked their feelings of being overwhelmed to their childhood losses. Their awareness of the importance of picking themselves up and finding strategies for looking forward was expressed in the interviews. Perhaps most touching was the statement by one young mother that what she most wanted for her son was that he would grow up with the feeling that even bad things can and do get better – a feeling she said that she had not had as a child and still had to struggle with for herself as an adult.

As children who had been exposed to severe stress in their early lives, it was not surprising that, however fortified most in the sample had been by their foster family's secure emotional and social base in childhood, as adults many continued to be rather fragile when their sense of self came under threat and would need to rush back for comfort and support, whether in person or by telephone. Those who did not have a family to draw on relied on friends or partners, resources which were also variable in the extent to which the young man or woman found their confidence restored. For them, lack of hope was most usually tied to a sense that they as people were somehow lacking something that other people had and they often despaired of knowing how to become more of a whole person. However, where adults did experience the combination of being secure emotionally, being effective, being reflective and being part of a family, this appeared to increase resilience and made adults leaving foster care more likely to adapt successfully and, on that basis, be more optimistic about their future.

Implications of this model for social work practice

This model of long-term foster care emphasises the role that foster care and foster carers play in promoting the well-being of children. However, although foster family life proceeds as family life does for most children, with the focus on the day-to-day activities of eating, sleeping, going to school, having holidays and so on, these children's family lives were conducted always within the bureaucratic framework provided by the local authority and within guidelines laid down by national government. With or without parental responsibility in law, local authorities had a duty to provide care and protection for these children. The local authority representatives, the social workers, were given the professional task of ensuring not only that procedural guidelines were followed, but that the children's welfare was safeguarded (CA, 1989 s24). As discussed elsewhere (Schofield *et al*, 2000), maintaining both support and monitoring roles is not an easy balance for social workers to achieve, particularly in long-term placements. Hoping for, valuing and supporting the *best* in foster care sits sometimes uneasily in practice besides fearing, looking for and preventing the *worst*. The model just described is a model of what we could learn from the study about what can contribute to good outcomes for children. But inevitably safeguarding a child's welfare also requires an awareness of what might be damaging or unhelpful in foster care. The translation of this theoretical model into practice must focus on what might be learned from good foster care experiences, but needs also to incorporate lessons learned from some of the more worrying stories of what happened in some of these foster and adoptive families provided by the local authority.

The model of long-term foster care practice that would logically arise from this psychosocial model for understanding long-term foster care (Figure 10.1) is set out in Figure 10.3. It includes some far from straightforward areas of social work activity, but most aspects will be recognisably linked to existing models of good practice. The main difference is perhaps that the theoretical drive is more explicitly developmental. For example, the importance of consulting children is often justified in terms of children's participation rights, whereas it is presented here in terms of the beneficial consequences for the child's sense of self-efficacy and the ability to think and reflect.

It is important to note that meeting children's needs and promoting their strengths in each part of the model requires social work activity in a number of different sites: with the child, with the carers, with birth families, with other agencies, and with the management of the looked after children system by social services departments. As Howe *et al* (1999) pointed out, what is needed when applying developmental theories to social work practice is to be aware of the numerous systems and environments that surround the child and the family and impact on development. It is this diversity which presents both the challenge and the rewards of good social work practice, because it is only the social worker who has the possibility of taking an overarching and ecological view of the child's progress through the care system.

Policy and practice in long-term foster care

There are some important messages for practice and policy from the study that will need to be given careful consideration in terms of how long-term foster care as a system can be understood, valued and supported in the future.

- ***Long-term foster care can provide a family for life***

The lack of biological, social or legal ties need not mean a lack of mutual family commitment into adult life in foster families. Practitioners need to be alert to the possibility that long-term foster family relationships can be meaningful as "real family" ties and treat their continuity as highly significant for the child and the carers. Even where no decision for "permanence" has been made, many carers continue to offer support to children and adults long after placements have ended.

In so far as policy directs, funds and supports practice, further thought needs to be given to ways in which policy and local authority systems can enable social workers and other professionals to offer the kind of thoughtful and supportive service to children, young people, their carers and their birth families suggested in the psychosocial model described above. Policy makers need to recognise that, if foster care can offer the family for life that looked after children need, they must build it into their planning for the looked after system – and cease the endless negative

Figure 10.3

Social work practice in long-term foster care using the psychosocial model

TO LOVE

- Recruit carers with the capacity to provide a secure emotional base/ contain the child's feelings and behaviour
- Support carers by reducing their own stress and increasing their emotional availability
- Monitor placements to ensure the child's safety and care/health
- Promote continuity of relationships through childhood AND into adult life
- Value all sources of relationships that could offer additional security for the child

Promoting felt security

TO ACT

- Support carers in valuing autonomy in the child, offering choices
- Support carers and child in promoting education, activities
- Promote self-efficacy in the child through appropriate consultation around decisions, reviews
- Promote awareness in other agencies of the importance of the child's perspective e.g. who does the child feel comfortable with at reviews?
- Promote routes to autonomy in adulthood while preserving the secure base

Promoting self-efficacy

TO THINK

- Recruit carers with some reflective capacity
- Reduce carers' stress/increase their thinking availability
- Work with children/help carers work with children to provide cognitive scaffolding
- Work with children/help carers work with children to make sense of the past/manage contact, multiple families, multiple identities

Promoting resolution of loss and trauma and developing reflective function

TO BELONG

- Recognise that this is the child's family as well as a local authority foster family
- Recognise that this is the child's family home as well as a foster placement
- Recognise that the child can be a member of more than one family
- Respect and use the child's terminology for birth and foster family members
- Manage the looked after children review system and leaving care system in ways that promote rather than diminish family membership
- Promote continuity of family membership into adult life

Promoting family membership in childhood and adult life

TO HOPE

- Identify strengths and difficulties in these different areas
- Promote self-esteem, self-efficacy, coping skills and adaptability through work with the child, the carers, the school, and other agencies

Promoting resilience

statements about the dire consequences for children who remain looked after, often made in order to press for policy development in other directions, such as adoption or placements with family and friends. What looked after children need is a range of positive options. What they do not need is to find themselves and their families the subject of further derogation and stigma.

- ***The development of the fostering service***

If it is to be accepted that foster families can provide "permanence", then this must become part of the current debate on the future of the foster care service. The drive towards professionalising the service is welcome in many respects, offering the very much overdue prospect of improving the status and employment conditions of foster carers. However, professionalism is not incompatible with parenting and family life. We should hesitate before devaluing the concepts of "parenting" and "family life" in favour of "caring skills" and "work" with children. Altruism and the wish to provide family care for children in adversity, whether on a respite basis or as a family for life, should also be welcomed and respected alongside our respect for the skills that foster carers undoubtedly need. Flexible thinking and integration of different but complementary models of foster care must be the way forward. This needs to inform all aspects of foster care policy – conditions of employment, recruitment, training and support.

- ***Flexible and creative approaches to planning for permanence***

Successful placements owe a great deal to serendipity, flexibility and opportunism in social work planning, with short-term and emergency placements, as well as long-term placements of very different kinds, leading to a family for life. Some children who stay long-term in a foster family may be described as "drifting", as "lingering" or as "languishing" in care, when actually they are at home with their family. We need to find ways, through professional assessments and planning systems, to distinguish between drift and continuing security.

Similarly, the balance between normalising foster family life and protecting children in placement is not easily achieved, but must be worked on flexibly in collaboration with the children, young people and their families. The reviewing system may itself need to be reviewed in order to achieve the right balance, avoiding intrusion and preserving the private family lives of children, while exercising the local authority's responsibility to safeguard their welfare.

• ***Transitions to adulthood***

The transition to adulthood during adolescence has great developmental and social significance. Family support and membership during this period can be critical. Late placements of children who have experienced a number of breakdowns can still lead to a family for life and a resource for adulthood. A supported lodgings carer can be a lifeline for young adults. Attachment theory should not be misused to suggest that secure relationships in new families are only achievable in early childhood. Continuity of family placement during this phase or the provision of a new family base can determine outcomes.

If family continuity is not available, the downward spiral out of placements, out of school and into drugs, alcohol and depression can create emotional vulnerabilities that last into adult life. Any suggestion that a young person who has a secure place in a family should be encouraged to move into independence may remove that young person's best chance of making a successful transition to adulthood and, most importantly, may put at risk the availability of ongoing family support in adult life.

• ***Belonging to more than one family***

Some involvement with and continuing membership of the birth family can exist alongside the commitment to membership in a new foster family. In many cases children, with the assistance of carers, comfortably manage this dual family membership. However, contact with birth parents who induce fear in their child or emotionally entangle them places stress on the child and the placement. Professional judgement needs to be exercised about contact in individual cases, following consultation with all parties, including the child. But flexibility about what family membership means should allow policy makers and practitioners to value the ways in which young adults may draw on kinship resources in several "families", including, in some cases, residential care.

- ***Understanding and applying developmental theory and research***
Social workers working with children, carers and birth family members would benefit from an understanding of developmental theory and research to help them make sense of the complex and varied developmental pathways that children take as they move through foster families and into adult life. As the analysis of these adult stories demonstrates, neither common sense nor professional wisdom alone can offer the depth of understanding that can be gained by applying theory and research to the life histories of those who need to find a family for life through foster care.

Attachment theory and ideas about resilience are very valuable. However, this study suggests that they can most usefully be seen as *part* of the picture. The models generated in this final part of the book would be incomplete without the concepts of family membership and kinship that are socially constructed but can interact productively with more psychological concepts. Such an integration of ideas can be seen as making a contribution to the broad-based psychosocial approach that is so distinctive of professional practice in social work.

Strengths and limitations of this study: the need for further research

This study has achieved what it set out to do in offering insights into the experience of long-term foster care and its meanings into adult life. One strength of the study has also been the connection made between developmental theory and the family placement concerns of social work researchers and social workers, which are woven through the analysis. Particularly significant, also, is the concept of kinship as applied to foster families, which emerged from the analysis and needs to be developed conceptually and in practice as part of the ongoing task of defining what family life can and should mean for children separated from birth families.

This study had some specific aims in its choice of research question, sample and methodology and was not intended to answer all the questions that face policy makers and practitioners in this field. A range of studies and methodologies are necessary to have the full picture and to press forward the boundaries of what we know. What this study has shown, through in-depth analysis of 40 cases, is the significance of a secure base as psychosocially defined and therefore what is possible for children who find a family for life in foster care. Since this is in contradiction to many current assumptions in policy and practice about permanence and foster care, this may therefore be its most important contribution. Further research is needed on just how well long-term foster care is being planned and supported in practice across the country, but what this study suggests is that such research needs to take place in the context of a belief that long-term foster care can play a necessary and vital role in providing families for life for very vulnerable children.

This research project was an attempt to capture the life experiences of 40 men and women in ways that can contribute to the major policy and practice debate about how best to offer security, in all its meanings, for children who are unable to grow up in their birth families. But along the way it has also offered insights, both harrowing and heartwarming, into what living in birth and foster families had meant to these young adults. The overall message is one of hope, to borrow a term from the theoretical model that has resulted. This is not because long-term foster care as a system has been universally successful in achieving families for life – it has not and cannot, any more than any other family form. But there is hope, because there is evidence here of the power of the human spirit, in children and foster carers, to overcome extreme adversity as a family, even in the face of inflexible views of what a family should be like. The messages about how this is achieved within foster families or how social work practice can facilitate the process are not simple and there are no guarantees of success. What the study particularly highlighted was the way in which young children who have experienced severe adversities have to manage the legacy of those experiences not only though childhood but also in adult life. This must reinforce the need to pursue the goal, through research, policy and practice, of ensuring that we are able to offer these children a secure base in a family which can support them with this life-long task.

Bibliography

Ainsworth, M D S, Bell, S and Stayton, D (1971) 'Individual differences in strange-situation behavior of one year olds', in Schaffer, H (ed.) *The Origins of Human Social Relations*, New York: Academic Press, pp 17–52.

Ainsworth, M D S, Blehar, M, Waters, E and Wall, S (1978) *Patterns of Attachment: A psychological study of the strange situation*, Hillsdale, New Jersey: Lawrence Erlbaum.

Allan, G (1996) *Kinship and Friendship in Modern Britain*, Oxford: Oxford University Press.

Allan, G and Crow, G (2001) *Families, Households and Society*, Basingstoke: Palgrave.

Bee, H (1999) *The Developing Child*, New York: Longman.

Beek, M (1997) *What does it mean to be adopted? A study of adoption through the eyes of adopted people*, Unpublished MA Dissertation, Norwich: University of East Anglia.

Berridge, D and Cleaver, H (1987) *Foster Home Breakdown*, Oxford: Basil Blackwell.

Bowlby, J (1969) *Attachment and Loss: Vol 1 Attachment*, London: Hogarth Press.

Bowlby, J (1973) *Attachment and Loss: Vol II Separation, Anxiety and Anger*, London: Hogarth Press.

Bowlby, J (1980) *Attachment and Loss: Vol III Loss, Sadness and Depression*, London: Hogarth Press.

Bowlby, J (1988) *A Secure Base: Clinical applications of attachment theory*, London: Routledge.

Bronfenbrenner, U (1979) *The Ecology of Human Development: Experiments by nature and design*, Cambridge, MA: Harvard University Press.

Carlson, V, Cicchetti, D, Barnett, D and Braunwald, K G (1989) 'Finding order in disorganisation: lessons from research on maltreated infants attachments to their caregivers', in Cicchetti, D and Carlson, V (eds) *Child Maltreatment: Theory and research on the causes and consequences of child abuse and neglect*, Cambridge: Cambridge University Press, pp 494–528.

Coffey, A and Atkinson, P (1996) *Making Sense of Qualitative Data: Complementary Research Strategies*, London: Sage.

Cresswell, J W (1994) *Research Design: Qualitative and quantitative approaches*, California: Sage.

Crittenden, P M (1995) 'Attachment and psychopathology', in Goldberg, S, Muir, R and Kerr, J (eds) *Attachment Theory: Social, developmental and clinical perspectives*, Hillsdale, NJ: Analytical Press, pp 367–406.

Crittenden, P M and Ainsworth, M D S (1989) 'Child maltreatment and attachment theory', in Cicchetti, D and Carlson, V (eds) *Child Maltreatment: Theory and research on the causes and consequences of child abuse and child neglect*, Cambridge: Cambridge University Press, pp 432–63.

Curtiss, S (1977) *Genie: A psychological study of a modern day wild child*, New York: Academic Press.

Department of Health (2000) *Framework for the Assessment of Children in Need and their Families*, London: The Stationery Office.

Department of Health (2002) *Looking after Children Statistics*, London: The Stationery Office.

Dunn, J (1988) *The Beginnings of Social Understanding*, Oxford: Blackwell.

Fahlberg, V (1988) *Fitting the Pieces Together*, London: BAAF.

Fahlberg, V (1994) *A Child's Journey through Placement* (2nd edn), London: BAAF.

Fanshel, D and Shinn, E B (1978) *Children in Foster Care*, New York: Columbia University Press.

Fetterman, D M (1989) *Ethnography: Step by Step*, Thousand Oaks, California/London: Sage.

Fonagy, P (1996) *Attachment and Theory of Mind: Overlapping Constructs?* Association of Child Psychology and Psychiatry Occasional Papers.

Fonagy, P (2001) *Attachment Theory and Psychoanalysis*, New York: Other Press.

Fonagy, P and Target, M (1997) 'Attachment and reflective function: their role in self-organisation', *Development and Psychopathology*, 9:4, pp 679–700.

Fratter, J, Rowe, J, Sapsford, D and Thoburn, J (1991) *Permanent Family Placement: A decade of experience*, London: BAAF.

George, C (1996) 'A representational perspective of child abuse and prevention: internal working models of attachment and caregiving', *Child Abuse and Neglect* 20:5, pp 411–24.

George C, Kaplan N and Main M (1985) *The Adult Attachment Interview*, Unpublished manuscript, Department of Psychology, University of California, Berkeley.

Gilligan, R (1997) 'Beyond permanence? The importance of resilience in child placement and planning', *Adoption & Fostering*, 21:1, pp 12–20.

Gilligan, R (2000) *Promoting Resilience: A resource guide on working with children in the care system*, London: BAAF.

Goffman, E (1964) *Stigma: Notes on the management of a spoiled identity*, Harmondsworth: Penguin.

Haggerty, R J, Sherrod, L R, Garmezy, N and Rutter, M (eds) (1994) *Stress, Risk and Resilience in Children and Adolescence: Processes, mechanisms and interventions*, Cambridge: Cambridge University Press.

Harter, S (1987) 'The determinations and mediational role of global self-worth in children', in Eisenberg, N (ed.) *Contemporary Topics in Developmental Psychology*, 9, New York: Wiley-Interscience, pp 219–42.

Howe, M (1998) 'Individual differences in factors that modulate storage and retrieval of traumatic memories', *Development and Psychopathology*, 10:4, pp 681–698.

Howe, D, Brandon, M, Hinings, D and Schofield, G (1999) *Attachment Theory: Child maltreatment and family support*, Basingstoke: Macmillan.

Howe, D and Feast, J (2000) *Adoption, Search and Reunion*, London: The Children's Society.

Jewett, C L (1994) *Helping Children Cope with Separation and Loss* (2nd edn), Harvard, MA: Harvard Community Press.

Kelly, G (2000) 'The survival of long-term foster care', in Kelly, G and Gilligan, R (eds) *Issues in Foster Care: Policy, practice and research*, London: Jessica Kingsley, pp 12–39.

Lowe, N, Murch, M, Bader, K, Borkowski, M, Copner, R, Lisles, C and Shearman, J (2002) *The Plan for the Child: Adoption or long-term fostering*, London: BAAF.

Main, M (1991) 'Metacognitive knowledge, metacognitive monitoring and singular (coherent) vs. multiple (incoherent) model of attachment: findings and directions for future research', in Parkes, C M, Stevenson-Hinde, J and Marris, P (eds) *Attachment Across the Life-cycle*, London: Tavistock/Routledge, pp 127–59.

Main, M (1995) 'Recent studies in attachment: overview with selected implications for clinical work', in Goldberg, S, Muir, R and Kerr, J (eds) *Attachment Theory: Social, developmental and clinical perspectives*, Hillsdale, NJ: The Analytic Press, pp 407–74.

Main, M and Goldwyn, R (1984–94) *Adult Attachment Scoring and Classification System*, Unpublished manuscript, Department of Psychology, University of California, Berkeley.

Mason, J (1996) *Qualitative Researching*, London: Sage.

Masten, A S, Best, K M and Garmezy, N (1990) 'Resilience and development: contributions from the study of children who overcome adversity', *Development and Psychopathology*, 2, pp 425–44.

Mollon, P (2000) *Remembering Trauma: A psychotherapist's guide to memory and illusion*, Wiley: Chichester.

Mrazek, P J and Mrazek, D A (1987) 'Resilience in child maltreatment victims: a conceptual exploration', *Child Abuse and Neglect*, 11, pp 355–66.

Murphy, L B and Moriarty, A E (1976) *Vulnerability, Coping and Growth*, New Haven, CT: Yale University Press.

Parker, R A (ed.) (1980) *Caring for Separated Children*, London: Macmillan.

Plomin, R (1994) *Genetics and Experience: The interplay between nature and nurture*, Thousand Oaks, CA: Sage.

Pugh, G (1999) *Unlocking the Past: The impact of access to Barnardo's child care records*, Basingstoke: Ashgate.

Pugh, G and Schofield, G (1999) 'Unlocking the past: the experience of gaining access to Barnardo's records', *Adoption & Fostering*, 23:2, pp 7–18.

Reissman, C K (ed.) (1994) *Qualitative Studies in Social Work Research*, London: Sage.

Richardson, L (1990) *Writing Strategies: Reaching audiences*, Newbury Park, CA: Sage.

Rowe, J and Lambert, L (1973) *Children Who Wait: A study of children needing substitute families*, London: Association of British Adoption and Fostering Agencies.

Rowe, J, Cain, H, Hundleby, M and Keane, A (1984) *Long-term Foster Care*, London: Batsford.

Rutter, M (1985) 'Resilience in the face of adversity', *British Journal of Psychiatry*, 147, pp 598–611.

Rutter, M (1999) 'Resilience concepts and findings: implications for family therapy', *Journal of Family Therapy*, 21, pp 119–44.

Rutter, M and the English and Romanian Adoptees (ERA) Study Team (1998) 'Developmental catch-up, and deficit, following adoption after severe global early deprivation', *Journal of Child Psychology and Psychiatry*, 39, pp 465–76.

Schofield, G (1994) *The Youngest Mothers: The experience of pregnancy and motherhood among young women of school age*, Basingstoke: Avebury.

Schofield, G (1996) 'Protection and loss: the impact of separation on the abused and neglected child', in Elsegood, J and Lindsey, B (eds) *Working with Children in Grief and Loss*, London: Bailliere Tindall, pp 150–61.

Schofield, G (2001) 'Resilience and family placement: a lifespan perspective', *Adoption & Fostering*, 25:3, pp 6–19.

Schofield, G, Beek, M, Sargent, K with Thoburn, J (2000) *Growing up in Foster Care*, London: BAAF.

Seale, C (1998) 'Qualitative interviewing', in Seale, C (ed.) *Researching Society and Culture*, London: Sage.

Silverman, D (1993) *Interpreting Qualitative Data: Methods for analysing talk, text and interaction*, London: Sage.

Sinclair, I, Wilson, K and Gibbs, I (2000) *Supporting Foster Placements*, Interim report to the Department of Health, University of York.

Sroufe, I A (1997) 'Psychopathology as an outcome of development', *Development and Psychopathology*, 9:2, pp 251–66.

Stanley, L and Wise, S (1993) *Breaking Out Again: Feminist ontology and epistemology*, London: Routledge & Kegan Paul.

Stein, M and Carey, K (1986) *Leaving Care*, Oxford: Blackwell.

Thoburn, J (1994) *Child Placement: Principles and practice* (2nd edn), Aldershot: Arena.

Thoburn, J (1991) 'Survey findings and conclusions', in Fratter, J, Rowe, J, Sapsford, D and Thoburn, J, *Permanent Family Placement: A decade of experience*, London: BAAF.

Thoburn, J, Norford, L and Rashid, S (2000) *Permanent Family Placement for Children of Ethnic Minority Origin*, London; Jessica Kingsley.

Toth, S L and Cicchetti, D (1998) 'Remembering, forgetting, and the effects of trauma on memory: a developmental psychopathology perspective', *Development and Psychopathology*, 10:4, pp 589–605.

Triseliotis, J (1980) 'Growing up in foster care and after', in Triseliotis, J (ed.) *New Developments in Fostering and Adoption*, London: Routledge & Kegan Paul, pp 131–61.

Triseliotis, J (2002) 'Long-term fostering or adoption: the evidence examined', *Child and Family Social Work*, 7:1, pp 23–34.

Winnicott D (1965) *The Maturational Process and the Facilitative Environment*, New York: International University Press.

Young, M and Willmott, P (1962) *Family Kinship in East London*, Harmondsworth: Penguin.

Index

abuse
- emotional, 142, 152, 166, 176, 180, 182
- physical, 37, 58, 93–5, 98, 108, 122, 145, 196–7, 208
- sexual, 16, 22, 38, 78, 97, 101, 108, 120, 122, 142, 151, 154–5, 163, 176

academic, 61, 66, 73, 76, 86, 92, 148, 208, 212, 235
activity, 16, 46, 64, 82, 122, 124, 196, 214–6, 237–8
adaptation, 10
adoption, 3–5, 12, 16–17, 21, 56, 62, 75, 80, 117, 130, 143, 145, 149, 154, 156, 158–9, 165, 175, 180, 185, 240
adoptive family, 4, 5, 16, 21, 27, 81, 85, 117, 142–4, 149–50, 154, 156, 158, 163–5, 169–70, 173, 177, 179, 184, 192, 194, 202, 204, 211, 224, 227, 237
adoptive parents, 21, 150, 154, 156, 163, 169, 177, 192, 194, 227, 248
adult attachment interview (AAI), 16, 42, 111, 189
affect regulation, 220
age
- adolescence, 15, 17, 27, 53, 65–6, 112, 117–8, 125, 127–9, 133, 139–41, 178, 197, 208, 226, 241
- infancy, 4, 9, 11, 22–3, 57, 59–60, 117–20, 122, 125, 132, 140–1, 157, 162–3, 185, 190, 208, 212–4, 218–20, 227, 233

aggression, 61, 167, 178, 180, 188, 212
anger, 8, 19, 22, 27, 58, 61–2, 64, 69, 75, 76, 92, 95, 100–1, 108, 113, 115, 118–9, 124, 128, 143, 146–7, 152, 156, 166–9, 171–2, 177–9, 183–4, 189–90, 202–3, 217, 221, 224, 226–7
anxiety, 8, 23, 33–4, 38, 44, 62, 84, 87–91, 93–5, 99–100, 102, 104, 108–9, 113, 115, 119, 124, 128, 132, 140, 143, 152, 163, 175, 179, 211–3, 218–20, 222, 235
assessment, 11
attachment patterns (childhood)
- ambivalent/resistant, 8
- avoidant, 8, 91, 211, 212
- disorganised, 8
- secure, 54, 65, 213, 216

attachment patterns (adulthood)
- dismissing/defended, 115
- enmeshed/entangled/preoccupied, 115

secure/autonomous/free to evaluate, 175, 218–9
unresolved, 115
autonomy, 174–5, 214, 216–9

bad dreams, 104, 121, 140, 143, 177, 208, 229
nightmares, 104–5, 121
night terrors, 121
being in care, 16, 50, 71, 89, 110, 117, 127, 128, 133–4, 170–1
birth parents, 5, 11, 21–2, 33–5, 40–1, 43–4, 52, 56–7, 61, 65, 68–9, 76, 78, 80, 83–4, 87, 91, 102, 104, 126–8, 132–4, 143, 146–8, 158, 166, 177, 179, 181–2, 199, 211, 223–7, 231, 233, 241

career, 20, 80, 86, 88, 90, 94, 109, 174, 208, 218
Christmas, 6, 22, 50, 57, 71, 83, 85, 101–2, 132, 152–3, 232–3
close relationships, 33, 42, 70, 81, 139, 211
cognitive appraisal, 145, 169, 223
confidence, lack of, 86, 100, 109
contact (with birth family), 20
controlling, 9, 10, 62, 65, 154, 157, 201, 211–12, 220
coping strategies, 184, 221
culture, 12, 20–1, 46, 69, 85–6, 218, 226, 228–9, 231–2, 234–5

death, 7, 23, 29, 36–7, 40, 77, 114, 120, 142–4, 162, 163, 219, 225, 233, 235
depression, 57, 70, 88, 118, 120, 132, 136–8, 142, 197–8, 201, 208, 225, 236, 241
development, 3–4, 6–7, 11, 16, 51, 59, 105, 177, 208–9, 212, 214, 216, 219, 222, 238, 240
discipline/punishment, 41, 49, 52, 151, 155, 180, 187–8, 191–2
distant, 26, 44, 73, 132, 212
downward spiral, 70, 117–8, 128, 131, 135, 139, 197, 241
drug taking, 6, 117, 131, 146, 178–9, 197–9, 201, 203, 208, 218, 241

eating problems, 143, 176
ecological approach, 11, 238
education, 6, 16, 28, 34, 54, 86, 196, 204, 213, 218, 235
graduation, 196, 232
school, 5, 8–9, 11, 23, 34, 36–7, 41, 44, 50–1, 53, 55–6, 59–60, 63, 71, 77–8, 80, 85–6, 91, 93, 99–101, 103, 108, 110–11, 113–7, 124, 128, 130–3, 143, 146, 148, 150–2, 154–6, 160, 162, 167, 170–1, 180, 186, 193, 203, 207, 214–5, 218, 225–7, 234, 237, 241
university, 18, 67, 86, 94,

109–10, 115, 179, 196, 218, 232, 234
employment, 28, 54, 218, 235, 240
environment, 3–6, 8, 10–11, 28, 38, 53, 86, 122, 139–40, 145, 173, 203, 208, 213–4, 220

family
membership, 11, 25–8, 38, 41–5, 48–9, 55, 67, 71–3, 92–3, 100, 106, 108, 115, 117, 141, 163, 178, 204, 207, 229, 231–5, 241–2
relationship, 229
ritual, 34, 67, 123, 132, 160, 229, 231–4
solidarity, 229–31
foster carers, 5, 17–19, 21–2, 24–6, 29, 33–4, 37, 40, 42–5, 47–9, 54, 56–7, 60–65, 67–8, 73–4, 80, 82–6, 93, 98, 100–109, 111–5, 117–9, 121–4, 127–34, 137, 140–2, 144, 147, 150, 152–3, 156–7, 160–74, 177, 181, 187–93, 195, 197, 199, 202, 204, 211, 213, 215–7, 219–20, 222–4, 226–8, 231–2, 234, 237, 240, 243
frozen, 102, 184

gender, 20, 215
genetic inheritance, "bad blood", 3, 66, 190, 226
grandparents, 57, 81, 118, 139, 141, 165, 226

home, feeling at, 38, 173
hope, 9, 15, 28–9, 79, 127, 135, 154, 178, 198, 209, 223, 235–6, 243

identity, 16, 43, 53, 71, 87, 167, 173, 191, 209, 224, 228–9, 232–3
independence, 35, 52–3, 56, 64–5, 74, 87, 90, 108, 141, 173, 216, 231, 235, 241
interdependence, 235
internal working model, 10, 62, 118, 143, 169, 204, 220

kinship, 229–31, 233, 241–2

leaving care, 18, 107, 173, 177, 197, 229, 231
legacy, 3, 8, 28, 34, 56, 73, 86, 90, 93, 118, 132, 143, 152, 166–7, 176, 179, 243
loss, 6, 16, 39, 88, 120, 141, 145, 147, 162, 181, 189, 217, 222–5, 228, 236
love, 69, 81, 85–6, 90–1, 101, 106, 120, 124, 126–7, 130, 144, 150, 163–4, 169, 171, 176–7, 181, 186, 190–3, 200,

202, 209, 212–3, 220, 223, 225–7
lying, 60, 65, 120, 212

maltreatment (see also abuse, neglect), 8, 10–11, 57–9, 61, 94, 142–3, 169, 221, 223–4, 226
manipulating, 10, 212
meanings, 15, 21, 26, 39, 165, 242, 243
memory, 33, 35–7, 48–9, 59, 63, 68, 74, 77–8, 85, 88, 97–8, 104, 109, 110–11, 119–20, 123, 130, 137, 140, 146, 147, 153, 158, 182, 185, 187–8, 193, 200, 215, 225–7
  episodic, 35, 37, 119, 121, 140, 158, 226
  procedural, 99, 226, 237
  semantic, 49, 99, 119–21, 140, 226
mental health problems, 6, 56–8, 61, 64, 68, 75, 78, 86, 98, 117, 131, 139, 166, 181, 212, 215, 227
mental representations, 8, 38, 42, 119, 141, 169

narrative, 16, 25, 95, 226
neglect, 6, 11, 22–3, 28, 34, 57, 60, 69, 84, 93–6, 117, 119, 121, 124, 141–5, 166, 211, 215, 225, 227–8
normal, 3–4, 7, 25, 39, 42, 45, 47–8, 50–1, 55, 61, 64–6, 69, 80, 87, 90, 92, 107, 111–2, 129, 149, 151, 159, 162, 173, 181, 190–1, 194, 199, 203, 222–5, 232, 236

parental responsibility, 5, 237
parenthood, 89–91, 174, 199–201, 235
part of the family, 12, 48, 66, 105, 121, 129, 159, 161, 165, 204, 229, 232
pathways, 3–4, 6, 14, 24–9, 31, 33, 48, 56, 61, 72–3, 93, 115, 117, 142–3, 178–9, 204, 207–9, 211, 213, 225, 229, 242
permanence, 13, 17, 21, 54, 70, 77, 115, 179, 207, 238, 240, 243
photographs, 23, 24, 232
placement, 5, 12, 17–18, 22, 25–7, 33, 39, 43, 54, 61–2, 66–8, 70–2, 81, 84, 86, 94, 99, 102, 107, 117–8, 125–6, 128, 131–2, 134, 141–2, 144, 147, 152, 156, 161–2, 166, 168, 173, 178, 179–80, 185, 187, 190, 192, 199, 204, 207, 212–13, 215, 222, 224–5, 230–1, 240–2
  breakdown, 71, 115, 117–8, 126, 131, 134, 162, 198, 211
professional, 5–6, 54, 73, 86, 231, 237, 240–2
psychosocial, 7, 9, 26, 207, 209, 235, 237–8, 242

racism, 12, 82, 85, 86
real family, 17, 41, 47, 52, 56, 63, 66, 73–4, 93, 100, 107, 123–4, 128, 130, 136, 139, 164, 171–2, 178, 181, 192, 208, 229, 231, 238
reflective function, 219, 235
rejection, 8, 56, 73, 76, 106, 135, 145–6, 149, 152, 153, 175, 180–1, 190, 195, 197, 213
singled out for, 93, 175, 182, 217
rescue, 95, 120, 142, 183, 222
residential care, 3, 5, 16, 178–9, 195–6, 199, 241
resilience, 8–11, 24, 28, 52, 55, 60–1, 65, 137, 140, 207–9, 216, 223, 235–6, 242
review, 16, 25, 159, 161, 171, 173, 207, 219
role models, 47, 52, 56, 64, 92, 196, 234

scapegoat, 133
secure base, 9, 44, 54, 71, 85, 92, 115, 133, 143, 173, 174, 178, 196, 202, 204, 207, 208, 209, 211, 212, 214, 218, 220, 221, 229, 235–6, 243
security, 26, 28, 38, 47, 70, 72, 80, 90, 93–4, 105, 177, 179, 207, 209, 211, 213–4, 219, 240, 243
self, 12, 16, 26, 35, 38, 58, 62, 70, 72, 76, 81, 84, 87, 95, 102, 104, 114, 118–20, 132–3, 135, 137, 140–1, 144, 156, 161, 167, 169, 173, 176, 179, 185, 198, 200, 203–4, 209, 211, 213–4, 220, 225–6, 228, 233, 236
separation, 6, 11, 15, 37, 65, 77–8, 85, 87, 115, 117, 132, 141, 144, 162, 170, 181, 217, 219, 222–3
sexual activity, 66
shared fate, 33, 50, 73, 147, 183
siblings, 7, 16, 18, 23, 29, 33–4, 36, 42, 44–5, 50–1, 54, 56, 67, 74–5, 77, 80–1, 83, 86, 90–3, 95–7, 99, 101, 103, 113, 124, 133–4, 140, 142–9, 152–5, 158, 161–3, 170, 172, 182–3, 186–7, 217, 223–4, 226, 232
social work practice, 3, 17, 25, 28, 108, 173, 194, 207, 237–8, 243
social work/social workers, 3–4, 9, 14, 16–20, 22–3, 25, 28, 33, 50, 52, 62, 78, 104, 107–8, 117, 124–6, 128, 130–1, 135, 140, 143, 146–7, 151, 154, 156, 159, 162, 169–73, 177–9, 182, 186, 192–4, 196–7, 204, 207, 213, 222, 224, 226, 227, 231, 237–8, 240, 242–3
stealing, 59, 65, 79, 115, 131, 178, 212, 217
stereotypes, 19
stigma, 28, 47, 51, 53, 124, 171, 228, 232, 240

suicide, 117, 131, 135, 136
supported lodgings carer, 140, 241
sympathy, 76, 80, 171

testing out, 56
transition, 105, 159, 184, 197, 222, 241
transracial placements, 85, 233
trauma, 14, 23, 94, 97, 106, 111, 137, 189, 224
turning points, 4, 28, 54, 61, 66, 70, 91, 115, 117, 134–5, 139–40, 159, 161–2, 177, 179, 199, 203–4

unresolved, 6–7, 16, 35, 94, 100, 114–5, 118, 144, 189

violence, 22, 35–6, 53, 58, 77, 94, 96–7, 99, 108, 121, 146, 178, 188

weddings, 29, 74, 232